Finding The Fallen

Dedication

To Lt Ralph Eugene Foulks Jr US Navy
Lost over Vietnam 5 January 1968

Finding The Fallen

Outstanding aircraft mysteries of the First World War
to Desert Storm investigated and solved

Andy Saunders

Grub Street • London

Published by
Grub Street Publishing
4 Rainham Close
London
SW11 6SS

British Library Cataloguing in Publication Data

Saunders, Andy.
  Finding the fallen : outstanding aircrew mysteries from the
  First World War to Desert Storm investigated and solved.
  1. Missing in action–Case studies. 2. Airmen–Biography.
  3. Aircraft accidents--Investigation--History–20th century.
  I. Title
  358.4'1338'0922-dc22

ISBN-13: 9781908117106

Design by Roy Platten, Eclipse, Hemel Hempstead
roy.eclipse@btopenworld.com

Printed and bound by MPG Ltd, Bodmin, Cornwall

Grub Street Publishing uses only FSC
(Forest Stewardship Council) paper for its books

Contents

Acknowledgements

MANY FRIENDS AND COLLEAGUES have greatly assisted me in writing this book. Without them, it is certainly the case that this account detailing various stories behind missing aircrew lost on operations in various conflicts would have been rather more difficult to put together.

I should like to thank, in no particular order of merit: Winston Ramsey, Martin O'Brien, Steve Hall, Ian Hutton, Arnaud Gillet, Martin Mace, Colleen Ijuin, Simon Parry, Chris Goss, Richard Allen, Marjorie Allen, Dirk Decuypere, Gordon Leith, Gerald Oury, Philippa Hodgkiss, Gerry Burke, Cynrik De Decker, Jill Craig, Don Bryans, Dave Stubley, Norman Franks, Emmanuel Bril, Dick Walker, Barry Hammerton, Sue Raftree, Amanda Berry, Terry Thompson, Larry Hickey, Richard Lyon, Peter Cornwell, Ruth Bloom, Geoff Carless, Joe Bamford, Melvin Brownless, Jiri Rajlich, Janet Lacroix, Dale Wait, Robyn Saunders, David Hinton, Peter Hess, Fred Hagan, Ken Rimmel, Walter Mankelow, Air Cdre Mulder, Jan Gnodde, Dick van Polen and Lt Col Erik Rab.

I must also add a special thank you to Richard Lyon who allowed me to quote extensively from his own research material that he used in the Wikipedia page he has set up for his uncle, Russell Lyon.

An equally special thank you must also go to Michael Rank for allowing me to quote from his work regarding Flt Lt Hinton.

Once more I must also thank John Davies and his team at Grub Street, including Emer Hogan, Sophie Campbell and Sarah Driver. I look forward to working with you all again.

Last, but by no means least, a big thank you to Zoe who has again put up with my absence whilst I was shut away in my study to prepare this manuscript. Your support and understanding has, as ever, gone above and beyond the call of duty!

If I have overlooked anyone who has had an input to this book then I extend to them my sincerest apologies. It will have been an entirely unintentional oversight on my part. Thank you again one and all.

Foreword

TWENTY-FIVE YEARS TO the day after he was lost, my brother, Lt Ralph Foulks of the US Navy, finally came home from Vietnam.

Our lives changed forever on 5 January 1968 when Ralph's plane was shot down, but our destinies took another twist on 5 January 1993 when the US Navy informed us that Ralph's remains had been positively identified and that he was now home. We never knew what had happened to him. Life went through phases during those many years. Until the war ended there was always the possibility that Ralph – 'Skip' to his buddies but always 'Bubby' to me – was alive. Even after the war was over, and the POWs came home, there were countless times when we said "what if?"

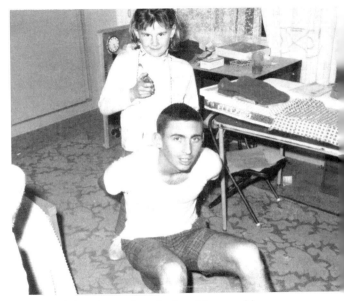

Colleen Ijuin's favourite photo of her and her brother Ralph. One of the last times she saw him.

when bits of news or movies would come out suggesting that POWs remained hidden in remote areas of Vietnam. That phase seemed to go on forever. Until he came home we never knew, but we always hoped there was some chance that he was alive, far-fetched as that idea may have been.

For many families the military knocking on the door had a sad finality and they knew their loved ones were dead. But for the families of those missing in action the haunting began. We carefully packed Red Cross POW care packages, diligently following the guidelines of what could be enclosed along with his favourite candy. It was as if the better the box was packed then the surer we would be that he got it. It was always painful to have the box come back marked 'undeliverable'. At the holiday season the Red Cross films of POW camps had us glued to the TV hoping that we would see Ralph and that the returned care packages were just a terrible mistake. I remember a letter from Ralph's wife saying she was sure she had seen him. Ralph had married just two months before deploying.

From the time Ralph went missing I replayed the scenes of our times together over and over in my mind, trying to keep him alive. During the years of having a loved one missing in action the recollections take on a greater-than-life importance and your very existence becomes just a period of endurance. Ralph's life was but one, and as deep as that hole was in our lives there were hundreds, if not thousands, of other families enduring the same. I'm sure the recollections are played over and over again

A typical all-American scene. Ralph Foulks, with Colleen (the youngest) and his other sister Debbie on the trolley.

in thousands of minds. Until the day they come home. And then a new phase begins.

Now, we can take flowers to Ralph's grave in Barrancas National Cemetery. We know that he is dead and although we still don't know the details of what happened to Skip we have him home. For the families who never have that new phase beginning it must be like torture if I think about it now. To have a loved one missing in action means you never give up hope. You just endure.

Having those who were found remembered in this book helps sustain those who bear that loss, and having them come home helps to heal. As you read here about those who were lost, including some who are *still* lost, the fact that the reader sees their names and remembers them brings a great deal of comfort to those left behind. I am so grateful to Andy Saunders for bringing back the missing as well as bringing them back from being forgotten. Each face here represents so many who still need to be remembered and found.

Colleen Ijuin

Colleen Ijuin
Sister of Lt Ralph Eugene Foulks Jr. US Navy
Lost in action over Vietnam 5 January 1968

Introduction

I N *FINDING THE FEW* (Grub Street 2009) and *Finding The Foe* (Grub Street 2010), I was able to tell the story of a number of RAF and Luftwaffe fliers lost over the UK during the Battle of Britain and later. Those two books, and the stories contained within them, proved to be exceptionally popular and there was an immediate clamour for more stories of the same genre. However, all of the missing aircrew losses for the 1940 period had been pretty much exhausted within those two books and thus it was only natural to look much further afield both in terms of timeframes and geographical location. Indeed, this book looks at cases from the First World War through to the second, into the Korean War to the Vietnam War and right up to the Gulf War. It is a fact that whenever and wherever aircrews fly off to do combat there will always be a percentage of those who will not return. Of those, there is yet a further percentage of fliers who have simply disappeared and this book looks at a range of such cases across a time span of almost ninety years. Some have been resolved satisfactorily. Others remain on the 'pending' list. Other cases yet will probably always remain a mystery.

In terms of the numbers of those aviators who are missing and unaccounted for from all nations and all conflicts it is impossible to put a figure, but if we take RAF and Commonwealth aircrew missing over north-west Europe alone we have a figure currently standing in the region of 20,300 names. Added to those, the losses of American air forces over north-west Europe who are still unaccounted for stands at a total of 5,126 whilst the Flying Services Memorial at Arras records the names of around a further 1,000 casualties of the First World War from the RFC and RNAS. In total, therefore, we have here around 26,500 allied fliers lost and missing in the European theatre alone during both wars – and this does not include an almost incalculable and unknown number of those from the Luftwaffe or Imperial German Air Service or Italian air forces, for example. Neither does it include, of course, the losses of all other air forces on a global basis. Quite simply, the numbers are staggering and it is hardly surprising that from amongst that huge number there continues to be ongoing finds of missing aircrew around the world that have been subject to discovery and identification, either by accident or intent.

From the very outset of aerial warfare there have been efforts to trace and identify the missing, and those efforts began with the work of the Imperial War Graves Commission and the Directorate of War Graves Registration and Enquiries in the immediate aftermath of the

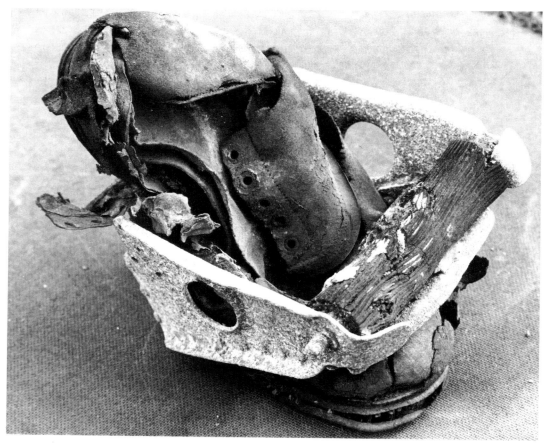

This incredible photograph shows a Typhoon aircraft rudder pedal that was found washed up on the foreshore at East Preston, near Littlehampton, West Sussex, just after the war. The story it tells is a chilling and yet an unknown one. Who was the unfortunate pilot of this Typhoon? Was he dragged to his death as the aircraft slid beneath the waves? Or did he struggle free, leaving just his boot behind in the cockpit? If he didn't survive the crash, then did the sea ever deliver up his body? If not, he must be one of just over 20,000 RAF and Commonwealth airmen with no known graves who were killed on active service over north-west Europe and who are commemorated by name on the Runnymede Memorial.

First World War. Indeed, our book logically begins with the very prominent case of Major Edward 'Mick' Mannock VC DSO MC whom I suggest lies in a grave marked to an unidentified aviator. It is worth considering, too, another case involving fliers from that conflict who were subsequently identified and given named graves in what must have been one of the very first post-conflict recoveries of missing fliers found in the wreckage of their shot-down aircraft.

In 1927 the Imperial War Graves Commission (now Commonwealth War Graves Commission) unexpectedly wrote to the family of Lt E H N Stroud of the Royal Flying Corps with astonishing news that their long-lost relative had been found. It stated:

"In the course of the work of removing the bodies of soldiers who were buried in isolated and scattered graves to cemeteries where their graves could be cared for and maintained, the remains of two officers were found in the debris of an aeroplane at a spot about one mile east of Zillebeke, which is south-east of Ypres, and in order to secure the reverent maintenance of the grave in perpetuity the remains were carefully and reverently reburied in Sanctuary Wood Cemetery, Zillebeke.

"A regimental button of the Royal Artillery and an aeroplane strut were recovered and are in this office and it has been ascertained from the markings on the strut that the machine was an R.E.8 type, and that the aeroplane in question was manufactured by the Coventry Ordnance Works during the period 15 March 1917 to 15 September 1918; also, the number of the machine was C.5037.

"From the investigations made it has been ascertained that Lieut Stroud and Captain C G White MC of the Royal Field Artillery, attached to 53 Squadron RAF, left the aerodrome at Clairmarais South flying an R.E.8 machine, No 5037, on counter-attack patrol duty, in the locality in which the bodies were found, but failed to return.

"A cross, with their names inscribed, has been erected at the head of the grave in Sanctuary Wood Cemetery."

Way before the advent of detailed scientific identification techniques then, we have here two lost fliers being named, and long after the event of their deaths, through basic detective work. This book charts a number of cases of missing airmen from the first and second world wars through to Vietnam, Korea and right up to the Gulf War. The passage of time has neither lessened the desire to bring home missing aviators nor has its importance diminished to those left behind. The detective trail can often be long and tortuous, but a satisfactory conclusion can mean just as much to relatives more than seventy years later as it did to those who have had to wait a considerably shorter while. We only have to look at the words of Richard Allen, brother of Fg Off Derek Allen (featured in Chapter 13), to appreciate that fact.

In writing this book I hope also to have kept alive the memory of those aircrew who are lost and still missing. Recently, a Lt Col Fullwood of the 2nd Batt, 9th US Marine Corps, said at a memorial service for a fallen comrade:

"A man dies first when his body expires, and second when his name is no longer spoken."

I hope this book will ensure that some of these men's names continue to be spoken, although by its very nature it can only deal with just a very small number of individual cases. There are many more stories such as these that yet remain to be told and many more names to be kept alive.

Andy Saunders
East Sussex, July 2011

Major 'Mick' Mannock, VC DSO MC, the highest scoring RAF fighter pilot of all time and who still remains officially listed as missing in action.

CHAPTER 1

The Enduring Mystery of Butter Lane

ONE OF THE MOST intriguing mysteries relating to missing fliers is the case of Major 'Mick' Mannock VC, DSO, MC and it has long been supposed that his grave *may* be that of the unknown airman buried in the CWGC cemetery at Laventie, France. That supposition was examined carefully by this author and Norman Franks in their book *Mannock VC* (Grub Street 2009) when the facts of the case were taken apart and re-assembled in forensic detail. Similarly, the case was looked at in the BBC2 Timewatch programme Aces Falling (2009) to which the author was a contributor. The conclusion reached was that the grave in question was, most likely, the last resting place of Major Mannock and on the back of the author's detailed case examination a submission was made to the Ministry of Defence requesting that the matter be looked at again. The result was a detailed thirteen-page assessment by the RAF Air Historical Branch with an outcome that perhaps ensures the enduring nature of this mystery. Before looking at that outcome and its implications we need to understand the complexities of the case.

On 26 July 1918 Private Edward Naulls was in the front line between Mont Bernechon and Pacault Wood and watched from his position on the ground somewhere near Hate Farm as a British aeroplane plunged to the ground in flames. In 1960 he wrote an account of what he had seen:

"I was with 'D' Coy, 2nd Battalion of the Essex Regt, on the Lys sector of the front. Stand-down was at 5am.

Lt Donald Inglis (right) of 85 Squadron was flying with Mannock when he was shot down in no-man's land and disappeared.

Shortly afterwards a Jerry monoplane (*sic*) appeared over no-man's-land. A little while later two British fighter planes arrived and engaged the Jerry in combat. I now know this was Major Mannock with Lt Inglis. A few bursts from their guns sent it crashing in flames behind Pacault Wood towards La Pierre au Beurre. Then Mannock dived to within forty feet of the ground. I think this is a fair estimate because the trees in Pacault Wood were not more than thirty feet high and Mannock's plane cleared them by just a few feet. Inglis circled at about a hundred feet.

"Suddenly, there was a lot of rifle fire from the Jerry trenches and then a machine gun opened up. I saw tracers enter Mannock's engine on the port side. In a few seconds a tiny bluish-white flame spread, enveloping the engine and cockpit, then a cloud of smoke and flame. With the propeller still turning the plane went down in a long glide and crashed towards Merville. A great column of black smoke shot up. Inglis started to climb away but his engine stalled (I distinctly heard it splutter twice before it stopped) and he forced-landed just behind the front line near St Floris."

From the account of both Inglis and Naulls we know that Mannock fell somewhere to the south of Calonne-sur-la-Lys and apparently near La Pierre au Beurre inside German lines. The clue as to exactly where, though, was provided by the Germans themselves who pinpointed the original grave location. So, we can be sure as to exactly where Mannock was buried in his original field grave. Or can we?

Certainly, the general location quoted by the Germans fits neatly with that indicated by Inglis and Naulls – although the reality is that we can now only be positive that the Germans confirmed his death and buried him. That is all. Unfortunately, much confusion across the intervening ninety years has caused a mystery to fall over what became of his body and its burial place. In that time some have tried to make sense of the confusion and to establish the current grave location for Major 'Mick'

A line-up of the SE5 aircraft of 85 Squadron during 1918, at about the time Mannock (the CO) went missing during July.

Mannock, VC, DSO, MC. Mostly, though, they have done so with incomplete information although when the Commonwealth War Graves Commission made available their extensive file on the Mannock case to his family, it became possible for the author to reach a

The headstone to an unknown aviator of the First World War in Laventie Military Cemetery, France, which the author contends is almost certainly the grave of the leading British ace, Major Mick Mannock.

conclusion that many believe is beyond any reasonable doubt. Indeed, when examining the case of Major Mannock during the early 1980s the Commonwealth War Graves Commission's own chief records officer, Major T.A. Edwin Gibson MBE, wrote an internal report for the commission suggesting the location of his grave to be in Laventie Military Cemetery, France, marked simply as an unknown airman. This suggestion was later published by Gibson in the 1989 HMSO publication *Courage Remembered*. The public airing of this theory had thereby gained at least a quasi-official stamp of approval and credibility.

It is important to appreciate that Mannock was but one of almost countless thousands of Commonwealth war dead during the period 1914-18. Of these, the vast majority had fallen in France or Belgium and amongst them were many thousands of unidentified servicemen and yet thousands more who had no grave at all – having simply been lost in the mayhem of the shell-torn battlefields. Therefore, and despite his heroic status, establishing the location of Major Mannock's grave was afforded no special prominence in the massive amount of work undertaken by the war graves directorate. This work included locating and recording the graves of service personnel and the identification and re-burial of the casualties from field graves.

In this respect, each man was dealt with on the basis of equality in death for all ranks from private to field marshal, although in the case of Mannock his long-time friend Jim Eyles was a constant correspondent and visitor to the Imperial War Graves Commission offices in the immediate post-war period. Tenaciously he harried the authorities for news as to the location of his friend's grave, and it was his constant badgering that has enabled subsequent examination of the salient points surrounding the case and to re-appraise it in detail. Were it not for Eyles then it is very likely that Mannock's place in the commission's records might be restricted to a single entry on a casualty card and the bland recording of his name on the Arras Flying Services Memorial to missing World War One aircrew. Instead, a weighty file exists in the Commonwealth War Graves Commission's Maidenhead HQ, thus making it possible to examine Jim Eyles's long-forgotten campaign. Significantly, it is correspondence from Eyles in January 1919, just three months after the end of the war, which opens the file.

Initially the Imperial War Graves Commission wrote him what might be described as a holding letter, stating that Mannock's grave had not yet been found, and "…in the final clearing up of the battlefields it is expected that the identity of many unknown graves will be established, and in addition many graves will be found which to date have not been

In the immediate post-war period search teams from the graves registration service found and recovered countless numbers of bodies from field graves across France and Belgium, including a number of fallen airmen. We know that such a search party found and recovered an unidentified airman from alongside Butter Lane at La Pierre au Beurre. This is the unknown airman now buried at Laventie and who the Imperial War Graves Commission in 1925 considered likely to have been Mannock.

reported and registered." (*The discovery of Lt Stroud mentioned in the introduction to this book being a case in point*) Thus, some crumbs of hope were offered to Eyles who waited patiently until the following year before enquiring again if any news was yet to hand. In the event, it wasn't – but it did prompt the commission to write to the Air Ministry asking if they had information as to the whereabouts of Mannock's grave. They didn't, and were only able to confirm the rough geographical location of his loss although for the first time it did spark enquiries to be made with the Directorate of War Graves Registration and Enquiries office in Berlin. Crucially, they were able to respond with what would be the first tangible clue to link Mannock with a field grave location, albeit that it then confused rather than helped clarify the actual place of burial.

The Flying Services Memorial at Arras Military Cemetery, France.

Responding in November 1920, Berlin wrote saying that the information contained in a report of an intelligence officer of the German 6th Army quoted the following:

> "Flight Captain (*sic*) Mannock, 85th Squadron RAF, was shot down on 28 July 1918 (*sic*). Machine crashed in flames. Body recovered and buried 300 metres NW of La-Pierre-au-Beurre on the road to Pacault."

Aside from discrepancies in detail as to rank and date of death, here at long last was some crucial evidence. Making sense of it, both then and now, could be described as challenging and it certainly taxed the minds of war graves directorate officials in determining what had happened when they wrestled with the problem during the early 1920s. Eyles would simply not let it go, however, and refused to be fobbed-off with being told that Mannock's grave could not be found. Besides, the posthumous award of the Victoria Cross (finally Gazetted 18 July 1919) had brought him into public awareness as an outstanding national hero.

Leaving matters be would simply not do, and so a concerted effort to unravel the case was embarked on by the Imperial War Graves Commission with the intention that he might at last be laid to rest, both in a physical and a metaphorical sense. Hopefully, the tenaciously persistent Jim Eyles could be given an answer that would finally satisfy him. As it would turn out, it seems that even when Berlin had sent their short note in November 1920, Mannock's original field grave had most likely already been unwittingly found and its then unknown occupant re-buried elsewhere.

It was probably map reading confusion, first by the Germans and then by the war graves service, that lies at the root of this mystery. Or, more accurately, it was not so much a map reading *error*, per se, that gave rise to incorrect grid references but rather a simple misunderstanding as to what the Germans, and later the British, were reading and interpreting on their respective maps.

When the war graves service re-examined the case and their files in light of the 1920 revelation from Berlin about the grave "300 metres NW of La Pierre au Buerre on the road to Pacault" they looked again at their maps – standard trench maps as used by the British Army throughout the First World War. At once they spotted something very odd. If the Germans had buried Mannock where they said they had, as quoted above, then this made no sense at all. They could see that 'NW of Pierre au Buerre' was **not** on the road to Pacault (a track known as Butter Lane to the Tommies) because Pacault was a settlement due *east* of La Pierre au Buerre. The geography and the bearings did not make any sense. However, things made a little more sense if one assumed the Germans had, perhaps, meant north-east. But did they really mean that? And does it *really* make any more sense? Either way, it was a possibility that the Imperial War Graves Commission considered and then ultimately dismissed.

Writing again of the case in 1923, another of the commission's officers observed that: "An unknown British aviator is shown in exhumation reports for Laventie Military Cemetery... and was exhumed from (Butter Lane) identified by a cross and wreck of plane. No date of death is stated." This report is significant in that it links, directly, a specific burial at Laventie Military Cemetery with the field exhumation at the Butter Lane location.

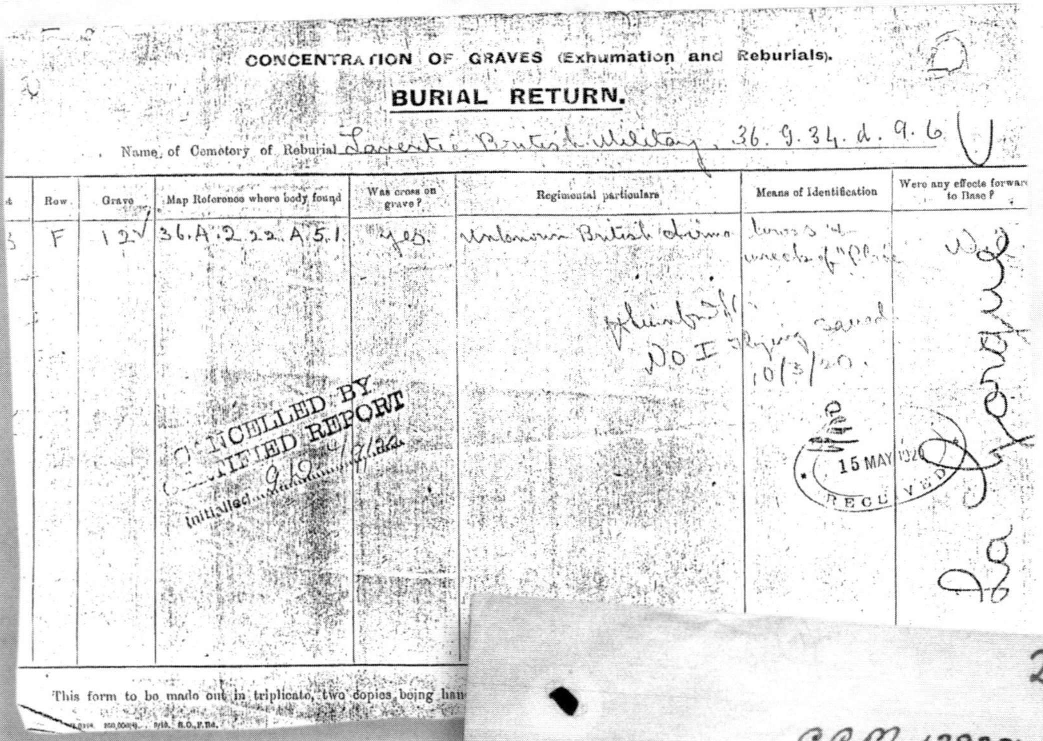

CONCENTRATION OF GRAVES (Exhumation and Reburials).

BURIAL RETURN.

Name of Cemetery of Reburial _Laventie British Military_, 36. 9. 34. d. 9. 6

Plot	Row	Grave	Map Reference where body found	Was cross on grave?	Regimental particulars	Means of Identification	Were any effects forwarded to Base?
3	F	12	36. A. 2. 22. A. 5. 1.	yes	Unknown British Airman	traces of wreck of "plane" ... NO I Flying ... 10/3/20	no

This form to be made out in triplicate, two copies being han...

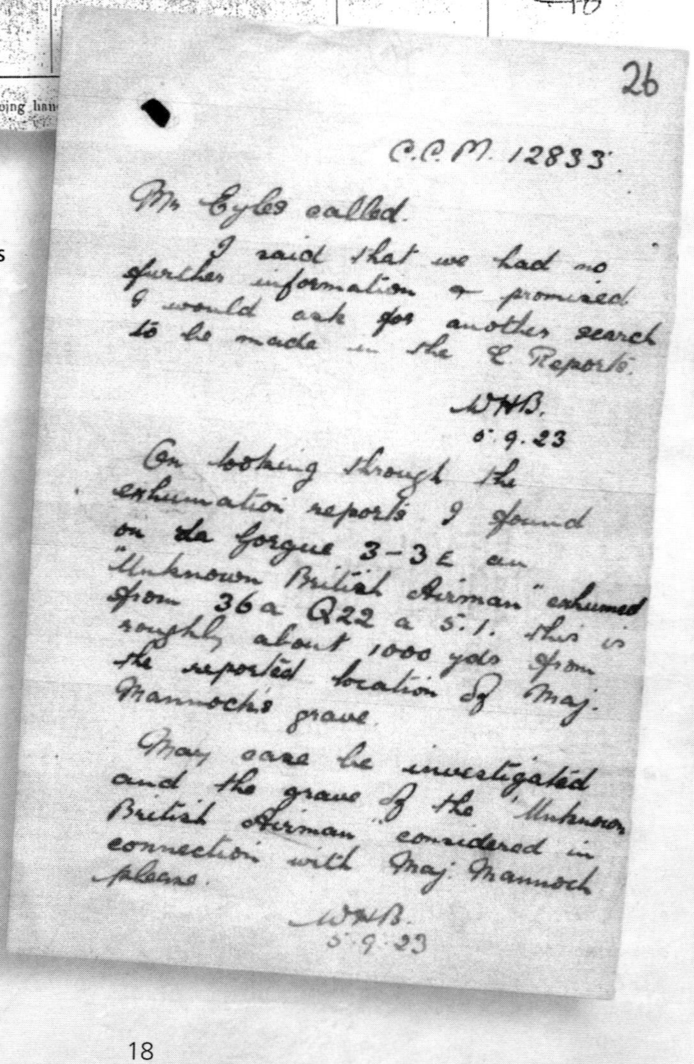

Above: When the unidentified aviator was removed from his field burial site at Butter Lane this was the commission's exhumation report. It is the crucial document that provides us with a link between the Butter Lane casualty and the Laventie burial and it also gives us a map reference for the location of that original discovery.

Right: Mannock's friend, Jim Eyles, persistently raised the question as to what had become of 'Mick', and the bulging Commonwealth War Graves Commission file on Mannock contains many notes and letters dealing with his tireless enquiries. This is one of the relevant file notes about Eyles's quest to find the grave, although it seems that he was never told about the original suspicions relating to the identity of the Laventie burial.

C.C.M. 12833.

Mr Eyles called.
I said that we had no further information & promised I would ask for another search to be made in the E. Reports.

WHB.
5. 9. 23

On looking through the exhumation reports I found on La Forgue 3-3 E an "Unknown British Airman" exhumed from 36a Q22 a 5. 1. this is roughly about 1000 yds from the reported location of Maj. Mannock's grave.

May case be investigated and the grave of the "Unknown British Airman" considered in connection with Maj. Mannock please.

WHB.
5. 9. 23

The report goes on to comment upon aeroplane wreckage seen nearby and suggests that this was *probably* linked to the unknown British airman. Further, the commission officer went on to say: "May this case be investigated and the grave of the Unknown British Airman (at Laventie) be considered in connection with Major Mannock please?" At last, the train of events that Eyles had first put in place in 1919 was given fresh impetus. Maybe answers to questions he had asked for so long might now be forthcoming.

At this point it is essential to examine where La Pierre au Beurre lay. Or rather where the German army and, later, the Imperial War Graves Commission evidently **thought** it lay. Herein lay the most important key to this whole conundrum. Clearly, the German army believed La Pierre au Buerre to be the name of a settlement or hamlet – or at least some fixed and tangible geographical location from where they had then measured a point 300 metres to its north-west as Mannock's burial place. The British trench maps show that the wording 'La Pierre au Beurre' lies adjacent to a small cluster of houses and, not unreasonably, this led the commission to conclude that these buildings were La Pierre au Beurre. Not so. The positioning of the wording on the map is purely coincidental, and La Pierre au Beurre is actually just an area of land a mile or so to the north of La Bassée Canal and to the south of Calonne-sur-la-Lys. The trap the Germans had fallen into, as would the commission later, was a complete failure to realise that La Pierre au Beurre was not a fixed geographical location. Consequently, it would never have been possible to plot a 'fixed' location (ie a point 300 metres to its north-west) from such a loosely defined geographical area anyway. The Germans, therefore, had also wrongly believed La Pierre au Beurre to be a fixed point just as the British did later. Had the commission sourced a German trench map, rather than just *assumed* (perhaps not unreasonably!) that to the Germans La Pierre au Buerre was in exactly the same place as it was to them, then confusion might well have been avoided. In all probability Mick Mannock would now have a known grave and all these years of uncertainty and debate could have been avoided.

Indeed, the German trench map (at a slightly different scale) also has the legend 'La Pierre au Beurre' but, very significantly, this is printed slightly to the east of where it had appeared on the British equivalent. Coincidentally, the inscription on the German map was also positioned adjacent to another group of buildings, but this time yet further off to the east. Without a doubt the Germans (who had only occupied the sector for a short while) must have believed these buildings to be La Pierre au Beurre. Measure 300 yards north-west of here and one reaches, almost *exactly*, the position where the unknown aviator had been found; and it was also '…on the road to Pacault' just where the Germans had described his burial!

And so the misunderstanding as to where and what La Pierre au Beure actually was was simply perpetuated. As they tried to unravel the mystery, so the commission deepened it through their failure to spot this geographical anomaly. And yet, time and again, they came so tantalizingly close to affording Mannock a marked grave. However, had they but realized it the position where the commission had assumed the Germans had originally buried Major Mannock would have been improbable anyway because that location was situated, quite literally, in the middle of no man's land and past impenetrable entanglements of defensive German barbed wire. Clearly, the field grave simply could not have been there or anywhere near that position!

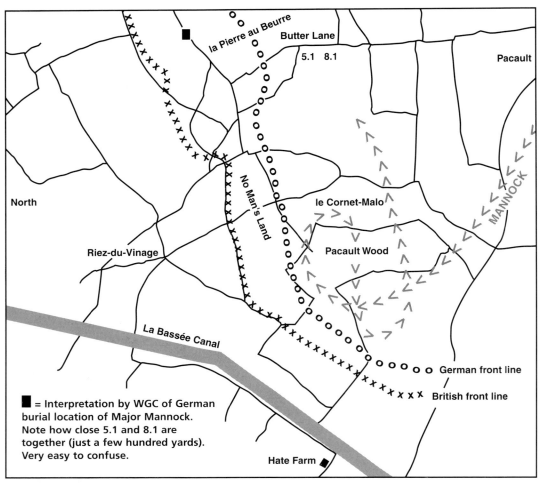

Map giving principal locations in respect of the crash of Mannock's aircraft and the reported field grave location.

In a memo of June 1924 another commission officer concludes, inter alia, that: "The unknown aviator in Laventie Cemetery from Butter Lane *is the only unknown that can be considered*. [author's italics and underlining] Had the location given by the Germans been 300 metres N. EAST of La Pierre au Beure then ….provisional identification….would probably have been justified, but as this discrepancy arises regarding the location then any cross action becomes rather difficult. Action please?"

With the case passed up the chain of command we subsequently find another officer writing a note to the registrar of the commission with some very definitive statements. First, he comments that: "I know of no other Air Force casualties in this area." Next; "The location….confirmed by Berlin is obviously incorrect. North East of Pierre au Beure is meant, and not North West." The second statement was clearly his attempt to make sense of the reported German location and explain away this puzzling discrepancy. From this point the file progresses rapidly to a blow-by-blow account of the facts unravelled thus far and finally goes on to state:

"In the circumstances it is suggested that the case be connected with Major Mannock and a provisional cross over Grave 12, Row F, Plot 3 in Laventie Military Cemetery (now marked Unknown British Airman) be erected. Is this justified please?"

The reply was unequivocal and seemingly final. "I think the case is not quite strong enough. He must be missing."

When Major Edwin Gibson compiled his 1980s report for the Commonwealth War Graves Commission the case was undoubtedly a convincing one. It was, however, still made without the benefit of any reference to German trench maps of the period but when the case was again picked up by the author a detailed submission, including all relevant maps and original documentation available to him at that time, was submitted to the commission and Ministry of Defence. The outcome was the afore-mentioned detailed thirteen-page report from the RAF Air Historical Branch (AHB) which concluded that the submission be rejected stating that "…the elements of doubt are too significant to ignore". Unfortunately, however, the MOD did not look at this submission with a view to considering the grave to be marked with a headstone inscribed 'Believed to Be'. Such inscriptions on CWGC headstones can be made where the evidence is strong but not absolute and would look for a test based around preponderance of evidence rather than 'beyond reasonable doubt'. However, what the AHB report did throw up was information that the author feels might *strengthen* the case rather than weaken it. However, it was information that seems to have been overlooked during AHB's assessment.

The report drew attention to and used information contained within the daily intelligence summary papers of the British 12th Infantry Brigade, which are to be found at the National Archives, Kew (under WO 95/1504). This source had not previously been accessed by the author or Norman Franks (co-author of *Mannock VC*) and thus an opportunity to review this document was taken at an early date after AHB had submitted their report. Significantly, the documents in WO 95/1504 place an approximate location for the Mannock crash just to the north of Pacault Wood. At twelve noon that day it is noted that Lt Garner and three other ranks of the 2nd Essex Regiment set out on patrol from the lines north of La Bassée Canal "to observe the enemy". The patrol worked north for about 300 yards from the lines and encountered an enemy wiring party and a party"…who appeared to be salvaging aeroplane debris". What is especially interesting is that the intelligence summary goes on to note that German soldiers (and possibly this same salvage party) were observed returning from the area of the crashed aeroplane until sight of them was eventually lost close to some buildings. Significantly, where these soldiers were lost to sight is almost *exactly* adjacent to the position where the field grave and aeroplane wreckage were later found.

It is not unreasonable to conclude that the party of Germans returned from the crash site with wreckage of Mannock's aeroplane and with his body. Further, it seems very unlikely indeed that they would have buried him in the exposed position of the crash but would have been much more likely to have returned with his body to the distant cover of the buildings. Whatever the facts it is certainly an interesting coincidence that the German party returning from the crash site are lost to the view of the British at almost the exact same spot where an airman's field grave and wreckage are subsequently found. The significance of this is not noted in the Air Historical Branch report; indeed, it is entirely overlooked and ignored.

The complexities of this case are significant and unravelling and detailing all of the arguments and counter-arguments within the context of this chapter are quite impossible. However, suffice to say that a response to that AHB report has now been submitted by the author requesting that the matter be looked at again. This is on the basis that some important evidence was missed, that some of AHB's counter-arguments were flawed and that other important facts had been misinterpreted or misrepresented. At the time of going to press with this book it is true to say that Jim Eyles's campaign, begun in 1919, had not necessarily been brought to a close by the January 2009 report on the Mannock case from the Air Historical Branch.

Relatives of Mannock have long believed that the Laventie burial is that of their illustrious ancestor. Here, his great-nephew Peter Burden lays a wreath on the grave during the 1989 remembrance week.

CHAPTER 2

"A Most Regrettable and Disturbing Incident…"

A N ISOLATED COMMONWEALTH WAR Graves Commission headstone to an unknown airman of the 1939-1945 war at Åndalsnes Cemetery in Norway hides not only his identity but the unfortunate story that most likely lies behind his death. It is a story that also remains hidden behind the captions to a series of British official photographs of a RAF Hudson aircraft that was badly shot-up by anti-aircraft fire over Norway in April 1940 and getting to the truth of a certain economy of facts that lie behind those photographic captions helps unravel the identity of the Åndalsnes grave.

Operation Primrose was the British codename for landings at Ålesund that were intended to secure ground to the south of Trondheim in the desperate situation that existed in Norway during April 1940, and it was on the 16th of that month that a mixed force of Royal Marines and Royal Navy personnel set sail from Invergordon in a hastily assembled group of four sloops; HMS *Black Swan*, HMS *Auckland*, HMS *Bittern* and HMS *Flamingo*. Their task was to seize and occupy the town of Åndalsnes and to take control of the vital rail head. Further, a force of four-inch guns were to be landed at Ålesund. So hasty had been the preparations that the force commander, Lt Col H W Simpson (Royal Marines) noted in his official report:

> "…The serious disadvantage of such hurried embarkation was that stores had to be embarked as they arrived, and it was not possible to embark in any pre-arranged or useful order, ie the first required to be the last embarked. When it became apparent that stowage was not possible for everything, certain essential equipment such as searchlights, generators and some HA ammunition had to be left behind."

As if that was not bad enough the weather reports were more than unfavourable and it was also noted that "no maps were available" of the town they were ordered to seize. It was not exactly an ideal situation. The worrying knowledge that the Luftwaffe was operationally very active in Norway and that no adequate RAF air cover could be provided presented an overall gloomy prospect for the operation named after the flower that gave the promise of spring. Primrose had been perhaps an over-optimistic name for a hopeless military venture.

Given the pressing demands upon the RAF elsewhere in Norway, and the lack of any available long-range aircraft or fighters to cover Primrose from the British Isles, thought was given as to what air assets *could* be provided to give at least some measure of cover. Ultimately, there was really only one possibility; Lockheed Hudsons.

Based at RAF Leuchars, 224 Squadron had primarily been engaged upon patrols over the North Sea to search for German ships since the outbreak of war but their range also allowed for anti-shipping operations off Norway after the German invasion. It was the available range of the Hudson that also made it suited (if not suitable!) to fly in support of Operation Primrose and on 23 April a battle flight of three Hudsons was despatched to RAF Wick where they were re-fuelled and armed for the long flight across the North Sea to Åndalsnes.

The forces of Primrose had been ashore since at least 18 April and, during that time, had already come under German air attack. However, the reality was that sending a force of three Hudsons over the town was nothing more than a rather impotent show of force. Indeed, the operations record book for RAF Leuchars accurately described it as a "demonstration". Nothing could really be achieved by the three Hudsons except, perhaps, to bolster flagging morale on the ground to show that the RAF were present. Unfortunately, it was an ill-conceived plan that was to have unfortunate consequences. Again, Lt Col Simpson takes up the story in his report:

"On 23 April occurred a most regrettable and disturbing incident.

"At about 11.00 hours I had met the Air Staff Officers at conference and had been informed that no British planes could be expected for at least 48 hours. Some little while afterwards I received a signal from HMS *Curacoa* saying 'Battle flight expected 16.00'. I discussed this with my adjutant and asked for a check from my own signal station. Lt Col Clarke, the War Office Liaison Officer, who was also at my HQ, also saw the signal which was interpreted to mean that we were being warned of enemy action at about 16.00. At about 16.05 three planes appeared and one, if not two, were shot down by either ships or shore anti-aircraft guns. As I did not see the actual shooting my evidence is only hearsay, but as the navigator and wireless operator of one of the planes who escaped by parachute were interviewed by me both said that ships guns opened fire on them. This was confirmed later by HMS *Curacoa*.

"At about 16.15 I received a visual signal from HMS *Curacoa* saying that the planes were friendly. I thereupon signalled to HMS *Curacoa* saying that the only signal I had received was the one quoted above and that I had been given no warning of the expected arrival of friendly machines.

"It then transpired through further signals that two signals had been made from the UK stating that a Hudson battle flight was leaving Wick and would arrive at about 15.30. HMS *Curacoa* informed me that the shortened signal 'Battle flight expected 16.00' was sent to me in that form '…to save time'. I afterwards learned that aircraft recognition signals were in existence, but these had never been transmitted to Primrose nor was I able to discover whether HMS *Curacoa* knew of these.

"The danger of sending a friendly flight into a battle area where no British machines had yet been seen, without the most careful co-ordination and planning, could not have been more fatally illustrated particularly when, seen in the distance, the planes sent were not noticeably dissimilar from those used by the enemy."

Quite what, exactly, had gone wrong is difficult to determine but it does seem that a combination of breakdowns in communications, misunder-standing and confusion had all played their part and, not least of all, faulty aircraft recognition. Clearly, we know that HMS *Curacoa* had expected what she knew to be a friendly battle flight at around 15.30 – notwithstanding the fact that the signal she sent to other elements of Primrose had been somewhat ambiguous and may have been interpreted to mean that the

Hudson N7264 being prepared for a flight.

aircraft expected at some time around 15.30 would be hostile. All the same, and despite *Curacoa* expecting friendly aircraft, it was her guns that opened fire on the Hudson aircraft, shooting one down and badly damaging another. There can be little doubt, and as Lt Col Simpson had intimated in his report, that the Hudsons were mistaken for Dornier 17 aircraft – their twin rudders, two radial engines, glazed noses and close approximation in size making the mis-identification quite understandable for edgy gunners little practiced in the finer arts of aircraft recognition. On board the Hudsons the hapless aircrew were perhaps a little less understanding of the navy's failure to recognise them.

The three aircraft that had departed Wick earlier that afternoon were piloted by Plt Off H O'Neill, Plt Of H G Webb and Sgt A James.

On board N7264 (QX-Q) was the pilot, Plt Off Hugh O'Neill, his co-pilot Plt Off Talbot Rothwell and AC Court and LAC McGhie. Hugh O'Neill would later write his own account of events over Åndalsnes:

"I had Plt Off T N C Rothwell as my co-pilot that day. He was a man of wry humour as he demonstrated post-war when he became the script writer for the Carry On comedy films. We were going to need a sense of humour!

"We made our landfall as planned at the entrance to Moldefjord at about a thousand feet, moved into line astern for our passage up into Romsdalsfjord and began to lose height. A naval vessel of some sort was anchored at the entrance to Moldefjord and she released a plume of smoke at our appearance – probably a warning blast on the hooter to warn those further up the fjord. Cloud cover in Romsdalsfjord had settled to below a thousand feet so that the sides of the fjord rose sheer into the cloud base. It had not been possible to determine beforehand exactly what we would do over Åndalsnes; indeed, we really did not know what to expect. As we were supposed to be fighters I wondered if the soldiers might appreciate some pansy formation flying and perhaps a noisy 'show the flag' type beat up. As it was, there seemed little room for manoeuvre and so I decided to run the formation in line astern up the north side of the fjord, make a fairly tight turn over Åndalsnes and then withdraw down the south side before making a second and possibly more runs. After that we would see how things developed.

"The anti-aircraft ship *Curacoa* lay alongside the fjord bank some distance from the town, so we took the usual precautions with a Verey pistol, Aldis lamp and by yo-yoing the undercarriage. There was no time for St Luke. Hardly had we arrived abreast of the ship and just short of the harbour in order to start our formation turn, when we received a shower of high explosive from both the ship and the guns on the jetty. Number two was immediately shot down into the fjord. Plt Off A B J Pearson was the sole survivor (*sic*) having made a miraculous parachute descent into the water. He returned to Leuchars some time later, wrapped in a naval blanket. I, on the other hand, found myself driving on one engine, full of holes and smoke and without room to turn. Rothwell appeared to regard the whole affair as a huge joke and we were both inclined to agree that our reception had been a little ungracious. We also agreed that our only course of action, without further delay, was to move forwards and upwards. There was a swift clipping on of seat-type parachutes and I pointed the aeroplane up into the cloud at the top end of the fjord muttering a quick prayer to St Christopher.

"Hurrah for the Wright Cyclone engine! Thumbs down for the propeller, though, which would only be put into positive coarse pitch. Up we went and broke cloud at about 4,000ft. A series of sharp-looking peaks stuck up out of the cloud all around us and so we must have sailed up some sort of groove. At any rate, we judged ourselves to have been quite lucky and set about the return journey deciding to make for the rigours of Wick. Halfway back across the North Sea and Sgt A James came alongside in the number three aircraft of the formation and I was delighted to see that he had extricated himself from the events in the fjord. He had a close look at our damage and reported by Aldis lamp. Although there were a number of sizeable holes, and plenty of oil and fuel leaks, the aeroplane seemed quite happy to fly manually straight and level. The auto-pilot was unable to cope with the stick forces needed to keep the starboard wing up. Rothwell and I chatted about landing tactics over coffee and we decided to approach without flap, ejecting the cockpit hatch as we crossed the hedge. This we did, after checking the undercarriage in the air. Finally, the aircraft settled on two burst tyres. I lowered the flaps as we lost speed on the ground and only one side came down – so we raised our glasses to what had been a sensible decision!

"Some time afterwards I just happened to run into the major of marines from the *Curacoa* in the Alexandria Union Club and so I was able to have a quiet word in his ear about aircraft recognition."

The safe passage back across the North Sea and landing of Hudson N7264 was little short of miraculous and it was an event that captured the attention of an official press photographer who took pictures of the shot-up Hudson and its lucky crew and also took close-up images of the damage it sustained. Within days the photographs were appearing in newspapers and magazines world-wide under the heading 'Lame Duck Gets Home!' The caption details were, to say the least, somewhat light on the detail stating "…shells pierced both wings and shrapnel spattered the fuselage, starboard engine and rudders and punctured the right tyre. A petrol tank was holed and many gallons of spirit were lost and

A group of photographs that hide a story of 'friendly fire' and of a missing RAF airman. One of the aircraft in the Åndalsnes episode was N7264, QX-Q, piloted by Plt Off Hugh O'Neill with his crew of Plt Off Talbot Rothwell, AC Court and LAC McGhie. Lucky to escape after being hit by Royal Navy anti-aircraft fire, the Hudson and its uninjured crew limped back across the North Sea and were later photographed as the crew posed to show off the damage. Wartime publication of these photos did not give away that this was a friendly-fire episode, merely stating that the Hudson had 'received direct hits from anti-aircraft guns when on reconnaissance over Norway'. Unluckier than O'Neill and his crew were those on board Hudson N7249 which was also hit by RN gun fire and brought down.

yet in spite of all these disabilities the machine was piloted home safely to her base on one engine but with her crew unhurt." Essentially, of course, this was factually correct although the official caption naturally failed to mention exactly *who* had put the shell holes in one very lucky Hudson!

Of the crew from the aircraft lost that day (Hudson N7249) only its pilot Plt Off Hector Garmen Webb lost his life. Plt Off A B J Pearson was rescued unharmed, as were the two other airmen or NCO aircrew on board. Unfortunately, the names of these two men are not recorded. The Hudson crashed at Toklegjerdet on the northern shore of Romsdalsfjord, and it was here in September 2004 that a Browning .303 machine gun was uncovered during construction work. Of Hector Webb, however, there officially remains no trace although there is certainly strong cause to link him to the grave of an unknown RAF airman in Åndalsnes cemetery. No other RAF casualty is known in this immediate area, and since Webb is still 'missing' with his name recorded on Panel 10 of the Runnymede Memorial it is very likely that this is his grave. Oddly, Webb's name does not appear in the published registers of the names recorded by the CWGC at Runnymede although it certainly appears on the memorial. It is also recorded on the war memorial at Ashford School, Kent, where Webb was educated.

23 April 1940 was a day of mixed fortunes for the Hudsons of 224 Squadron over Åndalsnes during the battle flight operation. Hugh O'Neill's crew knew they had had a most remarkable escape and can only have been reflecting ruefully on their good luck and the sad loss of a colleague when they jauntily stood in a casual and seemingly un-concerned pose for the photographer in front of their battered Q-Queenie. For Hector Webb, however, there is no marked grave and an absence from the published CWGC registers – an unfortunate omission.

Webb had been bravely doing his duty, and was called on to carry out a hazardous round-trip across the North Sea to a hostile enemy area. It was doubly unfortunate that he was killed in a so-called friendly-fire episode. That the grave at Åndalsnes is Webb's is beyond much doubt. However, there is insufficient evidence (aside from that which is circumstantial) to link Webb to the grave and the prospects of ever proving so are slim. As we shall see, there are very often graves to unidentified airmen where strong but inconclusive evidence points to a particular casualty. And there are also known crash locations of casualties for whom there are no known graves.

Bringing Bertie Home

SHORTLY BEFORE ONE O'CLOCK on the afternoon of Friday 24 April 1942, nine-year-old James Cleeland was walking with his parents up towards the town gates of the ancient settlement of Winchelsea in East Sussex. Young James, a keen aircraft spotter, detected the sound of a Spitfire flying overhead but its extreme altitude prevented any visual confirmation of his identification. Three quarters of a mile away across the Brede Valley, farmer's son Robert Mair was having lunch in a barn at Roadend Farm, Udimore. He too heard the Spitfire, but had taken little notice; the sight and sound of aircraft had by now become a routine event and it was probably an unusual day that saw no Spitfires overhead.

Suddenly, however, James Cleeland and Robert Mair took a much keener interest in the lone Spitfire as its engine note increased in pitch, getting louder and louder as it entered what would be a roaring all-out terminal dive. In the first few seconds the engine seemed to falter and splutter a few times before finally picking up and gathering a fearsome momentum. The sound of the screaming Merlin engine was a terrifying noise for those on the ground below who waited apprehensively for an inevitable climax to what was obviously a cataclysmic dive.

On Friday 24 April 1942 a photo-reconnaissance Spitfire PR IV of 140 Squadron, X4784, plunged vertically to earth at Winchelsea, East Sussex, taking its pilot, Plt Off C B Barber, with it. This is X4784 in its unusual and distinctive overall 'pink' camouflage paint scheme.

Many in Winchelsea and nearby Rye, fearing some awful catastrophe, hurriedly took cover although young Robert Mair, oblivious to any danger, rushed from the barn to see what the cause of all the noise might be. Searching skyward he saw nothing, although just at that moment there was a horrifying thud and his attention was drawn towards one of the fields in the valley below the farm. The silence after the horrendous din of the tortured Merlin was awesome; the terrible scream having stopped abruptly with the sickening thud of a crash. Across the fields Robert could see a huge pillar of water, smoke, mud, steam and debris plume skywards in a gigantic column that rose from one of the drainage ditches criss-crossing the Brede river valley.

Unlike young Robert, James Cleeland had briefly glimpsed the aircraft in its headlong plummet, having finally caught sight of it as it neared the ground in a flat-out vertical dive as the sun glinted from its cockpit Perspex and its light-coloured paintwork. A short while after it had impacted a fine spray fell gently across the western outskirts of Winchelsea; water caught and blown by the wind from the plume Robert Mair had seen thrown up by the impact. To young James those terrifying and momentous few seconds left a lasting and vivid impression; the sight, the sound, and then the feeling of the mist of water falling across James and his parents a few hundred yards away was a memory which never left him. In 1986 he said that it was something which he still thought of frequently. And he was not the only person whose thoughts had often turned to the events of that day.

Earlier that morning, Spitfire X4784 of 140 Squadron had taken off from RAF Benson, Oxfordshire, to conduct a high altitude photographic sortie of the French coastline between Calais and Boulogne, X4784 being a Spitfire PR IV photo-reconnaissance variant of the Mark V fighter. Basically, the airframe was an up-rated Spitfire Mk II fitted with a Merlin 65, its armament stripped out and extra 66-gallon tanks fitted in the wing leading edges. Under the wing was mounted an F.8 camera, whilst a double bank of F.24 cameras were housed in the fuselage behind the pilot's seat armour – the bank of photographic equipment able to capture oblique and vertical images. Almost incongruously perhaps, this particular Spitfire was painted overall a delicate shade of pink, an unlikely choice of colour for this sleek warplane. Pink, however, had been found to be a useful camouflage colour for use on high altitude work and against a cloud background. Seated at the controls of this rather pretty Spitfire was a young Yorkshireman, 22-year-old Plt Off Charles Bertram Barber. Whilst missions to Calais by PR Spitfire pilots were considered to be 'milk runs' and relatively safe, it was an operation from which Charles would not return.

Exactly what happened to Plt Off Barber in his final moments will never be known for sure, although the most likely explanation is that he fell victim to malfunction of his oxygen equipment, a common enough cause for the loss of RAF aircraft during the 1939-45 war. Barber's operating height would have certainly required oxygen, and any interruption or starvation of supply would have had dire and immediate effects. Presupposing that he had time even to realise what the problem was, he could well have been too weak or uncoordinated to open the canopy for baling out and considerable effort may well have been needed to push the stick forward for a deliberate dive to the less rarefied lower air. What probably happened is that he passed out and slumped forward over the stick, pushing X4784 into an all-out vertical dive with its throttles wide open. Had Plt Off Barber regained consciousness at a lower altitude it is quite possible that he would have been completely

A group of pilots and officers of 140 Squadron, photographed in 1942. Twenty-two-year-old Charles Bertram 'Bertie' Barber is in the back row, second from right.

unable to pull his aircraft out of its dive. In fact, it is more than likely he would have mercifully remained unconscious throughout the headlong plunge of his Spitfire.

The anoxia theory is not exactly borne out by the Air Ministry Form 78 for X4784 (the aircraft record card), however, which shows the cause of loss as a 'flying battle occurrence'. This, though, is not substantiated by surviving German records which do not show any Luftwaffe combats or claims which could account for the loss of Pilot Officer Barber and nor do witnesses on the ground speak of hearing machine-gun or cannon fire. It is, of course, just possible that Barber was hit by flak over the French coast and was returning home wounded when he finally passed out. The most likely explanation for the flying battle occurrence entry on the record card, though, is that it was automatically assumed that the cause of loss was through engagement with the enemy because it was an operational flight. However, its impact with the ground, and the depth at which the wreckage was embedded, prevented any examination of the aeroplane or its pilot to establish the exact cause.

The point where the aircraft had crashed was on the south bank of a drainage channel called New House Petty Sewer in Dumb Woman's Lane and about 800 yards west of Winchelsea Station. Although close to the town the crash was actually in the parish of Udimore, and police constables from both Winchelsea and Udimore attended the incident although it was left to Police Inspector Thomas Amos of Rye to file the official report. This document times the crash at 1255 hours, but Inspector Amos could only speculate as to the type of aeroplane involved, stating: 'Believed Spitfire Fighter'.

A few hundred yards to the south-west of the crash a River Authority drag-line dredger was at work clearing ditches when the Spitfire hit the ground and under the direction of the police, and the 16th Battalion Durham Light Infantry who were on the scene, the shaken drag-line operator was ordered to track his machine across to the crash site and commence an attempt to uncover the wreckage and pilot's body. The work was hopeless.

CRASHED AIRCRAFT REPORT

DIV. REF. _C/17/42_   H.Q. REF. _RA7 115/5/42_

Parish ___Udimore___   Date ___24 April. 1942___   Time ___12.55 hrs.___

Exact Location ___On bank of dyke in marsh land 800 yards west of Winchelsea___
Map Reference ___330.368___   Railway Station.

British, Allied or Enemy ___British___   Type ___Believed Spitfire Fighter.___

Condition of Machine ___Totally wrecked and buried.___

CREW

Killed _____ Seriously injured _____ Slightly injured _____ Unhurt _____

Not traced ___1 (presumed)___

Disposal of crew ___Pilot apparently buried in wreckage. Awaiting arrival___
___of R.A.F. Crash Party.___

Which R.A.F Station notified ___Hawkinge___

Time and Date of notification ___13.50 hrs___

I. P.—20183

Detail of Occurrence

A British aircraft, believed to be a Spitfire Fighter, was seen to crash from a fairly great height, at a fast speed, into to ground. The aircraft was completly buried. Efforts were made to remove part of the earth, but the water from the adjoining dyke prevented any succesful result. No crew were seen to bale out of the machine.

Military, Fire Service and Civil Police attended. Military Guard provided by 16 Bn. D.L.I.

All services, excepting military guard, withdrew at 15.30 hrs.

EAST SUSSEX CONSTABULARY
25 APR 1942

Time and Date information received by Police   1300 hrs. 24 April. 1942.

Signature ___Thomas Amos.___   Insp.

The East Sussex Police report detailing the occurrence of 'Bertie' Barber's Spitfire crash at Winchelsea on 24 April 1942.

The point of impact had clearly been on the bank of the twenty-foot-wide ditch rather than in the water itself, and although digging operations were carried out down to a depth of some twelve to fifteen feet, the excavation flooded and no wreckage was uncovered. In fact, they were a long way from being able to reach it.

Young James Cleeland, curious to see what had happened, managed to make his way to the crash site but all he could see were piles of mud and no trace of the aeroplane that had

The visit of a Post Office telegram boy was dreaded by families of British service personnel. During World War Two it was the first notification that a loved one was killed, injured or missing. This is the telegram informing Mr & Mrs Barber that their son was missing as the result of air operations. Initially, the exact circumstances of 'Bertie's' fate were unclear.

once been. Robert Mair, however, remembers a few shreds of evidence lying on the river bank with the most substantial being two undercarriage assemblies. At 3.30 that afternoon the work was halted, the site being left under guard by the Durhams. Later, a team from 49 Maintenance Unit, RAF Faygate, arrived to inspect the site but they too realised the task was beyond them and merely collected a few remaining pieces of surface wreckage and departed. Amongst the items collected were the remains of at least one of the wing-mounted F.8 cameras; evidence enough to link the disappearance of Pilot Officer Barber with this crash.

It was some while, however, before the authorities established that this particular crash was X4784, and on the afternoon of Saturday 25 April the CO of 140 Squadron, Squadron Leader Mesurier, was only able to tell Charles Barber's father by way of a telegram that his son was missing. In a follow-up letter to Mr and Mrs Barber the next day, Mesurier still had no further details as to Charles Barber's fate and even held out hope that he might be a prisoner-of-war. That sentiment was echoed by the Air Ministry who, in a letter dated 30 April, stressed that he was only missing as a result of air operations and that this did not necessarily mean he was killed or wounded. For some odd reason it took the Air Ministry a further five months to confirm to the anxious Barber family that Charles's aeroplane had been found in a tributary of the River Brede at Udimore, although this had certainly been deduced shortly after the crash. Furthermore, the letter went on to tell the distraught parents that their son's body had not been recovered owing to the great depth at which the aircraft was embedded. Just to prolong the agony, they were informed that six months would have to elapse before death could be presumed.

Unwilling to accept that the recovery of his son's body was impracticable Mr Barber questioned the Air Ministry's decision not to proceed with any salvage operation. As soon as the six-month period stipulated by the Air Ministry had elapsed, Mr Barber took up the case with his Member of Parliament, The Right Hon. T. Williams, who was also Minister for Agriculture and Fisheries, urging that something should be done to recover Charles's body. Taking up the matter on his behalf, Williams wrote to the then Parliamentary Under Secretary of State for Air, Captain Harold Balfour, and received a reply on 26 November 1942 which held out no hope of any action being taken. It read as follows:

When it became clear where Plt Off Barber's Spitfire had crashed, and that he was still entombed in the cockpit, his parents pressed to have the wreck recovered in order that they could properly bury their son. This was the disheartening letter from Lord Balfour at the Air Ministry stating that recovery would be impossible. Mr and Mrs Barber maintained pressure on the Ministry of Defence to recover the wreck right up to the 1960s, but were consistently told it was both impossible and impracticable. Later, his brother Raymond Barber took up the campaign to have his sibling re-covered and decently buried.

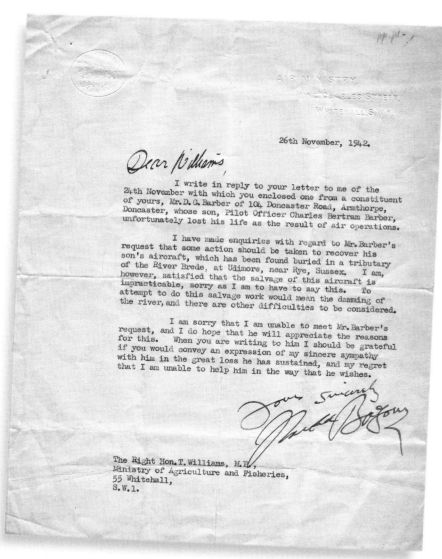

As events have since proved, the Air Ministry's view in 1942 that recovery was impossible had probably been a fair assessment given the ground conditions on site and the rudimentary machinery available at that time. The Barber family's rationale for pursuing their request to make salvage attempts was simply that they could not believe that the Air Ministry could say this work was impossible when aside from one almost half-hearted attempt minutes after the crash no other effort had been made to ascertain that the task was indeed 'impracticable'. Once the winter of 1942-43 was over Mr Barber again embarked on his campaign to have his son's body recovered and decently buried.

In February 1943, the Air Ministry, responding to a request from him, took the unusual step of sending the family an ordnance survey map of the Hastings area on which they had marked the exact crash location. Wearing his Home Guard officer's uniform, Mr Barber made a lonely pilgrimage to visit the spot where his son had died, meeting up with the farmer, Mr Mair (senior) who had first-hand knowledge of the crash. Although saddened by his journey to Sussex, Mr Barber had satisfied himself that he had seen the spot but, nevertheless, still refused to accept that recovery was impossible. For the time being, however, no further requests to carry out a salvage operation were made.

With the end of the war in Europe, the

A section of the map supplied by the Air Ministry to Mr Barber indicating where the Spitfire crash site was located.

Commonwealth War Graves Commission were charged with the erection of memorials to the airmen of the British Commonwealth and Empire who had no known grave. The memorial covering those who had lost their lives in the United Kingdom and within Europe was located above the Thames at Runnymede and bears 20,547 names: amongst them, on Panel 68, that of Plt Off Barber. In the register of names he is shown as: 'BARBER, Pilot Officer Charles Bertram, 47734, R.A.F. (V.R.) 140 Squadron, 24th April, 1942. Age 22, Son of D. George Barber and Edith Barber of Armthorpe, Yorkshire'. On 17 October 1953, HM Queen Elizabeth unveiled the memorial in a dedication ceremony attended by many relatives of those commemorated there. The still-grieving parents of Charles Barber were not among them. Instead, they chose to hold a small memorial service on the site of the crash, officiated over by the Rector of Udimore. Both were still unable to accept that Charles could not be properly buried, and the line taken by George Barber in 1942 was followed by the family right up until the deaths of both parents during the 1970s.

Charles came from a family of four, having two sisters Molly and Dorothy, and a brother, Raymond. A native of Yorkshire, Charles was brought up in the Doncaster area and lived in the family home at Armthorpe where he attended nearby Thorne Grammar school. In 1935 he expressed an interest to join the expanding Royal Air Force as a boy aircraft apprentice, and on 5 November 1935 he sat the qualifying examination and in 1936 joined up to commence his training at RAF Halton. At the outbreak of war, and having completed his trade apprenticeship, he applied for aircrew selection and was accepted as an officer candidate for pilot training, being sent to No. 21 Elementary Flying Training School, RAF Booker.

From here he graduated to the Flying Training School at Hullavington. Unfortunately, his training took a setback when he suffered a non-flying accident resulting in a broken leg although he made a speedy recovery to eventually earn his wings during the early months of 1941. Writing home he excitedly told his parents of the great thrill he had had when flying a Hurricane for the very first time. His eagerness to fly fighters caused him to persist in trying to get a posting to an operational squadron, and it was a dream-come-true when he was posted to 140 Squadron, an army co-operation squadron, based at Benson, Oxfordshire, and flying Spitfires.

On the morning of Friday, 24 April 1942, Charles Barber was detailed for a flight to the Pas de Calais area and took off from Benson in Spitfire X4784 at 1030 hours with full fuel tanks and cameras loaded and set. From here on nothing further is known of Barber's last mission, but in view of the duration of the flight up until the crash near Winchelsea it must be concluded that he had flown his sortie over France and was on the return leg home. What happened after X4784 had been lost to the sight of ground crews at Benson and right up until it vanished into the ground before an astonished James Cleeland and Robert Mair will always remain a mystery.

Interest in aviation archaeology in the south-east corner of England had, for many years, been rife since the early 1970s and it was to be expected that requests to excavate the crash site would have been made to the landowner, now Mr Robert Mair, who was the young man having his lunch at Rodend Farm when the aircraft had crashed. In about 1970 the Brenzett Aeronautical Museum approached Robert Mair but were turned down flat on the not-unreasonable grounds that the wishes of the next of kin were unknown to both the Brenzett team and the landowner. Furthermore, the task of recovery was judged to be very difficult if not well nigh impossible. There the matter rested until the author set about trying to contact the Barber family.

In view of the fact that Charles Barber had no marked grave it was felt that it would be an appropriate gesture to have a memorial erected on or near the crash site, and this was a scheme to which Robert Mair gave his enthusiastic support. Along these lines, an appeal was therefore placed in the *Doncaster Star* on 27 November 1985 asking for members of the Barber family to get in touch with the author. The response was immediate. His brother Raymond and sister Dorothy, together with various cousins, immediately made contact. Charles Barbers's closest next of kin was his brother, Raymond, and whilst he welcomed the interest and the plans for a memorial he revealed an amazing saga dating back to 1942, since when the family had persevered with their efforts to have Charles's body recovered. As recently as 18 October 1968 the then Minister of Defence, Merlyn Rees, had written to Raymond re-stating the previous official view that a recovery was impossible. Whilst the 1942 decision could, no doubt, be vindicated, the 1968 decision must be called into serious question given the existence of more sophisticated equipment and more freely available manpower. According to Merlyn Rees, there was little hope of finding more facts and, whilst the possibility of salvaging the buried part of the machine had been considered, he said that this was impracticable and the aircraft remained struck off as a total loss. This letter, said Raymond Barber, ".......destroyed the last remaining flicker of hope that we as a family had to lay our Bertie to rest, properly, back home."

On 6 February 1986 Raymond Barber travelled down from his Yorkshire home to visit the crash site. During the war he had not had the opportunity to do so as he was himself in the forces, serving with the 8th Army in North Africa. He had also been unable to attend the post-war memorial service at the crash site. His visit, therefore, was an emotional one. As he surveyed the snow-covered crash scene and the wooden shuttering put on the bank to stabilise the soil after the crash, he satisfied himself that he would continue his efforts to have his brother recovered. As he walked away from the scene with Robert Mair he muttered quietly: "Cheerio Bertie, we'll try not to leave you there for much longer."

Robert Mair, whilst not relishing the disturbance to his field and river bank that an excavation of the spot would bring, had nevertheless readily acceded to Raymond's request for an attempt to be made. Consequently, this was accepted as a project under the auspices of the Tangmere Military Aviation Museum and led by the author, one of the museum's founders and its curator. Without delay a site meeting was held with the Southern Water Authority's river board engineer on 11 February 1986, who agreed to the excavation proceeding even though this would mean damming the river and pumping it dry before the virtual destruction of the river bank and bed at the crash site. Without any doubt the operation would be of epic proportions and cost, and with no guarantee of any successful outcome.

Coincidentally, the contact which had been made with the Barber family came at a time when Michael Mates (Conservative Member of Parliament for Hampshire East) had proposed his private member's Protection of Military Remains Bill. This bill, if it became an Act of Parliament, would make it an offence to interfere with the wrecks of military aircraft or sunken military ships unless a licence for such work had been granted by the Ministry of Defence. Introduced on 4 December 1985, the bill finally became law on 9 September 1986, having passed through all stages of parliament and been given Royal Assent on 9 July. In the light of the long-running controversy over the recovery of wartime airmen by private individuals and groups and diving on sunken Royal Navy warships, the legislation was intended to give the government tight control over all such sites and thus prevent problems arising in future over discovery of human remains or bombs. In such cases where finds of this nature were suspected, a licence would not normally be granted.

Whilst the recovery team working on the Barber project had no wish to fly in the face of published parliamentary proposals, it was clearly an option to go ahead immediately with the recovery plan – given that both the family and the landowner wished the excavation to proceed. At this time there were absolutely no legal requirements for permission to be sought from the Ministry of Defence for recovery operations, although the ministry's pre-existing 'Notes of Guidance' stated that permission *should* be sought. Given the prevailing circumstances, therefore, the recovery team wrote to the minister of defence seeking official view of a situation where a particular aircraft crash site could be positively identified, where the pilot was still missing and where the next of kin wanted recovery to take place. The response from Michael Berkeley, assistant private secretary to the minister, was set out in a letter dated 18 March 1986, in which it was stated that, in such cases, 'Licences would not unreasonably be refused'. Heartened by this positive response, the team therefore elected to apply formally for permission to recover Pilot Officer Barber's aeroplane in a letter to the Ministry of Defence on 23 March.

On 11 April, having satisfied themselves that the site under question was indeed the wreck of X4784, the MOD wrote to Charles Barber's next of kin, Raymond, asking for confirmation that he wished approval for the recovery to be given to the Tangmere Aviation Museum and for proof of his relationship to Pilot Officer Barber. Whilst satisfactory answers were speedily provided to these questions the matter thereafter appeared to get bogged down in red tape, there being no further response aside from numerous telephone conversations until a letter was received from the ministry to the recovery team dated 24 July. This merely stated that consultations relating to the case had taken longer than anticipated, but that a firm decision was expected in the 'not too distant future'. However, the ministry's representative verbally informed the author that a decision was expected "within the next few days". Unfortunately, this imminent decision was not forthcoming.

By 4 August nothing further had been heard by either the recovery team or by Raymond Barber, who was now becoming anxious for an early decision and therefore wrote to the ministry's Department S10 (Air) requesting early action. This was followed by a letter from the author on 20 August urging that the matter be concluded without any further delay. It was pointed out to the ministry that time was running out from the point of view of organising a recovery to fit in with the farmer's calendar, the river authority and rising water levels that could be expected with the onset of autumn. Of course, time was also running out if the excavation were to be completed inside the law and without the need for a licence and with the effective date of legislation on 9 September looming near.

The project to recover Plt Off Barber from his Spitfire involved damming and emptying a stretch of river and its ultimate success flew in the face of continued Ministry of Defence assertions across many years that such a recovery was impossible. Here Dick Walker and Andy Cresswell construct the dam.

By 28 August no approval had still been received and after much deliberation, the recovery team decided to go ahead, putting the necessary wheels in motion for an attempt to be made over the period 29 to 31 August. Tangmere museum stated that it was with regret that a decision to move on the recovery in the absence of official approval had had to be made, but that the team felt that they were morally obliged to do so because if they had waited until after 9 September, and the Ministry of Defence had then refused a licence, the wishes of the family would never have been carried out unless in direct contravention of the law.

In view of the location of the crash site, it was anticipated that immense difficulties would be encountered during the operation; the biggest problem being with water. The river authority, most helpful throughout the project, confirmed that they were able to control water levels to a limited extent but that in all probability it would be possible to isolate the stretch of water involved and for the pumps at the downstream pumping station to all but empty the river of its water. However, as this could not be guaranteed, it was decided to drive a steel piling dam across the river several yards upstream of the crash site and to dam off the river about 120 yards downstream where it passed through a narrow culvert under a bridge between two fields. This spot would make an ideal location to place large water pumps, lifting the water up from the isolated section of river and across to the downstream side of the bridge. Fortunately, there was little water flowing downstream, so it was not foreseen that there would be a problem with water backing up against the main dam.

From Wednesday 27 August the river authority pumping station had been working flat out to reduce the water levels, and with some measure of success. However, problems were experienced with large quantities of river weed being drawn into the water intakes and choking the pumps. More serious, though, was the problem of water seeping back into the pumped section from sluices downstream which had less than effective boards. Despite herculean efforts by the staff of the water authority the problem could not be resolved, and by the evening of Thursday, 28 August, it was clear that the water level would only be reduced by about ten or twelve inches. This, at least, was better than nothing and even these few inches represented many thousands of gallons of water over the stretch of river which had been pumped. From this point on it was entirely down to the recovery team to deal as best they could with the water problem.

The main period scheduled for damming and pumping was on Friday 29 August and by 09.00 a hired mechanical excavator was on site and working to place the steel shuttering across the stream. Once the piling had been driven into place, a polythene sheet was stretched across the 'wet' side of the dam by team member Dick Walker in his wetsuit, and an earth bank piled against the 'dry' side of the dam. With the bridge culvert closed downstream, both pumps were then put into operation, each one moving an astonishing 12,000 gallons an hour. Not surprisingly it wasn't very long before an appreciable difference in the water levels could be discerned.

Whilst pumping continued, preparations were made at the actual crash site by way of removal of topsoil and the digging of a ramp down to the anticipated excavation area on the embankment. During this operation numerous small items came to light which indicated that the actual impact point was exactly on the bank and waterline just as indicated by Mr Mair and the Sussex Police report. One major clue was the discovery of two

With the dams in place and pumping underway the crash site is prepared for excavation, supervised on the right by Robert Mair who had witnessed the crash as a young boy.

wing-mounted gun blast tubes; one just into the field from the bank and the other found nearby in the bed of the still-flooded river. Both items had been buried vertically, and their separation distance meant that each had come from different wings. Although X4784 was an unarmed aircraft it would have been jigged up and built basically as a standard fighter, and therefore the blast tubes would have been fitted although they would have remained empty. Unless the two tubes had been moved subsequent to the crash they were, therefore, an important indicator of the exact position of the buried wreckage, estimated from these two items to be on the bank with the wings forming a 45-degree angle across the embankment and into the water.

By late afternoon on 29 August the level of water had been reduced to almost a trickle but with the movement of water, the earth on the downstream side of the main dam had begun to slip on the black muddy bed of the river. If this movement continued then the stability of the dam would obviously be compromised, especially with such enormous pressure of water building up against it on the upstream side. Surplus steel shuttering left over from the dam construction was therefore hastily assembled as a retaining wall for the earth bank and was driven deep into the river bed. Fortunately, this prevented any further movement and thus saved the dam and the entire project.

Having left the river almost drained on the Friday evening, it was a bitter blow to the team to discover at the 6.30 am. start on the Saturday that the culvert dam had failed to remain watertight overnight, allowing water to flood back into the drained section from downstream. Fortunately the main dam upstream had held and remained watertight. Hastily, the leaking dam was made good and the pumps brought back into action although this hitch delayed for some time the start of digging operations.

Although every indication was that the impact point was below the bank it was obviously unwise to commence digging before first exploring the river bed with the excavator bucket. Had the team done so, and had the excavation below the bank proved fruitless, it would then have been difficult, if not impossible, to move the area of operation to the river bed from the bank itself as the excavated hole would have meant that the machine would have got itself out of reach of the centre of the river. However, with very little indication of wreckage or disturbance in the bed of the river itself, the excavation was shifted to the landward side of the original timber shuttering that had been placed along the bank line in 1942. At about ten feet or so the signs were rather more promising; small fragments of airframe, a strong smell of aviation spirit and, at that depth, some large baulks of timber which must have been placed in the hole when it was excavated in April 1942 by the river board drag-line. With renewed enthusiasm digging continued on this spot and with all excavated soil being carefully sifted for wreckage.

Very soon a considerable amount of the aircraft was being uncovered including parts of the instrument panel, one rudder pedal, the camera control box, rolls of exposed film that confirmed he had completed his mission, the tail wheel, radio equipment, head armour, the pilot's escape kit and lastly

Bogged-in! Whilst not impossible, the recovery task was certainly challenging and difficult as this image of a stranded mechanical excavator illustrates. Despite nearly having lost his machine the plant hire operator successfully retrieved his valuable equipment and manfully carried on with the work in hand.

the de Havilland propeller assembly. Evidence of human remains and uniform also came to light and were placed carefully into a specially prepared container and Sussex Police immediately notified by the team. Nothing positive, however, had come to light to identify clearly the pilot or aeroplane, save for one gold cufflink and some numbering pencilled onto a piece of the radio equipment. This read '4?84', with the digit between the number four and eight having come away with flaking paintwork. However, this could well relate to X4784, the aeroplane's serial number. Obviously more evidence would be needed if any formal and positive identification were to be made, and it was plain by late afternoon on Saturday that a considerable amount of significant wreckage was still buried. Furthermore, it seemed that not all of the remains of the pilot had yet been found and officers of Sussex Police who had been called by the team were both supportive and keen that operations should continue. Unfortunately, it was at this point that the excavator became firmly bogged down in the soft sub-soil and all efforts to free it only made matters worse. The prospects for continuing looked very bleak indeed, but despite a staggering twenty-seven-foot-deep hole not enough had yet been recovered to identify properly the aircraft or pilot.

However, with the machine bogged in on the edge of a

Amongst the items and artefacts recovered from the wrecked cockpit was this engraved cigarette case (a gift from his father) and a set of gold cufflinks. Most important, though, was the discovery of an identity disc bearing Plt Off Barber's name, rank and number. It was all that was needed for official confirmation that 'Bertie' was no longer missing.

very unstable and deep excavation, the work had to be terminated overnight by a more than anxious recovery team and excavator owner-driver. If the dams did not hold overnight then the problems would be enormous and if water flooded back now it would fill the excavation and submerge the excavator. Worse still, if the highly unstable bank supporting the machine should give way, as seemed likely, then the machine would end up almost thirty feet below ground level and under water as well. Needless to say, a sleepless night was had by one and all, although the pumps were kept running and fuelled overnight.

Fortunately, pumping out the residual water which had seeped back through the culvert ensured that the river remained drained and it was a relieved team who discovered that the excavator was still sitting high and dry on the bank the following morning although it had visibly sunk further into the glutinous grey mire. Strenuous efforts by the team, and the arrival of a caterpillar tractor, eventually freed the digger and work was re-started. However, the depth of the excavation was now beyond the reach of the digging arm and consequently yet another deeper working ramp had to be excavated in the same position. By now it was late afternoon and time was running out but with the machine now teetering on the edge of the hole at an alarming angle, digging work got underway again.

Very soon the pilot's seat armour was exposed at the bottom of the hole and, after little more than three scoops of the excavator bucket, the last remaining items of wreckage reached the surface. Careful sorting revealed a large quantity of fragmented human remains and these were taken charge of by Police Constable Wallis. The police also removed another gold cufflink and silver cigarette case engraved with the initial 'B' which had been found in the pocket of a pair of RAF trousers that were lying together with the perfectly packed and preserved parachute. Minute examination of the last three or four bucket loads of soil satisfied the recovery team and the police that all the bodily remains had now been accounted for.

These searches also revealed one particularly significant find; amongst all the black mud was one of Pilot Officer Barber's identity tags still in good condition and still quite legible. As a result of this discovery the police were fully satisfied as to the pilot's identity and informed the salvage team that the Yorkshire Police would be contacted immediately with a view to letting Raymond Barber have the news of the discovery without delay. The operation successfully over, it only remained to fill in the excavation and clear up the site, reinstate the embankment and remove the dams to re-flood the river. This work was carried out on Monday 1 September, the fourth and final day of what had been an epic operation and one that many had deemed impossible.

Raymond Barber had been formally notified at his Doncaster home on Sunday evening that his brother's body had at last been found, and he immediately telephoned the author to offer thanks and his gratitude to the team for the hard work they had carried out. Undoubtedly, the speed with which Mr Barber had been notified was unprecedented. Often the contacting of next of kin in such cases is a long delayed affair, with protracted official enquiries and checks being made beforehand and contact then normally being made by way of the nearest RAF establishment. Almost immediately, however, a serving RAF officer was assigned to the case, Flight Lieutenant Stephen Howard from nearby RAF Finningley who visited Raymond Barber every few days to keep him abreast of developments and to plan the funeral arrangements. At first it was considered that Brookwood Cemetery in Surrey would be Charles Barber's last resting place, alongside a number of fellow airmen who had been discovered in recent years. However, the family were finally adamant that they wanted him taken home and opted for interment in St Oswald's churchyard, the wartime burial ground for RAF Finningley and which literally borders the airfield.

On 3 September PC Anthony Barnard, HM Coroner's officer at Hastings, was able to announce that an inquest would not be held and on the same day released the remains to Wing Commander Bell at RAF Halton. By odd coincidence, it was at Halton that Charles Barber had joined the Royal Air Force in 1936 from his Yorkshire home fifty years before and it was from here that his remains were prepared for the final journey back home to Yorkshire and a military funeral at RAF Finningley on 15 October 1986. Had he lived, Charles Barber would perhaps have risen to high office in the Church of England into which he had been intending to take holy orders at the war's end. But, in the words of his brother Raymond: 'It was obviously not God's will that this was to be. To me I can never think of Bertie being sixty-seven, or how he might now be all these years later in 1986. In my mind he will always be twenty-two."

Whether the MOD would ultimately have granted a licence to recover Charles Barber and his Spitfire is a matter for speculation. However, immediately after the event they wrote to the author saying that they were on the point of making their decision known when the recovery went ahead. They did not, however, reveal their hand as to what that decision might have been. The view of the recovery team was that they had to proceed when they did in order to ensure that bringing Charles Barber home to his family was not thwarted by officialdom once the Protection of Military Remains Act had come into force,

D. Cert.
R.B.D.

CAUTION—It is an offence to falsify a certificate or to make or knowingly use a false certificate or a copy of a false certificate intending it to be accepted as genuine to the prejudice of any person, or to possess a certificate knowing it to be false without lawful authority.

CERTIFIED COPY   **OF AN ENTRY**
Pursuant to the Births and   **Deaths Registration Act 1953**

DEATH	Entry No. **59**

Registration district
Sub-district   HASTINGS AND ROTHER   HASTINGS AND ROTHER

Administrative area
COUNTY OF EAST SUSSEX

1. Date and place of death   *Twenty fourth April 1942 Road End Farm, Udimore*

2. Name and surname   *Charles Bertram BARBER*

3. Sex   *Male*

4. Maiden surname of woman who has married   —

5. Date and place of birth   *3rd October 1919 Doncaster, South Yorkshire*

6. Occupation and usual address   *Pilot Officer, Royal Air Force. Officers' Mess, R.A.F. Benson, Oxfordshire*

7. (a) Name and surname of informant   *Stephen James HOWARD*

(b) Qualification   *Causing the body to be buried*

(c) Usual address   *South Oak Cottage, Dams Lane, Belchford, Horncastle, Lincolnshire*

8. Cause of death   *1 a Unascertainable*

9. I certify that the particulars given by me above are true to the best of my knowledge and belief.
S. J. Howard
Signature of informant

10. Date of registration   *Fourteenth October 1986*   *On the authority of the Registrar General*

11. Signature of registrar   *K.W. Cook.*   *Registrar*

Certified to be a true copy of an entry in a register in my custody.
Registrar   *14.10.86* Date   **IX**   **401076**

Forty-four years after his death, a certificate was finally issued on the authority of HM Coroner for East Sussex, Mr Alan Craze. Unfortunately, it came too late for Charles Bertram Barber's parents who had long-since passed away never believing that their deep desire to have their son given a Christian burial would come to fruition.

notwithstanding the fact that they and Raymond Barber had consistently worked with the MOD in the run-up to eventual recovery and had thus acted within the spirit of the impending legislation and parliament's intentions. However, when interviewed for the BBC2 documentary Splendid Hearts (transmitted 23 October 1992), which looked at some of the stories of those recorded on the Runnymede Memorial, an emotional Raymond Barber revealed how an MOD official had threatened that he faced arrest and prosecution if he were to proceed regardless with any attempted recovery of his brother after the act was in place. If anything, it stiffened Ray's resolve to bring his brother home. Thankfully, the combination of efforts by a dedicated recovery team, Sussex Police, plant hire operators and the local river authority ensured the success of a project that the family had long been told was impossible.

To many it still seemed incredible that missing RAF aircrew could be found within the UK and, indeed, that they could be located and identified by private groups and individuals whilst the MOD (or that ministry's predecessors) either could not find them, were unable to find them or had said that recovery and identification was either impossible or impracticable. To an extent, part of that problem lay with a failure by the then Air Ministry to execute any kind of search within the UK for missing or unaccounted for airmen at the war's end in the manner in which such searches were officially carried out on the continental mainland of Europe.

Taken home to Yorkshire for burial, Charles Barber was buried with full military honours in the churchyard alongside the then operational RAF Finningley. All flying was stopped for the duration of the funeral, apart from a lone Spitfire of the RAF Battle of Britain Memorial Flight which flew a moving single low pass in salute over the grave as the coffin was lowered. 'Bertie' had finally come home.

CHAPTER 4

The Post-War Search

I N THE IMMEDIATE POST-WAR years it was evident that all former enemy territory in Europe, and indeed on a world-wide basis, would need to be scoured for missing RAF aircrew. This would be a search that looked for unburied remains in wrecks, tried to identify remains buried as unknown casualties or solved anomalies with existing burials where recorded names or dates made no sense when compared to RAF records. It was a mammoth undertaking, and perhaps some sense of that scale may be judged by the fact that over 40,000 RAF casualties were unaccounted for in north-west Europe by 8 May 1945. Equally, some idea of the work carried out by post-war investigations may be gained when one considers that at the end of the work by these specialist teams the number had been reduced to 20,547 casualties who remained unaccounted for. In the space of just a few years almost half of the total had been found or identified and this work was primarily carried out by RAF missing research and enquiry units, or MREUs for short. However, other units were involved, most notably 3 Base Recovery Unit (RAF) who operated in the recovery and identification role between 1945 and 1947 in France, Belgium, Netherlands and Germany. Since the work of the MREU teams has already been covered splendidly in Stuart Hadaway's excellent book *Missing Believed Killed*, it would seem appropriate, here, to look at the work of 3 BRU since their activities were certainly germane to many of the cases examined in this book.

The 3 Base Recovery Unit teams ranged out across Europe as they were tasked to undertake individual enquiry cases, or 'arisings' as they are referred to in contemporary reports. The tasks were co-ordinated centrally via the Air Ministry Casualty Branch, Dept P.4 (Cas), which had centrally administered all RAF casualties throughout the war on a world-wide basis. Generally, these could be broken down into the following categories:

- Confirmed killed and grave location known
- Missing presumed dead but grave location unknown
- Missing, but later confirmed prisoner of war

Of course, many in the first group had been killed and buried in 'friendly' territory, but a number had been killed and confirmed dead with their burial details transmitted to the UK via the International Red Cross and this category was only of any relevance to work by RAF recovery units insofar as such burials might provide clues to unidentified airmen that might be linked (eg, other crew members) or crashes nearby where there might still be missing casualties. However, it was of course those who were missing and presumed dead but for whom no grave location had yet been identified, who were of prime concern to the search teams; and as the allies moved across the continent and eventually the war in Europe drew to a close, so the exact position regarding those unaccounted for began to emerge. Even so, it was a very patchy picture. That picture, to an extent, began to become even more muddled as the advancing armies found aircraft crashes and graves and the information coming into P.4 (Cas) started to build.

By December 1944 the first Missing Research and Enquiry Unit (No 1 Section) had been mobilised and sent to France. The case load was colossal, and perhaps partly because of the scale of the task there seemed to be no particular objection when a non-MREU officer, Fg Off Vivian Oury, took on what he later described as a "self-appointed" role in recovering and identifying missing RAF aircrew. His 3 Base Recovery Unit, part of 83 Group RAF within the British Air Forces of Occupation, received its tasks direct from the P.4 (Cas) at the Air Ministry in London or from 2 and 4 MREU in France and Germany. With limited resources, Oury's men carried out scores of investigations across what had previously been enemy-held territory. The work was arduous, relentless, difficult and for the most part gruesomely unpleasant. However, Oury's dedication to what he rightly viewed as vitally important work can only be marvelled at in the face of frequently challenging circumstances. Often undermanned, Oury also complained of inadequate transport and of his Jeep being un-roadworthy. Not only that, but he felt that his parent unit were not always supportive of his activities. As if all of that were not enough, he also had cause to complain when an officer from one of the MREUs 'stole' his credit for a particularly successful recovery and identification. This involved a deeply buried Spitfire at Dranoutre, near Ypres in Belgium, although the report of the MREU officer whom Oury claimed misrepresented the facts is an interesting insight into the grim and difficult tasks undertaken. It reads:

Fg Off Vivian Oury was one of the band of personnel and officers who scoured Europe in the immediate post-war years looking for missing RAF, Commonwealth and allied aircrew who had been lost between 1939-45. His single-minded determination to solve cases was second to none and resulted in a good many hitherto missing aircrew being accounted for.

"Fighter. Date reported missing: 5 May 1942. Dranoutre. Date: 20 July 1946. Further to the above-mentioned enquiry and preliminary report I have to state that the recovery of the body of the pilot of this single-engined fighter shot down at Dranoutre on 5 May 1942 was attended by me.

This was the gaping crater at the Dranoutre crash site that confronted Oury and his post-war recovery team when they arrived. The force of impact has driven the wreckage deep underground, with just a few portions of wing structure showing.

"On 15 July the body was recovered at a depth of 21ft 6 inches. It was found amongst the remains of the cockpit in a mutilated condition but very well preserved probably due to the heavy clay subsoil in which the aircraft was embedded. The hair was dark brown/black and the left arm bady mangled.

"No documents or identity disc found. There was slight evidence of fire (this was confirmed by local inhabitants who saw a trail of black smoke when the aircraft crashed), three small holes having been burnt in the battledress blouse in the left breast and sleeve.

"The deceased pilot was wearing blue RAF type battledress, trousers size 7 and blouse size 8 on which was found RAF pilot's brevet and a sergeant's chevrons. On the underpants a laundry mark in red cotton: A/ML. He was also wearing brown brogue shoes.

"Other objects found included:

1) Irvin type parachute (rip cord not pulled) No SS 84011
2) Dinghy number 2299
3) Mae West type flap – size medium, serial no. unknown but on the inside was written in indelible pencil T27. NB – the number 7 was a continental one
4) 20mm cannon Mk II serial no. 11830 with 05614s on barrel
5) Propeller no. believed to be 7053

Personal objects found included:

1) One chromium oblong cigarette case probably machine turned with the inscription 'Js McD' on the front and on the inside was engraved 'Jackson Trophy 1939'
2) One cigarette lighter "ORLIK SPORT" Made in London
3) Chrome wrist watch (large size) screw on front and back cover – this watch was stopped at 16.08 hrs
4) Part of silk lining of flying gloves bearing number in ink – 787431
5) Stainless steel penknife with two blades and one spike
6) Small ivory elephant slightly charred
7) Small leather purse containing:
   a) One brass button marked 'Legion Etrangère'
   b) Three Czech-Slovakian coins
   c) One Palestinian 2 mils copper coin
   d) Two half crowns
   e) One two shilling piece
   f) Two sixpences
   g) Six half-pennies
   h) One farthing
8) Key chain and ring to which was attached:
   a) 1 Yale type latch key marked 'Made in Canada' with 'RON' scratched on the back
   b) I Yale drawer key marked 'Made in England'
   c) One trinket-box-type key
   d) One rubber bag attached to key ring marked:
      (FRONT) Don't forget your RED-X Tune-up when topping up the sump
      (BACK) RED-X Tune-up Club
9) Emergency fob box – perspex type
10) 15 x 100 French francs
    8 x 50 French francs
    10 x 10 French francs

"In conclusion, unintelligible painted letters which were on the twisted metal of the fuselage might have been 'B' (for the first letter) and either 'K', 'N' or 'R' for the second letter.

"The body was put in a coffin and placed in a communal vault at Ypres civil cemetery pending identification of pilot by Air Ministry as there was no suitable vault or mortuary at Dranoutre."

Whilst containing much graphic detail, this report gives a dramatic portrayal of the challenges faced by the recovery teams and well illustrates the sometimes confusing clues that were unearthed. In this case, the cigarette case might well have indicated a British casualty, perhaps with initials 'Js McD', or else somebody known as 'Ron'. In fact, these were red herrings and might well have been property inherited from other previous casualties – or even won during a game of cards! In this instance the only significant clues were the known date of the crash (5 May 1942) and the number 787431 on the flying glove silk inners. Both of these details provided P.4 (Cas) with a perfect match; Sgt Karel Pavlik of 313 Squadron who had gone missing on that date in Spitfire Vb BM261 whilst escorting Bostons to Lille on 'Circus 157' and had been shot down by Hptm 'Pips' Priller of JG 26. (Note: Although Oury had organised and carried out the recovery of Pavlik's body the actual crash site was re-excavated on 29 June 1997 by the Belgian Aviation History Association and a number of remaining artefacts, including the Rolls-

Sgt Karel Pavlik. His was one of the cases solved by Oury and thanks to his work he now lies buried at Ypres. Here, Pavlik paints a good luck symbol on his Spitfire although, unfortunately, his luck ran out on 5 May 1942.

Royce Merlin engine, were recovered. The association later organised the placement of a memorial to Karel Pavlik close to the crash site.)

Ultimately, Pavlik was laid to rest in Ypres town cemetery (Grave 4-A-41) although the fall-out from the MREU report did not lay things to rest for Vivian Oury. On 26 July 1946 he wrote:

"On delivering [*my report*] personally I found a report [*by a MREU Squadron Leader*] already on the file and on the point of being sent to Air Ministry by Sqn Ldr Hussey. The date of investigation was given as 17.7.46 and the name of the search officer was given as another officer, not me. The report begins 'Further to the above-mentioned enquiry and preliminary report I have to state that the recovery of the body of the pilot of the single-engined fighter shot down at Dranoutre on 5.5.42 was attended by me.' That statement is untrue. This Squadron Leader paid a short visit to the site on the first or second day in the preliminary stages and did not put in another appearance until the job was completed. He neither saw the hole nor the body on the second occasion and the only sight of 'the body' he had was when I delivered the sealed coffin to Ypres Cemetery on Thursday 18th at which point I handed it over to him. His report was based entirely upon information obtained from me. I can think of no possible excuse for such a deplorable breach of etiquette."

Pavlik fell to the guns of Hptm 'Pips' Priller who survived the war, only to die of a heart attack in May 1961.

The frustrations for Oury mounted with his case-load, although by April 1946 he reported that he had been working on the task for ten months and in that time had recovered

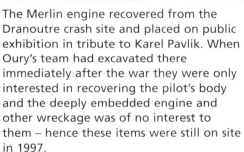

The Merlin engine recovered from the Dranoutre crash site and placed on public exhibition in tribute to Karel Pavlik. When Oury's team had excavated there immediately after the war they were only interested in recovering the pilot's body and the deeply embedded engine and other wreckage was of no interest to them – hence these items were still on site in 1997.

twenty-three aircraft with crews, twelve of them bombers and the remainder fighters. From these, thirty-seven bodies had been recovered and thirty-three of those identified. However, and notwithstanding the 'arisings' issued by the Air Ministry, the work of Oury and his team attracted the interest of the *London Evening Standard* who featured his various undertakings in an article on 24 June 1946. It was hardly surprising that this interest by the press resulted in a flood of enquiries from relatives asking if Vivian Oury could help find their loved ones. As early as the next day Constance Earnshaw was writing to Oury:

The impressive memorial placed close to the scene of Pavlik's crash.

*81, WEST ST.
DEPL
KENT
25/6/46*

*Flying. officer Oury.
Dear Sir.
Having read
the Evening Standard
of Monday the 24th
June. of you tracing
Missing airMen. I
wonder if you could
help me. My husband
Pilot officer Reginald
Earnshaw. Plt. 142946
of bomber Command
Pilot of a Halifax*

*bomber. was reported
missing on the night
of the 27 april 1944
after setting out to
Montzen on the borders
of Belgium, and
Germany.
Four of my husbands
crew were found dead.
my husband and the
other two as above
stated reported missing
If at any time in your
quest for missing airmen
you should find any
trace of place of*

*itemment. I would be
eternally. gratefull to
you. if you could
let me Know
I Remain yours.
Sincerely
Constance*

*PS. The names of those
of the bodies found.
were Nav. Royer
Sampson Sgt. Hinton.
Sgt Pullen. Tail gunner.
The other two names. I
am not sure of.*

The pain, unwritten between the lines, is almost palpable in this plea to Fg Off Oury to help a grieving wife find her husband. In the event, however, Oury had to reply saying that he could only carry out investigations tasked to him by the Air Ministry and instead suggested that Constance write direct to P.4(Cas), although he had also clearly referred the matter to them himself. Whether or not this enquiry prompted some early action to investigate the case it is very difficult to judge.

What is certain, though, is that by 15 July 1946 the casualty branch was able to report on investigations carried out at Dinteloord cemetery in the Netherlands. Here, it was found that the Germans had buried four of Earnshaw's crew; Plt Off J Riordan (bomb aimer) and Sgt R J Sampson (navigator) plus two unidentified bodies. By the simple expedient of exhuming the graves it became apparent that there were more inter-mingled remains than just these four men, and it became possible to conclude that all seven of the crew were buried there. Consequently, these seven men were re-buried in a collective grave at Bergen-op-Zoom cemetery in the Netherlands under a named headstone. Constance Earnshaw finally knew where her husband lay.

It is clear from some of Vivian Oury's writings that he felt passionately about the work he carried out, and even after he had left the service he was being contacted by the MREU operations in Europe to help out with cases that were being re-examined. One in particular, a Lancaster crash at Vouziers in France, was a case that he had never been able to action to any conclusion. Answering a query from the Air Ministry in 1947 after he had retired elicited this comment from Mr Oury:

"If I had had half a chance to work on that crash I would most certainly have done so, with or without authority, because I feared then as I fear now that nothing short of excavation at the scene of the crash will establish positively the identity of that aircraft. In fact, if I were asked to action that aircraft now I would not hesitate to volunteer to do so."

If Vivian Oury's passion for his work, and its importance, was something that he wore on his sleeve then the same could be said nearly seventy years later of Erwin Kowalke, a sixty-nine-year-old German who has made it his business to search for missing casualties (mostly soldiers) around Berlin. In 2004, for instance, he found the remains of five RAF airmen whilst searching woods at Gerbisbach near Wittenberg, just to the north-east of Berlin. Of course, this was an area in the former Soviet-controlled territory and thus access by MREU teams had never been possible. Kowalke discovered that the crash site was that of yet another Halifax of 640 Squadron, flown by fellow crew members of Plt Off Earnshaw. It had been shot down, he established, on 24 March 1944 and the remains were duly handed to the British authorities. In his quest, Kowalke is single minded about his purpose: "My job is to give the dead a face. My work is also my way of trying to make amends for what Germany did."

Whilst the Gerbisbach site could never have been accessed by MREU teams, it is a sad fact that the MREU investigations were finally wound up on 30 September 1949 when much work remained to be done. The discovery of RAF and allied aircrew remains across Europe, on a regular and annual basis, is testimony enough to that fact. However, doubtless the authorities decided that a line had to be drawn somewhere under the ongoing official searches and there were also clear financial pressures by HM Treasury to cease these operations. Even so it must have remained absolutely clear, even as the Runnymede Memorial was being completed in 1953, that there were still casualties out there to be found. No less than nine others were located and identified after the names for inclusion on the memorial had been finalised.

Certainly, many of the names listed at Runnymede will forever be 'beyond reach' as the Air Ministry then described them. Some, at the time, were beyond reach because they lay in the communist east although the majority of the 'unreachables' had been lost at sea or so completely consumed by fire and explosion that no earthly trace of them will ever be found. However, Herr Kowalke's persistence had paid off in his determination to see that the seven-man crew of a former enemy bomber that had come to pound his home city were identified and decently buried.

On 1 September 2005 the remains were buried in Plot 14, Row K, Grave 8 of the 1939-45 Berlin War cemetery. Unfortunately, positive individual identification of the remains proved impossible, and it was established that in fact only five sets of remains were present from the seven missing crew. However, that crew can be named as Plt Off W C McLeod, Sgt N L Cooper, Sgt S W Wheeler, Sgt J C Burdett, Sgt A P Webb, Sgt J N Boston and Sgt R A G Turner. Consequently, in view of the impossibility of naming the individual remains and the fact that they had died together as a crew it was decided that the remains would be buried in a collective grave under a single headstone. Unusually, the CWGC pattern headstone bore the following poignant inscription, and without any individual names:

Five Airmen of the 1939-45 War
24 March 1944
Members of the crew of Halifax LW430
Known unto God

No longer, however, do the British authorities pro-actively seek out wartime casualties, and that role has fallen to volunteers like Erwin Kowalke or the recovery teams and individuals whose work is described throughout this book. Of course, the stance of the British authorities in respect of searching for their missing is in direct contrast to that of the Americans. For them, the search is never ending and an almost sacred duty.

CHAPTER **5**

Finding 'Francie II'

THE WAR FOUGHT BY American forces in the Pacific was an unforgiving one on many levels. First, the Japanese enemy was a determined, tenacious and often ruthless foe who sometimes had little regard for the American war dead. Second, the terrain over which the war was fought was equally unforgiving. Vast tracts of mountainous jungle and an expansive and empty ocean meant that aircrews in distress who were forced down or who had crashed into either jungle or sea often stood little chance of survival. Even if they had survived the initial crash, then the chances of remaining alive and being discovered by friendly forces were not always high. And capture by Japanese forces did not always ensure survival, either. Taking all of these factors into account, it is hardly surprising that there are a very high number of American war dead in the theatre that have never been accounted for. Many of these are still being found by dedicated American search teams, however.

The 389th Bombardment Squadron, 312th Bombardment Group, were a newly-assigned A-20G Havoc unit posted to Gusap airstrip, Papua New Guinea, during March 1944 with fifteen aircraft arriving there on the 13th of that month. It was on that same date that the 312th flew its first combat mission. Their squadron patch bore the legend 'Roarin 20s', clearing alluding to the A-20 aircraft with which the unit was equipped. Taking off at 08.30hrs, nine aircraft of the unit headed out for an attack on Alexishafen led by Major Wells with each two-man crew carrying out a bombing and strafing run using the powerful punch of four nose-mounted 20mm cannon and two .50cal machine guns. With the strike successfully completed, the formation turned back for Gusap and home.

However, the aircraft flown Major Wells had been hit by anti-aircraft fire and had crash-landed into the sea, although one of the other aircraft, flown by Col Strauss, circled overhead until Wells and his gunner, S/Sgt Jack Bachelder, had been picked up from liferafts by a navy Catalina. Col Strauss had ordered Lt Hedges to lead the rest of the formation home, but the seven remaining A-20s flew into bad weather on their way back to Gusap.

Hedges was running low on fuel and he figured the safest thing to do would be to cross the Finnesterre mountains and glide into Gusap if necessary. When there was a break in the clouds, Hedges could only see three other aircraft instead of six. 2/Lt Calvin Slade was a pilot in one of the remaining aircraft, but as he was having trouble keeping position in the bad weather he decided to leave the formation and turn back. Relying on his instruments, Slade flew out to the ocean where the cloud bank ended and from there he managed to follow the coastline and eventually find his way to the Ramu river and thence home to Gusap. It had been an eventful and costly 'blooding' of the 312th and unfortunately three of the A-20s that had been in the formation never made it back.

The next day, the Squadron began looking for the missing crews or plane wreckages but could not find either. The searches continued for a week before they were called off and it was concluded that the crews had either run out of fuel and crashed into the mountains or the sea. By 27 January 1946 the men were presumed dead and their remains were determined as 'non-recoverable' by 24 August 1949. Nearly forty years later, however, the aircraft belonging to 2/Lt Henry J Miar and gunner S/Sgt Harley A Spear was discovered in the Finnesterre mountains near Saidor. Over the next few years searchers also found the other two planes flown by 2/Lt Valerie L Pollard and his gunner Sgt Dominick J Licari and the aircraft of 2/Lt Hansen and his gunner, Sgt Bustamante. All had flown into the mountains in formation, but it is specifically the case of Hansen and Bustamante which this chapter will examine.

The US Army Central Identification Laboratory, Hawaii (CILHI) was a specialist unit set up to conduct search and recovery operations in the Pacific for World War 2, Korean War and Vietnam War dead – as well as searches elsewhere in the world as and when required. Deploying highly specialised teams that included anthropologists, archaeologists, odontologists and forensic experts, CILHI was unique on a world-wide basis, tasked with the carrying out of a mission that was succinctly spelled out by former President Reagan when speaking of his nation's duty in respect of the repatriation of its war dead:

> "I renew my pledge to the families of those listed as missing in action that this nation will work unceasingly until a full accounting is made. It is our sacred duty and we will never forget them."

It was that 'sacred duty' that led to CILHI following up reports in October 1988 from a Papua New Guinea resident who had told them he had located the wreck of an aircraft. Tellingly, he also reported that it had the number 42-54117 still clearly marked on its tail fin. If the number was correct then there could be no mistake about the aircraft or its crew; this was the A-20G aircraft called 'Francie II' that had been flown by Hansen and Bustamante. With reports that the aircraft was relatively intact, there was clearly promise that the long-missing remains of the two

Sometimes, discoveries of crashed aircraft can be dramatic. Here, the virtually complete wreck of an A-20G Havoc lost in Papua New Guinea during March 1944 emerges from the dense jungle. Investigators found the tail, marked with the aircraft constructor's number; 42-54117. This alone was sufficient to identify the date and details of its loss and to establish that its two crew were still listed as missing.

men might be present and identifiable. So, despite the problems associated with the task, an expedition to the crash site in dense jungle four kilometres south-west of Zawan village in the Madang province of Papua New Guinea was duly mounted by CILHI during 1990.

It was an operation that required the construction of a helicopter landing pad in the jungle, but even then a two-hour hazardous trek to the site from the helipad had to be undertaken by the team in order to reach the impact point which was situated on a steep slope with a 70° incline. Nonetheless, and despite these difficulties, the pledge given by President Reagan was one that CILHI would see met whenever and wherever humanly possible.

The full CILHI report into the loss of 42-54117 has been made available to the author by the American authorities and is demonstrative of the level of care, attention to detail and the extreme effort that is often expended to ensure a satisfactory conclusion to such cases. The report of the archaeological recovery begins with a brief summary of the crash site.

Cockpit area

Gunner's Position

A general view of the crash site taken by the investigating team, showing how intact and remarkably well preserved the aircraft actually was. The annotations were added by the American CILHI recovery team.

"The site is in a high canopy area of the upper montane forest zone, with a zone of grassland and shrubs developing towards the crest line. Although rainfall is frequent it is seasonal, the vegetation not being in moss forest conditions. The area is uninhabited, although the crash site is adjacent to a hunting trail. A high rock overhang is just above the helicopter pad, a frequently used shelter for the hunting parties. There are no major drainages, although there are numerous small run-off gullies that cut through the ridge and down the slope.

"The A-20 crashed into a steep slope. There was limited dispersal of wreckage, much of the plane staying intact though damaged. There was major damage to the front of the aircraft, with the cockpit and nose crushed on impact with large rocks that were the face of a narrow ledge. The area where the gunner was positioned also slammed into a large boulder that penetrated the under belly of the aircraft. The aircraft was pointed north, head on into the slope. An observer with experience with aircraft crash sites in this region described the crash as a probable 'pancaking', with the nose pointed up and the engines at full throttle."

When the recovery teams arrived at the site there could be no doubt as to the aircraft type or its specific identity as large portions of it remained substantially intact and with the paintwork etc in good condition. One of the sections that remained very well preserved was the tailfin, bearing the aircraft number; 42-54117. There was thus no difficulty at all in positively confirming the identity of this aircraft from the appropriate missing aircrew report which gave the crew as 2nd Lt Carl Hansen (pilot) and Sgt Ernest Bustamante (gunner). The aircraft had been named 'Francie II' by its pilot, whilst it also emerged that air-gunner Ernest Bustamante was flying his very first combat mission. As we now know, it would also turn out to be his last.

Working on site between 18 and 23 August 1990, the CILHI team was faced with first clearing the extensive vegetation that surrounded it in a twenty-square-metre area. This was followed by the creation of a buffer zone before surface cleaning and inspection could be carried out. This included the separation into pieces of the major portions of the aircraft and close inspection and photography of these sections. Thereafter, excavation of the cockpit area, the gunner's position and an area beneath the port wing was undertaken. In respect of the port wing area, this was a location of interest in view of the fact that some remains and effects had evidently been placed there by visiting hunters and passing villagers. The forensic detail with which the investigation was conducted is borne out in the narrative of the CILHI report:

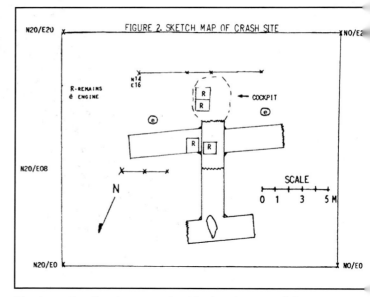

The investigating team made this sketch map of the wreck site as part of their forensic investigations, including details of the alignment of the A-20G and where human remains were found.

"The aircraft was disassembled where possible, starting at the rear fuselage. Each piece of metal and the ground around and beneath it were inspected. The left wing and attached gunner's turret were left in place. While that was taking place two teams cleaned debris from around the cockpit and left wing, the dirt being placed into buckets, then inspected and dumped beyond the buffer zone to the right side of the aircraft. By doing these tasks portions of aircraft could be excluded from further consideration and areas sensitive for human remains could be prepared for final archaeological excavation.

"Systematic controlled excavation of the cockpit and portion underneath the left wing near the fuselage within a one by one meter or one by two meter grid square was carried out. Each of the two areas sensitive for remains were excavated around and down to sterile conditions using pointed flat mason's trowels and paint brushes. All dirt was placed into buckets and then inspected before being dumped. The cockpit area, being a mangled tangle of wires, glass and metal compacted and mixed with remains and personal effects was excavated primarily with dental picks. Remains and personal effects were placed in plastic bags and/or on aluminium foil. Personal identifying media such as dog tags and rings were partially cleaned in the field. Each bag or parcel was numbered in sequence for the cockpit and gunner's position."

With the recovery of two sets of remains from the cockpit and gunner's area, along with identity dog-tags associated with each set of remains, there could be no doubting that Hansen and Bustamante had been recovered and their discovery certainly matched the information contained in missing aircrew report number 5675. For Hansen, his dog-tag number was 0-803612 and for Bustamante it was 39280277 although it is interesting to observe that for both men their dates of death are recorded with the American Battle Monuments Commission as 27 January 1946. This date is the date at which they were officially presumed dead by the American military, rather than an *actual* date of

Personal effects recovered from the crash site included coins, a pen, air gunner's 'wings' and a graduation ring engraved 'US Army Air Corps Advanced Flying School 1942'. These effects, coupled with the aircraft tail number and the discovery of two named and numbered dog-tags, enabled a positive identification to be made of the two crew.

death. Post-recovery, the remains and effects were transferred to the CILHI laboratory in Hawaii for forensic examination and formal identification prior to turning over to families and next of kin for burial.

Here then, in the case of 42-54117, are some important areas where procedures adopted by the Americans somewhat differ from the approach of the British authorities. First, and as we have already seen, there are no longer any official and pro-active searches for war dead by the British authorities. That aside, the date of death in the case of British casualties is presumed in all cases to be that on which the casualty disappeared rather than the date when death was formally presumed as was the case with Hansen and Bustamante. Next, in the case of British casualties who are sometimes found overseas, any repatriation of their bodies home (as with American casualties) is never an option and the remains are always buried at the nearest 'open' British Military CWGC cemetery in the theatre of operations where the casualty was lost.

After more than sixty years, Carl Hansen and Ernest Bustamante were found and appropriately returned to their families. However, the case of another bomber and its lost crew in the Far East, this time a RAF B-24 Liberator, has thus far witnessed significantly different and sometimes controversial developments. It is a story that has been ongoing for many years and even now is not yet resolved.

CHAPTER 6

Liberator KL654

I N JUNE 2011 THE Ministry of Defence Joint Casualty and Compassionate Centre were asked by the author about news and internet reports relating to the discovery of a RAF B-24 Liberator in the Far East, KL654. Their response was brief, and summarised the position at the time of going to print with this book:

"In October 2010, the Ministry of Defence was provided with a report and photographs regarding Liberator KL654, detailing the results of a privately funded expedition that took place the previous year (August 2009) to the crash site. This explained that some 100 bone fragments had been recovered and were now held by the Malaysian authorities. After liaison with officials in Malaysia and the families of the crew members, through their representative, staff at the Joint Casualty and Compassionate Centre have agreed that the bones are the remains of the crew of this aircraft. Discussions are ongoing with the families' representative over their wishes regarding identification of individual crew members and the planning for a funeral service in Malaysia. This will hopefully take place either at the end of 2011 or in 2012."

The back-story, of course, is rather more detailed than the information contained within that statement from the JCCC although it rather pointedly highlights the differences between the recovery and identification of British and Commonwealth casualties and those suffered by American forces. On the one hand, as in the case of Liberator KL654, we have a 'privately funded expedition' to recover the entire crew of a British bomber lying in a far-away jungle whilst on the other we have the American government expending vast amounts of money and committing

The wreck of a B-24 Liberator lies in a Malaysian jungle and was clearly identified from engine numbers, a fuselage code letter and its RAF serial KL654 which can be faintly made out on this portion of rear fuselage.

considerable resources to search for and recover their war dead. This is certainly not implied or intended as any criticism of the JCCC or its staff who work tirelessly to ensure that cases like those involving KL654 are brought to a satisfactory and dignified conclusion. However, it is impossible within a book of this nature not to present the distinct contrast between the position of the British and American governments with regards to missing casualties. In this context we have already seen the stated US position to leave no stone unturned in that nation's quest to bring home the missing. On the other hand, the British position (set out in Appendix I) is entirely opposite in its approach.

Lying in and around the wrecked Liberator were the remains of its missing eight-man crew who had been ignored over successive years by HM governments. In October 2010 a privately-funded expedition recovered around one hundred bone fragments and these will ultimately be appropriately buried. However, a private expedition of the nature described can hardly have been carried out in the scientific manner of investigation employed by official American teams in the recovery of US personnel in such circumstances – the matter of Hansen and Bustamante in the previous chapter being a case in point. Here, in a recent view, the interior of the wrecked fuselage shows just how much of KL654 survives on site.

To a very large extent it is likely that this is all driven by economics and available resources, and it is very clear that the accessibility of defence funding and manpower to complete such a tasking is readily available to the American military. It is also the case that there is a political will and resolve on the part of the American government to give this undertaking such a high degree of prominence. In part, that might have been driven by the POW/MIA lobby and campaign in America to one way or another properly account for those service personnel missing in Vietnam, and where questions hung for so many years as to whether the missing were actually dead or still held captive. To an extent, that lobby still exists and comes to the fore once again in the penultimate (and militarily most recent) case examined in this book. Either way, the British official position tends to suggest that the reason for not pursuing their missing war dead is not financial but instead is both practical and ethical:

> "It is no longer feasible or possible to methodically excavate all known crash sites/ battlefields using official resources. The MOD discourages the disturbance of crash sites and battlefields other than where necessary......"

Applying financial considerations when presenting the MOD's case for not pro-actively taking up cases like Liberator KL654 would, perhaps, be viewed somewhat negatively by the British public – notwithstanding the financial climate of 2011 and the severe constraints placed upon military and public spending. It is easy to see that elements of the British media would have a field day if it were suggested that Britain could not afford to deal with its war dead and that those who paid with all they had were simply being left in 'some foreign field' because a grateful nation couldn't afford to do anything other than abandon them. The MOD, it seems, are between a rock and a hard place when it comes to presenting its case in relation to missing casualties. Whilst the position set out by them is clear there does seem to be some ambiguity when comparing that stance with the recent and ongoing work with the World War 1 Fromelles battlefield casualties as well as the fact that the MOD are often quoted as stating they are pleased when long-lost casualties are accounted for.

For example, when Flt Lt Gabriel Ellis and Sgt William Reidy were found in the wreck of their Mosquito in The Wash during 2005 an MOD representative stated: "It is good that we are still finding bodies of servicemen sixty years later because it gives families closure after all these years." To an extent, then, the apparent MOD position regarding Fromelles and the recent discovery of missing RAF aircrew might be viewed as being at odds with the official MOD and governmental position towards missing casualties as set out in the JCCC statement. At best, it is all the product of muddled thinking. That said, if there is any fault then it lies with the *policy* and certainly not with the JCCC staff in their dealings with such casualty situations as they arise. However, there is an inevitability that the official policy will sometimes spill over into controversy.

Such is the case with Liberator KL654 and this is highlighted by the Malaya Historical Society who state: "Since 1945 the wreck has been reported to the British authorities on twenty separate occasions from 1949 to 2007 and on each of those occasions the British government have refused to acknowledge or offer to send investigators."

In looking in detail at the story of KL 654 and the aftermath of her discovery the starting point has to be the official entry in the operations record book for 356 Squadron. It reads:

"23 August 1945. Cocos Islands. Three aircraft successfully dropped in the briefed receptions. Aircraft 'R' is missing but believed successful. The cause of this loss is not known.

Liberator VI
KL654 'R'

Fg Off Watts J S (Pilot)	Flt Sgt Turner A (W/Op)
Fg Off Mason E D (2nd Pilot)	Fg Off Bromfield J T (A/Bmbr)
Flt Sgt Blakey J (Flt Engr)	Flt Sgt Towell R A (Front A/G)
Fg Off Dover W K (Nav)	Flt Sgt Ross W (Rear A/G)

Aircraft took off at 10.30hrs."

How or why Liberator KL654 crashed into the dense Malayan jungle on a ridge of Gunung Telapak Burok mountain is unknown, but what we do know is that it was taking part in an operation to drop two officers or agents in order for them to locate small groups of British and allied prisoners of war and to liberate them and assist in their journey home. Officially, the war against Japan had ended six days earlier and thus there is no reason to suppose that KL654's loss was anything other than a tragic accident. That said, the crew on board were still very much war victims. However, we do know that KL654 left the Cocos Islands, flew to Toborjoeng then on to Kuala Selangor, dropped her 'supplies' on the target area of Post Langkap in the jungle of Kuala Pilah, Negri Sembilian, and from that point on made no further contact although the crash position would seem to be thirty miles or so off-track from her intended route home.

Clearly, there has been much debate and controversy down the years about the wreck of this aircraft and her crew. Was it really KL654? And did her crew actually die on board or did they survive the crash and perish somewhere in the jungle? And should an official expedition be mounted to search for and recover these missing men? They are controversies that have embroiled individual researchers, enthusiasts, newspapers, veterans, the British authorities in Malaya and the MOD back home as well as the Malaya Historical Society. Ultimately, however, the answers have now been provided and clear evidence that this is KL654 has been found at the site. Nothing could be more conclusive than the RAF serial KL654 still painted faintly on the fuselage, along with a large letter 'R' painted in red. Not only that, but scatterings of bones and personal effects like rings have told their own story. As we now know from the MOD, a privately funded expedition (it is understood by a military helicopter pilot and a retired police officer) have established that a large number of bones have been recovered and it has been accepted that this indeed is KL654 and her crew.

The final chapter in the story of this missing RAF Liberator is yet to be told or written, but it seems certain that relatives of the crew will now have the satisfaction of knowing that their kin are accounted for. Furthermore, the remains will ultimately be given the sanctity of burial in a CWGC plot, albeit the route to that conclusion has been long and tortuous. Sadly, had these airmen been American servicemen then it is certain they would have been brought home long ago.

CHAPTER 7

The Finding of Lakeside Green Three

T HERE CAN BE NO doubting that a very considerable percentage of the missing aircrew commemorated on the RAF and Commonwealth Air Forces Runnymede Memorial and at the Madingley American Military Cemetery Wall of Missing must have lost their lives in either the coastal waters around Britain or else in the further reaches of the English Channel, North Sea or the surrounding oceans. Consequently, there can be little hope of most of those ever now being accounted for. However, one of the 5,126 names engraved at Madingley was indeed one of those who went down over the sea but by a remarkable chance find, and the diligence of researchers, he is no longer missing.

On 12 December 1944, three P-51 Mustang aircraft of the 479 Fighter Group, 435 Fighter Squadron, took off from their Wattisham base in Suffolk to engage in a training mission off to the south of the airfield and over the Thames estuary. The sequence of events that followed was set out by one of the other squadron pilots on that flight, 1st Lt Billy C Means:

When 2nd Lt Robert B Hymans disappeared on 12 December 1944, fellow pilot 1st Lt Billy C Means was able to report back on Hymans's inexplicable disappearance. Here, Means is photographed with his P-51 Mustang and ground crew.

"On the morning of December 12th, at approximately 10.45 hours, three of us took off from the home field on a high altitude training mission. We climbed to 21,000ft where my engine began to surge from 40 to 60 inches of Hg (mercury; author). I tried several times to get by this point, but to no avail. We then chased some bombers south for a short while and then began to simulate combat. At approximately 11.30 hours I pulled out of a shallow dive right on top of a cloud deck. Up to this time, Lt Hymans had been right on my tail, but on looking back I could note but one plane and it was piloted by Lt Hill. I immediately called Lt Hymans but received no answer. Lt Hymans was Lakeside Green Three, and at one time I thought I heard Colgate in contact with a Lakeside Green Three and giving him a steer of 200 plus degrees to a clear spot, but that is all I could understand. Lt Hill and I circled the spot where we had last seen Lt Hymans for about five minutes, and then we took a 90 degree heading and held it for approximately ten minutes. After we had been on this course two to three minutes we received four or five bursts of flak off to our left. We then let down through a break in the clouds and saw that we were over water. We took a 290 degree heading and in about five minutes we made landfall in at Southend. We then turned north and flew up the coast to Ipswich Bay, then home, where we landed at 12.30 hours."

As was so often the case in these incidents, Hymans had simply vanished from under the very noses of Hill and Means; one moment he was there, the next he was gone. What happened to him, exactly, is now just a matter of speculation. Either he suffered an oxygen malfunction and, unconscious, fell from the sky in his out-of-control Mustang or else experienced some form of structural or mechanical failure. Perhaps, even, he may have simply lost control during aerobatics. On the other hand, the possibility cannot be excluded that the 'friendly' anti-aircraft fire encountered by the other two pilots had struck a fatal blow on Hymans's Mustang although it would seem likely that such an event would have been noticed by his fellow pilots.

What we do know, however, is that the Mustang in which Hymans was flying, number 43-7157, (fuselage codes J2-7) was an old P-51 B model which was no longer an operational front-line machine but instead serving as the squadron 'hack'. As such, the possibility of some major failure to this war-weary bird can probably not be excluded. However, when Means reported back regarding Hymans's disappearance the duty officer, Major William B Hugill, telephoned round to 11 and 12 Groups, RAF, and the Observer Corps for news of the missing Mustang. There was none. By 15.33 hours Hugill had implemented 'overdue action' and began the paperwork for the relevant missing aircrew report.

During the July of 1997, Southend fisherman, diver and aviation archaeologist Dick Walker was returning from a fishing trip when he noticed something looking very much like a piece of aircraft wreckage sticking out of the water about two miles from land due east of Shoeburyness on Maplin Sands. Marking the spot, Dick decided to investigate further and on the next low tide, Tuesday 15 July, he returned to the site with colleagues Barry Hammerton and Gordon Ramsey and discovered a mass of compacted wreckage, stainless steel oxygen cylinders and .50 calibre machine-gun ammunition laying around. Quite clearly, this was an American aircraft although beyond that the team could tell very little at this stage. However, as the trio pulled the propeller blade from the mud it dislodged a rudder pedal with what appeared to be a fragment of bone adhering to it. By now, however, the tide was on the turn and gave only a short 'window' of a maximum of one and a half hours at the site. There was nothing for it but to return on another low tide.

Aviation archaeologist Dick Walker located the crash site of Robert Hymans's P-51 Mustang off the Essex coast in July 1997. Here, he gropes in the muddy, water-filled excavation pit searching for remains amongst the sharp and jagged edges of torn airframe and engine wreckage as the tide comes back in. As with most of the cases covered in this book it is illustrative of the extreme lengths to which teams, official and unofficial, are prepared to go in order to account for the missing.

Two weeks later and Dick and his colleagues returned, only this time a flying boot emerged from the mud. Inside was the grisly skeletal evidence of the pilot who had once worn it. Clearly, the situation had now changed dramatically from a pile of as yet anonymous and unidentified aircraft wreckage to a site potentially containing the remains of a missing pilot. With the provisions of the Protection of Military Remains Act 1986 to consider, Dick made a spot decision. Thus far, the team had taken nothing away from the site but were very much conscious of the fact that if they wished to proceed with any form of recovery, a licence under that act would be required. Although a licence to excavate there was unlikely now to be granted, given the likely presence of human remains, this no longer particularly mattered to Dick. To him, the primary consideration was for the pilot whose remains he had accidentally stumbled upon. Before he headed back to shore, he photographed the numbers on a .50 calibre Browning machine gun he had discovered and then consigned the weapon back to the water in order to avoid problems with UK gun laws. As things turned out, recording the gun numbers would prove to be a good decision and whilst he left the gun behind he reasoned that he could not do the same with the skeletal parts he had found. The action of the tide could well make them non-recoverable before anyone could visit the remote spot again. Instead of leaving them there he carefully preserved them and took the finds directly to the local coroner once he was ashore before telephoning the US Embassy in London to report the discovery.

With responsibility for foreign servicemen resting with their respective governments, the coroner was happy for matters to be turned over to the USAF Mortuary Service in Germany who, in turn, notified the Central Identification Laboratory at Hawaii of the find. As a result, forensic anthropologist Richard Harrington was sent to Europe in order to organise and co-ordinate investigation of the site and the potential recovery of any remains. With the crash located on the army firing ranges at Maplin Sands, Richard Harrington made arrangements with Major Gerry Collins of the Defence Test and Evaluation Organisation at Shoeburyness for the necessary work to be undertaken urgently, since there were concerns that the site may be lost due to tidal action or through the wreckage submerging into the sand and leaving no visible trace. After interviewing Dick Walker on 1 September, and having been shown the site two days later, Harrington organised plant, a team and equipment for the next suitable tide on 17 September.

After Dick Walker had notified the US authorities a full-scale dig was organised by the American CILHI team, using Dick Walker and his colleagues to assist and with digging equipment borrowed from the nearby army test ranges.

Making use of the early morning low tide the party set out across the sand, following the water out as it receded and reaching the crash site, already marked out by Dick Walker and Richard Harrington on 3 September, just as sections of crumpled and impacted wreckage emerged from the sand. Unfortunately, however, the tracked mechanical excavator that had been promised did not materialise and instead the team was provided with a rubber-tyred digger accompanied by a tracked vehicle in the form of a 'Lance' missile carrier. Whilst transit out to the site across the relatively hard sand was not a problem it was clear that excavating a pit might well be an issue since excavators of this type rely on extending hydraulic stabilising jacks before digging from the back-actor arm. As expected, once the jacks were extended they simply pushed into the wet sand and at once the machine began to get bogged in. Two miles from shore, and with a tide not far off the turn, the situation was not good.

Nonetheless, and with extraordinary focus on the task in hand, the digger driver set-to digging out portions of wreckage whilst a wet-suit-clad Dick Walker groped in the crater for wreckage and remains. The emergence of a parachute and shroud lines told its own story, and it was not long before Richard Harrington had secured quantities of human bone sufficient, at least, to say that Robert Hymans was no longer missing.

Now, the focus turned to trying to retrieve the excavator and return to shore ahead of the incoming tide. However, despite the best efforts of the tracked vehicle (and another that had been sent out to join the rescue!), the digger was stuck fast and sinking and before long was up to its cab in rising water – illustrative of the hazards and perils not infrequently encountered in the course of recovering the missing. Ultimately, the machine had to be abandoned as a total loss and was eventually salvaged on another tide the next day. However, the prime objective to recover Robert Hymans had been achieved.

Events subsequent to the recovery of Hymans's remains from Maplin Sands are a little hazy, but it is known that they were transferred to the CILHI laboratory in Hawaii where tests confirming the remains to be his were carried out. Ultimately, it was established that these were indeed the mortal remains of 2nd Lt Robert B Hymans, O-719350 who had been officially missing since 15.33hrs on 12 December 1944. He has subsequently been laid to rest at Arlington National Cemetery in the United States, although it is not known if he had any surviving kin or, indeed, if they were ever traced. It was a satisfactory conclusion, although another very similar case investigated by Dick Walker and Barry Hammerton, and not too far away from the crash site of Hymans's P-51, had an outcome that was both surprising and sad albeit that it drew a line under the mystery of another wartime airman's disappearance.

During his investigations of submerged ship and aircraft wrecks in the Essex and Thames estuary areas, Dick was made aware of scattered wreckage of what was believed to be an American aircraft on the tidal mud flats about a quarter of a mile out from Dengie Marshes. Visiting the site in 1980 he discovered a scattered mass of wreckage which he was able to identify as having been a P-47 Thunderbolt, although his further investigations revealed that the site had previously been investigated by the Essex Aviation Group. Evidently, that group had identified the wreck as a P-47 D, 42-26057, from 63rd Fighter Squadron of the famous 56th Fighter Group.

The aircraft had been lost on 18 September 1944 along with its pilot, 2nd Lt Elwood D Raymond of New Jersey. Indeed, Raymond was yet another of the names listed on the Wall

This mechanical excavator became bogged in during operations to retrieve Robert Hymans from his P-51 Mustang off the Essex coast. It had to be abandoned and left to be claimed by the incoming tide.

of Missing at Madingley as no trace of him had ever been discovered. Clearly, there was a strong possibility that Raymond was still with the wreckage of his Thunderbolt – just like Robert Hymans. However, extensive digging operations at the site (which pre-dated the implementation of the Protection of Military Remains Act 1986) revealed a mass of wreckage including the pilot's back armour, head rest and seat. Inside this crumpled ball of wreckage Dick found a leather flying helmet with its oxygen mask and leads still attached. Given the nature of this find, and Elwood Raymond's status as still missing in action, it looked

This is the Wall of Missing at the Madingley American Military Cemetery, Cambridgeshire, showing the panel on which is recorded the name of Robert B Hymans. In cases where casualties are subsequently accounted for, names on this memorial are marked with a gold rosette (as here) to signify that the casualty is no longer missing in action but confirmed killed on active service and now with a known and marked grave.

Right: The very same aircraft in which Raymond was lost, photographed over almost exactly the same stretch of water where both aircraft and pilot went missing.

Below: The trail of aircraft wreckage across mud flats at Dengie, Essex, discovered by Dick Walker in 1980.

very much as if the digging team might well be confronted with the remains of this American pilot.

In the event, they weren't. Despite carefully excavating and examining all that remained of the cockpit wreckage, there was simply no trace of Raymond and it was concluded that he must have baled out, landed in the water and drowned. This theory was given some weight by the discovery of the unfastened seat harness straps. So, either the sea had never delivered up his body or perhaps it had been washed ashore some while later and not been identified. As for the flying helmet and mask, this is easily explained by the fact that the standard procedure for baling out of such aircraft was always to remove all headgear in order to avoid entanglement with the leads etc when leaving the cockpit. Indeed, there are several instances of wrecks being recovered in which the flying helmets have been found exactly where they had been left behind by aircrew as they abandoned the aircraft.

Finding the flying headgear was a discovery that at least drew a line under solving the fate of Elwood D Raymond. However, and unlike the case of Hymans, it is unlikely that Raymond's name on the Wall of Missing will ever be marked by a gold rosette to signify a change of status from missing in action to killed in action. The possibility that

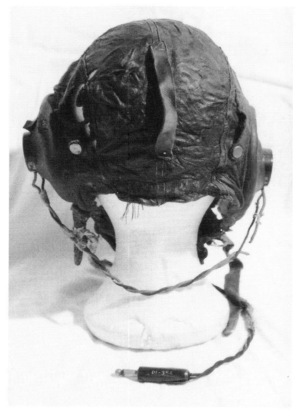

When Dick Walker and his team investigated the crash site between tides they came across this perfectly preserved flying helmet in the cockpit.

he will ever be found must be considered extremely remote. Indeed, those lost over water are the least likely of all missing aircrew casualties to be discovered and surely represent the most significant proportion of all such losses. In many cases, these included complete crews although sometimes one or two members of such crews would be found at sea or on coastal shorelines whilst their comrades were never located. Such is the case with a slightly mysterious and secretive loss of an RAF flying boat off the coast of Norway in 1941 which also reveals a sad husband-and-wife double tragedy.

CHAPTER 8

Special Recce to Tromsø

THE COMMONWEALTH WAR GRAVES Commission register entry for Sgt Kenwyn Charles Lawry RAF (VR) at the Runnymede Memorial hides a tragic story which saw a husband and wife both killed by enemy action just one year apart from each other. It reads:

"LAWRY, Sgt Kenwyn Charles, 959601, RAF (VR) 413 (RCAF) Sqn 22 October 1941. Age 28. Son of Charles A Lawry, and of Agnes Lawry, of Richmond, Yorkshire; husband of Winifred Lawry (nee Carroll), killed by enemy action at Eastbourne, 1940."

Sgt Kenwyn Lawry (left) and his wife Carol (right).

The story behind that almost bland detail can only leave us to guess at the dark sadness and empty loneliness that must have engulfed Kenwyn as he struggled to get on with life after the loss of his wife. War brought tragedy to countless millions of families between 1939 and 1945 and in varyingly awful ways, but the loss of a wife or girlfriend to enemy action must have been especially hard to bear for a serviceman who had to get on with the war without the support of the woman he loved. In this case, Kenwyn (or Ken, as he was more usually known) had also to endure the further pain of knowing that his wife was pregnant with their child at the time of her death.

Carol Winifred Lawry had enlisted in the Women's Auxiliary Air Force as early as 23 September 1939, just over two weeks after the declaration of war. Quite probably this was typical of the outgoing and adventurous girl that she was – climbing, hiking and caving being among her passions. Indeed, she had been the first woman recorded to have climbed Mount Kenya in February 1938 and her lively spirit no doubt prompted her to join up and do her bit. However, mustering as a clerk and being promoted to ACW1 on 1 June 1940 she had found herself posted to RAF Kenley, Surrey, and on 18 August she was at the end of a ferocious Luftwaffe attack against that airfield. Ken, meanwhile, had joined up on 3 April 1940 to begin his training as an air observer and with postings to initial training wings throughout the spring and summer of 1940 he was relatively safe whilst Carol was very much in the front line.

The pair had married in Torquay on 18 July 1940 and at thirty-seven Carol was ten years Ken's senior although, by all accounts, she was an exceptionally fit and youthful-looking woman. Family members recall how very much in love the pair clearly were, and it must have come as a relief to Ken to know that his wife was getting away for a few days leave from 8 October in their marital home town of Eastbourne where she was to spend some time with her mother-in-law. Here, he reasoned, she would be away from the danger of being on an operational fighter station with the ever-present threat of attack.

With his recent posting to No 9 Bombing and Gunnery School, for the core part of his training with effect from 1 September 1940, Carol's leave period in Eastbourne was a weight off Ken's mind. Late in the afternoon of 8 October she stepped off the train at Eastbourne where her mother-in-law met her and they set off for home via the shops. As the two women walked through the town centre, Ken was preparing for what was only his fifth training flight since joining 9 BGS at far-away Penrhos – a local flight with Flt Lt Thomas in a civilian Fokker (G-AFXC) which had been impressed into military service.

As he was doing so, hundreds of miles away, almost without warning, a German air attack scattered bombs randomly across the town centre at around 16.15 hours, with one heavy-calibre bomb detonating in Lismore Road just outside Messers Bobby's Department Store as Carol and her mother indulged in a spot of window-shopping. As the bomb whistled down, Carol grabbed her mother-in-law and flung her to the ground throwing herself on top of her just as the bomb detonated. Sadly, Carol was struck by shrapnel and was seriously injured being taken at once to St Mary's Hospital where she died of her injuries the following morning. Mrs Lawry (sen) was shaken but unharmed, her life having been saved by the selfless actions of her daughter-in-law.

By the time Ken landed back at Penrhos at around 18.30 hours that same day the telegram saying that his wife had been seriously injured was already on its way, although

This was the bomb site in the street outside Bobby's Department Store, where Carol Lawry was killed.

by the time he could get away from Penrhos airfield in North Wales for the long journey home Carol had died. He was now returning for his wife's funeral, and not coming back to be a comforting presence at her bedside as he had imagined. With the funeral in Eastbourne over, Ken was obliged to return to his unit and ongoing training and by 16 October he was back flying and trying to cope with his devastating loss as well as the crushing knowledge, gleaned *post-mortem*, that his Carol was also carrying their child. In 1988 Ken's niece, Jenny White, said: "When Carol died, Ken apparently lost interest in living and he volunteered for secret and dangerous missions in the RAF."

By 8 March 1941, now a sergeant, Ken had been posted for several weeks of training with an operational training unit and then, fully fledged, he was assigned his first operational squadron on 21 May. This was 236 Squadron at Carew Cheriton, a Blenheim squadron, with whom he flew a number of operational flights up until the end of June. Then, in mid-August, he was posted to 413 Squadron, RCAF, a Catalina flying-boat squadron, operating first at Stranraer and then out of Sullom Voe. Here, he flew only local flying trips and on air-to-sea firing sorties. His first operational flight with 413 Squadron was on 22 October 1941. It was also his last.

According to squadron records a signal had been received by 413 Squadron to the effect that photographs of five specific points of interest in Norway were urgently required: Simavik power station, Skarfjord power station, Vagfjord power station, Skattora seaplane base and Tromsø harbour. The crew, it is understood, were all volunteers and in view of the special nature of the operation the squadron CO, Wg Cdr R G Briese, flew the sortie on Catalina AH566, QL-G, along with:

Fg/Off C C Proby (Pilot)	Sgt R E Austin	AC2 W Benson
Sgt W H Martin	Plt/Off W J Hoover RCAF	AC1 T H Atkin
Sgt K C Lawry	Sgt L J Harris	AC1 A H Agus

Such long-range recce trips in Catalinas were, recalled Lawson Randall a former 413 Squadron pilot, not for the faint-hearted. The type, he believed, was entirely unsuited for this kind of operation and, in his opinion, Wg Cdr Briese went along that night because he had grave reservations about the Catalina's suitability for the job. If his men were being expected to fly on such dangerous operations, then so should he.

After the aircraft had departed at 02.35 hours on 22 October nothing further was heard of it. Initially, however, this was not a matter of any concern since strict radio silence had been ordered and it was not until some hours had elapsed past its due return time that AH566 and her crew were declared overdue. At dusk the following evening, and throughout that night until dawn, a flare path was laid out on the water anticipating the

Although not of the same squadron, this is a scene typical of a Catalina crew returning from an operational flight as they come ashore for breakfast. Sadly, there was to be no return for the traditional bacon and egg breakfast for Ken Lawry and his crew-mates.

The Canadian commanding officer of 413 Squadron, Wg Cdr Richard Briese of Lanigan, Saskatchewan, flew in the Catalina on which Lawry and crew were lost. Concerned about the risks faced by the crew on what was to be a hazardous operation, he decided to fly the mission himself in order to look out for his men. Briese is photographed here in the cockpit of one of 413 Squadron's Catalina flying boats.

return of Briese and his men. However, they were not coming home. Ken Lawry had flown his last operation, still deeply mourning Carol and his unborn child, caring little for his own survival but bent on carrying the war to the Germans if at all he could. The last entry of any significance in the diary he had left behind was poignant. On 9 October 1941 he had written 'Carol's death anniversary'.

By a quirk of fate the body of Wg Cdr Briese was the only one of the crew which was ever found, the Norwegian Red Cross reporting that he had been recovered from the sea and buried at Trondheim (Stavne) cemetery. The men he had been anxious to protect and shepherd, so far as he was able, had all been taken by the cruel sea although it is tempting to speculate that two of the eleven unknown airmen buried at Stavne close to Briese might be men from Catalina AH566. Sadly, there is no evidence that they are or even might be, and it would not be right to speculate given the lack of any information about them. However, it is impossible not to wonder.

Throughout this book we have looked, primarily, at casualties who have been lost and subsequently found. At least, we have examined cases where the location of missing crew can be convincingly established if not proven. Each one of those losses represents a personal tragedy to their close family members and nearest and dearest. Indeed, the 20,463 names recorded at Runnymede each represent an equal number of stories of tragedy and enduring grief. In this chapter I have tried to look behind the bland recording of just one man's name at Runnymede, Kenwyn Lawry, and the unbearable tragedy behind his name and his loss. In this instance, to some extent at least, a small mercy exists in the fact that there was no widow left behind to grieve for her man across the following long decades. It seemed appropriate, somehow, within the context of this book about finding the fallen to consider fully at least one of those cases. In many

The headstone for Carol Lawry in Eastbourne's Ocklynge Cemetery with its inscription also remembering Kenwyn. Buried here lies Carol and the couple's unborn child. Of Sgt K C Lawry, widower and erstwhile expectant father, no trace was ever found.

instances, of course, somebody is left behind to care when casualties from the distant past are found. In other cases, there isn't anyone. And in all instances, as with the story of Ken and Carol Lawry, the stories behind those casualties can be heart-wrenchingly tragic.

CHAPTER 9

The Corsairs of Lake Sebago

L UCRETIA DOUGLAS WAS TWENTY-NINE years old when she heard the familiar roar of Corsair aircraft over Lake Sebago, Maine, on 16 May 1944. So familiar was the sight and sound of Fleet Air Arm aircraft operating out of HMS *Sakar*, Brunswick, USA, that she barely gave a second glance at the aeroplanes so frequently overhead. Suddenly, there was a loud boom that drew attention to the area over the lake. Witnesses saw a fireball on the water. Then nothing. When investigators ventured out to the scene by boat all that could be found was a headrest and radio antennae mast floating on the lake. Despite an intensive search of the water and shoreline over subsequent days no further trace of either aeroplane or their two occupants was ever located.

Aside from a general belief that the two machines were Corsairs, nothing further of the incident seemed to be known in the locality of the lake and the facts were never reported upon (at least, not in any detail) in the wartime local press. With the passage of years all memory of the event had dimmed or been lost although a few, like Lucretia Douglas, remained able to tell investigators during the late 1990s a basic outline of the story. Sufficient, at least, to whet appetites amongst the US-based wreck-hunting fraternity. Here lay the possibility for salvage of one, if not two, World War Two fighter aircraft believed to be Corsairs from a freshwater lake. By any standards this was a tempting prize.

By 1998 sonar imagery had located promising images of a wreck 300ft beneath the surface of the lake, and the California-based Historic Aircraft Recovery Corporation owned by Dave Tallichet and Fred Hagen were immediately keen to locate and recover it. Under US law the pair took out a lawsuit to 'arrest' the submerged aircraft and thereby stake a claim to salvage and eventual title. This procedure is a familiar one in the USA and in the event that the lawsuit is upheld in the claimant's favour, the wreck is marked with a 'No Trespassing' sign and a court docket number.

In the case of the Lake Sebago wrecks, United States Magistrate Judge Margaret Kravchuck granted the arrest order of the Corsair in favour of Tallichet and Hagen on 20 June 2003. But it was only the opening shot in what would turn out to be a rather more protracted legal battle. However, on 21 June 2003 US Marshal John Cooper collected his statutory fee of $681.30 from Historic Aircraft Recovery Corp. and duly had a sign and airtight container attached to the wreck by robotic arm. Unfortunately, it was the wrong aircraft and not a Corsair at all! As things turned out this was a sunken post-war

During World War Two many RAF and FAA pilots were trained in the USA. HMS *Sakar* was situated at Brunswick, and it was from here that the Royal Navy trained its F4U-1 Corsair pilots in the relative safety of non-hostile airspace. That safety, however, was certainly only relative as a number of pilots under training lost their lives in flying training accidents there. Here, a training flight of Corsair aircraft operates out of HMS *Sakar*.

amphibious aircraft – its bent wings having unfortunately served to mimic the inverted gull-wing shape of the Corsair's wings on the radar imagery.

Subsequent to the ill-fated attempt to 'arrest' one or other of the two Corsair aircraft, Historic Aircraft Recovery Corp. were able to conduct further investigations at Lake Sebago during July and using a camera-equipped remote operated vehicle (ROV) they were able finally to locate, film and identify one of the two Corsairs. Standing on its nose, its Pratt & Whitney R-2800 engine and propeller embedded in mud, stood a Chance Vought F4U-1 Corsair. Emblazoned on the rear of its still painted fuselage were the words ROYAL NAVY above the aircraft serial number, JT160. Here was all that was needed to identify the aircraft and the story behind it in detail.

Deep in the icy black waters of Lake Sebago, investigators using remotely operated vehicle mounted cameras located and filmed a sunken Corsair wreck.

The wreck located has been identified as the machine in which nineteen-year-old Sub Lt Raymond Knott was lost. The serial number JT160 still clearly marked on the rear fuselage tells us that this is Knott's machine. The remains of Knott, and of his colleague Gill, are believed to still be in their respective cockpits.

As the camera moves further along the fuselage, the code letters 3BH almost look to have been freshly painted.

Although massively rugged, the folding wings of the sunken wreck of JT160 seem to have been torn from the fuselage and engine. They probably lie nearby on the lake bed. This shot shows to advantage the unique gull-wing shape of the Corsair carrier-borne fighter and also demonstrates its folding-wing configuration.

Lake Sebago seemed to attract a number of Fleet Air Arm Corsair accidents, this one coming to grief on the shoreline in another unrelated incident.

JT160 was one of a pair of Corsairs from 732 Squadron FAA engaged in low-level flying on 16 May 1944 over Lake Sebago. The other was JT132. Flying JT160 was nineteen-year-old Sub Lt Raymond Laurence Knott, RNVR, from Grantham in Lincolnshire. Piloting JT132 was Sub Lt Vaughan Reginald Gill, of whom no further details are recorded by the Commonwealth War Graves Commission. Both men were killed in the accident and both are shown as serving with HMS *Sakar* although, sadly, no trace of either pilot could be found. Consequently, the names of both are remembered on the Lee-on-Solent Memorial at Hampshire in the UK. Their deaths, however, were far from unusual in this region of North America with no less than 177 British-operated Corsairs being lost in Maine alone. Indeed, the CWGC plots at Miami (Woodlawn) and Corpus Christie (Rose Hill) Memorial Park in the USA hold the burial plots of many other HMS *Sakar* pilots from Brunswick and they comprise a not insignificant proportion of the total 642 British and Commonwealth casualties of WW2 buried in the United States.

Once word emerged as to the specific identity of the Corsair aircraft that were the subject of the Historic Aircraft Recovery Corporation's interest, matters became somewhat more complicated. Almost immediately, the State of Maine moved to reverse the earlier arrest orders secured by Tallichet and Hagen, with Assistant Attorney General William Laubenstein III asking the court to dismiss HARC's earlier lawsuit. In addition, the Maine Historic Preservation Commission slapped an emergency protection zone around the supposed location of both Corsairs under archaeological protection rules. By the time the matter reached the court of US District Judge George J Singal it had further been complicated by input from the Ministry of Defence in the UK who objected to the possible disturbance of the remains of the two pilots. Not only was the wreck of JT160 wrapped up in fishing line it was now entangled in red tape, too. When the matter finally reached a hearing, Judge Singal decreed that the basis of the claim by Tallichet and Hagen for the right of salvage and finds over the Corsair(s) rested within US Admiralty Law and found that, in this instance, Admiralty Law did not apply:

> "Sebago Lake is considered a 'great pond' and the lake, its contents and the land underneath it are held in trust by the State of Maine for the public. From approximately 1830 until 1870 it was possible to navigate from Sebago Lake to the Atlantic Ocean via the Cumberland & Oxford Canal. However, for well over a century Sebago Lake has been essentially landlocked and navigation is limited to other connected bodies of water within Maine. For Admiralty Law to apply, the piece of water must be navigable within the meaning of that law. In this case that piece of water is not navigable, and thus the basis of the claim by Historic Aircraft Recovery Corporation cannot stand."

Essentially, Judge Singal pronounced that it was not his place to decide and in dismissing the case he effectively ruled for the State of Maine and the British government. JT160, possibly with the remains of Sub Lt Knott, (and JT132 with Sub Lt Gill wherever they lay) would for the time being at least rest on the bottom of Sebago Lake.

In making his clear decision that Admiralty Law could not apply to Sebago Lake, Judge Singal may well have only temporarily avoided further legal arguments and submissions –

matters that even yet might surface in a court of appeal before either of the Corsairs can surface in the lake. For instance, what of the question as to title to these two aeroplanes – whatever the restrictions on salvage or interference? Both were supplied to the UK government under the lend-lease arrangements. When the Lend-Lease Act was passed by Congress on 11 March 1941 it stipulated that aircraft remained the property of the USA and must be returned at the end of World War Two. To account for Lend-Lease materiel, US field commissioners were established in various theatres of operations and after the cessation of hostilities all US-owned equipment was offered back to Britain. Aircraft lost in accidents and by enemy action had been noted and it became the responsibility of the appropriate field commissioner to decide on the disposal of surviving Lend-Lease aeroplanes.

What, then, of the Sebago Corsairs? As both were 'lost', and have remained so ever since, does title to the newly discovered wreck revert back to the US under the Lend-Lease rules? Certainly, they were US property at the time of their loss and so it is hard to see how the UK-based Ministry of Defence are in a position to influence a court in the USA to exercise some control over them at their behest, unless the airframes in question have now specifically been gifted to the UK government. Either way, these are doubtless all arguments that will yet be rehearsed in court should the matter go to appeal. There are, though, issues relating specifically to the two missing pilots (although doubtless it is the pilots that are the primary matter of concern for the UK Ministry of Defence) that cannot be ignored here.

Of course, within the UK the Protection of Military Remains Act 1986 would serve to protect the crash sites and the unfortunate aircrew although clearly this does not apply in another sovereign state. However, a strange dichotomy is thrown up in this case which involves two 'missing' aircrew from Britain who most probably lie within the wrecks of their respective aircraft within the United States. On the one hand we have a government in Britain that generally stands opposed to recovery of missing airmen such as Knott and Gill and have fought to prevent any such recovery taking place. On the other hand, we have two missing aircrew lying within the United States – a country that vigorously and pro-actively seeks out its missing from all conflicts and from all around the globe. Indeed, as recently as 22 October 2009, the US Senate and House passed the National Defense Authorization Act of 2010. The bill now goes to the president for signature and instructs the secretary of defense to "implement a comprehensive, coordinated, integrated and fully resourced program to account for the Missing from WWII through today, and to triple recovery rates to 200 per year by 2015." Had Knott and Gill been US servicemen there can be little doubt that, by now, an official recovery by the US CILHI team would have been undertaken and the two men repatriated to their families.

In pursuing their case to prevent any further interference or recovery of these two aircraft, it is likely that the State of Maine and the Ministry of Defence might well have had concerns relating to the propriety of such sensitive recoveries and been mindful, too, that this was essentially a commercial venture. Despite the moral and ethical issues at stake here, it is a matter of fact that these airframes *do* have a commercial value. To pretend otherwise would be foolish. Indeed, The Historic Aircraft Recovery Corporation have been up-front about their aims and would clearly need to invest a great deal of money to recover – let alone restore – either of the Corsairs. However, they are also clear as regards to their obligations to the two pilots and state that they are intent on working to ensure their proper and reverent recovery, identification and eventual burial.

So far as Hagen and Tallichet are concerned, Sub Lts Knott and Gill are their primary consideration in all of this and it is fair to say that the Historic Aircraft Recovery Corp have an impressive record when it comes to finding and recovering the missing. In a mission to Papua New Guinea, Hagen was looking for a B-25 in which his uncle had been lost but managed to find instead four other wrecks with the remains of US pilots. In each case the authorities were duly informed and American teams subsequently recovered the remains, notified families and had the men buried back home in the USA. Thus, there is no reason to suppose that Hagen and Tallichet would act in anything other than an honourable way in the case of the Sebago Corsairs. Indeed, the recoveries would doubtless be conducted in the glare of publicity when the salvage team's actions and methods would be subject to the closest public scrutiny. In fact, HARC have made it clear that they would welcome official co-operation in the project should it ever go ahead. For the time being, however, the project has stalled. So, what of the future?

The underwater film footage secured by the Historic Aircraft Recovery Corporation shows remarkable and dramatic imagery of the one Corsair so far found. Incredibly, it still retains its original paint and markings and with fabric still attached to control surfaces, although both of the main-planes seem to have separated from the fuselage. With its cockpit canopy open and, apparently, locked back it is possible to view ROV images into the cockpit. Remarkably intact, there is clearly a collection of unidentifiable material lying across the instrument panel and control column. Whilst it is difficult to ascertain what this might be, it is possible that it could be a parachute pack and flying overalls. Certainly, the whole of the instrument panel is obliterated by something and an object lodged above the gunsight on the cockpit coaming might well be a femur.

Viewing these images it is difficult not to take the view adopted by the US government in such matters – ie that the missing should be found and accounted for. Peter E Hess, the Admiralty & Maritime lawyer acting for Hagen and Tallichet, is emphatic about what is the right thing to do and about his client's intentions.

> "The pilot is still in the cockpit, with fishing line strewn all around and lying forgotten 300ft on the bottom of a lake and a long way from home. Can that be right? All the time it is also vulnerable to damage from people or the environment. This is not a fitting resting place for a brave soul like Sub Lt Knott. The right thing needs to be done – lay Sub Lt Knott to rest and preserve his airplane in his memory. And only the Historic Aircraft Recovery Corporation know exactly where the Corsairs are and have the means to salvage them."

For the time being, all that is on hold. National Geographic have meanwhile expressed some interest in film rights to a documentary with plans already laid, although not yet furthered, to dive during the winter ice period when underwater biological conditions are at their best. Cutting a hole immediately above the located wreck, free swimming divers in heated suits would descend to the Corsair and, for the first time inspect and film the aeroplane close-up. The other Corsair, not yet located, cannot be far away and the Historic Aircraft Recovery Corporation are confident of their ability to find it shortly. Until then, we must content ourselves with the remarkable pictures already acquired whilst awaiting any further legal moves that might take the project forward. In the interim, Hagen and Tallichet would dearly love to establish contact with any family members of Knott or Gill, but so far relatives have not been found.

Lucretia Douglas, one of the last surviving witnesses of the fatal crash, recently expressed the view that it should not be up to courts, governments or individuals to determine these things. Ultimately, she felt, the families should decide. Indeed, should the families express the desire for further work then this would spur the Historic Aircraft Recovery Corporation to take forward the court appeal and also for them to strive to work together with any appropriate agency to secure the desired result. In the words of lawyer Peter E Hess, and echoed by Lucretia Douglas, "….the right thing needs to be done."

Unlike RAF aircrew casualties who are missing with no known grave, Sub Lts Gill and Knott are not remembered on the Runnymede memorial but instead have their names recorded at the Lee-on-Solent memorial in Hampshire. Raymond Knott's name is also to be found on the war memorial at his old school, Kings, in Grantham, Lincolnshire.

CHAPTER 10 Beyond All Reach

THAT 'RIGHT THING' TO which Lucretia Douglas referred in relation to the two Corsair pilots is, of course, the proper recovery, identification and reverent burial of remains wherever it can be achieved. In the case of the Corsair pilots that may never be possible. Like many missing aircrew they may simply be beyond all reach anyway, and that is certainly most probably true of the majority of missing airmen from all nations and all conflicts. Of course, many who have previously been considered beyond such reach have been recovered in recent years with the discovery of Plt Off C B Barber (Chapter Three) being a case in point. However, there continues to be a surprising number of RAF airmen still classified as missing with no known grave and who perished on home soil. Whilst these are men who were deemed, not unreasonably, to be beyond all reach it is a fact that the situation that sees them still classified as missing almost seventy years later is, in part, compounded by the policy of non-disturbance and non-recovery by the UK's Ministry of Defence. One such relates to a memorial to a still missing Lancaster crew near Boston, Lincolnshire. The memorial, alongside a narrow road between Bicker and Algarkirk reads:

To the Glory of God
And in Honoured Memory
Of
Flt Sgt D J Farran
Sgt R H F Malthouse
Sgt J B Bannan
Sgt J W Nixon
W/O R T Lord
Flt Sgt A I G Hunter

Who lost their lives when Avro Lancaster ND820 of 635 Squadron crashed here whilst on a flight from RAF Downham Market, Monday 10 April 1944 and who now lay at rest in the surrounding fields. Their names are commemorated on the Runnymede Memorial to the missing.
Also in memory of crew member Fg Off T F Wilson buried in
Stonefall Cemetery, Harrogate.

Above: The crash site of Lancaster ND820. It is understood that the wreck of the aircraft, together with the missing crew, lies buried alongside and under the small road. The memorial is just to the right of the road with the tree on the left sheltering a very lucky farm worker from harm when the Lancaster impacted.

Right: Flt Sgt Joseph Bernard Bannan of Head's Nook, Cumberland, was one of the crew on board Lancaster ND820 which dived into fields between Bicker and Algarkirk, Lincolnshire, on 10 April 1944. The entire crew, apart from the rear gunner, remain missing and lie buried somewhere at the crash site. A roadside memorial to the crew has been set up, albeit that it incorrectly records Bannan as a Sergeant instead of a Flight Sergeant.

Here, then, are commemorated six airmen who still lie in unmarked graves on British soil. Whether they are still truly beyond reach in 2011 it is perhaps difficult to judge, although another Lancaster loss over Britain is most probably within that category. It also contains the remains of missing aircrew. This aircraft is a Lancaster I (W4890) of 1667 Heavy Conversion Unit which took off from RAF Lindholme at 12.25 hours on 10 February 1945 for a cross-country exercise with a crew of seven on board. The pilot, Flt Lt G A Liversedge, had been briefed to avoid and therefore not enter expected cumulus-nimbus cloud but high over RAF Thorney Island on the West Sussex coast Liversedge edged his Lancaster into the lethal cloud formation.

It is believed that the Lancaster initially suffered icing before breaking up in the violent forces within the cloud formation, and then being seen to plummet out of the cloud base on fire before major portions of the rapidly disintegrating airframe plunged into the upper reaches of Thorney Channel just south of Prinsted village at 14.50 hours. At once, the wrecked centre section, cockpit, wings and engines vanished beneath the tidal mud and water of what is part of Chichester harbour along with all seven crew members and was immediately lost to view.

A terrific shot of a Lancaster in flight.

In its terminal fall earthwards the twisting, turning, diving and tumbling wreck must have exerted terrific centrifugal forces on the crew and there could have been no hope of escaping from their crew stations, let alone exiting the disintegrating aircraft, during those awful few moments in the plunge of W4890. When the spray and swirling foam had subsided, just patches of petrol and small bits of floating debris bobbed on the receding tide above a muddy and oily patch of the channel. The water here is relatively shallow even at high tide, and at low tide the mud bed of what is part of Chichester harbour is exposed. When the tide had fully gone out just a black gash in the mud was evident, with scattered and jagged bits of silver aluminium and black and camouflage painted airframe all that was visibly left of the Lancaster.

Over the following days, personnel from the adjacent RAF station at Thorney Island undertook salvage operations at the site and later boats and divers joined the efforts. Initially, three bodies were found but ultimately the bodies of five members of crew were recovered; Flt Lt G A Liversedge, Fg Off C D Callum, Sgt H Netzger, Sgt P B Kellegher and Sgt C B Darby. Of Sgt C Woodhead and Fg Off S J King, however, no trace could be found although salvage operations were still ongoing by 24 February Eventually, the search was called off and a service was conducted by the RAF Thorney Island chaplain from a boat moored over the site. The five recovered airmen were buried at various locations in the UK, although Fg Off Charles Callum, the flight engineer, was buried at Thorney Island very close to the spot where he had lost his life.

Ultimately, Woodhead and King were commemorated on the Runnymede Memorial and it is probably true to say that considerable efforts were made to find them in 1945, albeit without success. There can be little doubt, therefore, that Colin Woodhead and Harold King lie somewhere, beyond all reach, in the murk of Chichester harbour. However, it is certainly likely that a concerted search effort of the type undertaken by the American recovery and identification teams would most likely find them but such an operation can probably be considered as unlikely. That said, Harold's sister Phyllis Webb, writing to the author in 1987 articulated her feelings on the matter:

"It is a great comfort to me to know that there is someone interested in what happened on 10 February 1945. My parents were devastated and never got over the shock. To me, it is an everlasting sorrow. I do not like to think of Harold lying lost and forgotten in that harbour and I hope that one day he might be found and laid to rest for the sake of his mother and father. It would be the right thing. I hope one day that 'right thing' can be done."

Surprisingly, the two Lancasters detailed above are far from the only such aircraft of that type still missing with their crews over the UK and at Sibsey in Lincolnshire there stands yet another memorial to the men lost when Lancaster ED503 of 9 Squadron crashed whilst on fighter affiliation practice. The memorial, situated in a field two miles north-west of the village, reads:

Here lies the crew of a Lancaster bomber which
crashed on 29 January 1943.
This memorial is their families' tribute of love
and remembrance.
Ronald A Brown
Charles W H Cocks
John Doran
Thomas S Henry
Bobby F Lind

The wording of the memorial is slightly ambiguous in that it is not the entire crew as the sixth man, the rear gunner, was the only crew member found; Sgt T Wishart being buried at Dalkeith. Naturally being at the rear of the aircraft, his body was found on or near the surface whilst the rest of the Lancaster with its six occupants became deeply embedded and out of reach in the soft ground.

An interesting element associated with all of these Lancaster crashes is that they were lost on training flights as opposed to operational sorties, and it is certainly the case that an overwhelming majority of RAF casualties in the UK were sustained through flying accidents and training. In relation to such losses to RAF Bomber Command, author John Terraine in his book *Right of The Line* has the following to say:

"From first to last, 1939-45, the Royal Air Force lost 70,253 officers, NCOs and airmen killed or missing on operations, the overwhelming majority of them being aircrew. This was the price of its victory, and of it by far the largest share fell to Bomber Command between Sept 1939 and May 1945: 47,268. This great number is the grim total of those lost on operations; it was the unique hazard of the airman's trade that a further 8,305 Bomber Command aircrew lost their lives in non-operational flying – training or accident. In addition, 1,570 ground crew (RAF and WAAF) were killed or lost their lives from other causes during that period, making a full total of 57,143."

This, of course, is not the overall total of RAF casualties lost in the 1939-45 war with that figure standing at a staggering 116,000. Included in that latter figure are obviously those lost to non-operational causes in other commands; coastal, fighter and training commands. The latter command saw at least one RAF aircrew member posted as missing over the UK after his aircraft crashed in Shropshire; the name of its under-training pilot LAC John Toplis Carr, 1252426, being inscribed on Panel 56 of the Runnymede Memorial. He is recorded as the son of Charles Watson Carr and Elsie Margaret Carr and at just nineteen years of age he is the youngest missing casualty dealt with in this book. He was lost during a solo training flight in a Miles Master trainer.

John Carr was doubtless inspired by the exploits of pilots from RAF Fighter Command who, during the Battle of Britain, he must have almost daily seen in action above his Eastbourne home on the East Sussex coast. His selection for pilot training on joining the RAF must have therefore been cause for great excitement and celebration to the aspirant teenage pilot. Having got through his basic training and its attendant square bashing and lectures at an initial training wing, he had progressed through to an elementary flying training school and thence on to 5 Flying Training School at RAF Tern Hill, Shropshire.

It was from here, on 10 April 1941, that Carr took off in Miles Master T8827 for a cross-country flying exercise that took him from Tern Hill to RAF Sealand, then down to Great Malvern and from there back to Tern Hill. Carr was doubtless congratulating himself on completing his milestone task successfully and was settling down into the landing pattern at his home airfield and probably engrossed in his pre-landing checks, running through undercarriage selection, airspeed, flap settings and the like. The cross-country solo had been another major way-mark on the road to the eventual award of his pilot's wings. Life was doubtless good and the dream of becoming an RAF pilot was just around the corner. It was a dream, too, for another young LAC airman, Dennis Hartley, at that moment taking off from RAF Tern Hill in another Master, T8439, to carry out a similar training flight to the one just completed by John Carr. Hartley was also just nineteen years of age.

Quite what occurred is open to some speculation, although somehow the trainee pilots apparently did not see each other. As Hartley was concentrating on his take-off and Carr on his landing both aircraft collided in mid-air in the Tern Hill circuit. Hartley's Master crashed, out of control, at nearby Stoke Heath and the young trainee pilot was killed on impact. Carr's aircraft, however, plunged into a swampy and waterlogged piece of land at Helshaw Grange Farm, Tern Hill, and immediately vanished almost totally from sight. Just part of the tail-plane was visible above the surface and farm worker Bill Ashley was first on the scene and aghast at what he could see – or rather, at what little he could see. To him, it seemed incomprehensible that a whole aeroplane could have simply vanished from view, with just a small part left showing.

The Miles Master was a standard single-engine two-seat RAF trainer aircraft of World War Two. Here, one of these aircraft is looked over by fighter pilots from an American Eagle Squadron during October 1940. It was in an aircraft of this type that trainee pilot LAC John Carr was lost.

Shaken by what he had seen, and knowing that the pilot had not escaped, he guided an RAF rescue and recovery team to the site. Of the pilot, there was simply no trace although efforts were at once begun to haul the aircraft out of the bog using farm horses harnessed to ropes and chains. Inevitably, the attempt was futile and only succeeded in pulling off part of the tail section as the rest of the Miles Master sank deeper still into the sodden peat. According to the Ministry of Defence, writing in 1978:

"Considerable efforts were made by Royal Air Force Tern Hill to locate the remains of LAC John Toplis Carr in aircraft T8827. It is recorded that the Royal Engineers declined to undertake the salvage and the Station Commander, RAF Tern Hill, reported that there was considerable danger of loss of life to his salvage party through continuing subsidence. They were down to sixteen feet underground in the swamp and because of the danger authority was sought and given to abandon the salvage."

Whether or not Mr and Mrs Carr were told as to exactly where their son's body lay entombed is not known, although they were eventually notified that his name would be recorded on Panel 56 of the Runnymede Memorial. As for Dennis Hartley, his body was extricated from the wreckage of his aircraft the next day and taken to the station mortuary at Tern Hill. From here, he was taken home for burial at Basildon (St Bartholemew) Churchyard although there was to be no burial back at home for his colleague John Carr.

In 1977 the Wartime Aircraft Recovery Group became interested in the crash site of the aircraft at Helshaw Grange and although this long pre-dated the requirements of the

Protection of Military Remains Act, the group sought and obtained on 11 October 1977 the authority of the MOD to carry out an excavation and recovery at the crash site. Under the leadership of Donald Matthews from Shrewsbury, the WARG chairman, the team began an excavation at the crash site on Sunday 22 October 1978 by hand, although they only succeeded in recovering a few inconsequential parts. It was clearly apparent that witness Bill Ashley had been right and that the bulk of the aeroplane was deeply buried in the soft ground.

The memorial to missing RAF and Commonwealth air crew who have no known grave is situated overlooking the River Thames at Runnymede, near Windsor. Amongst them Leading Aircraftman John Toplis Carr.

The following Friday, 27 October, the team returned with a mechanical excavator and managed to extract the rear fuselage (clearly marked T8827), the cockpit area and the Rolls-Royce Kestrel engine. Also discovered was a data plate confirming the aircraft serial number to have been T8827. Not surprisingly the team found the shattered remains of the pilot amongst the cockpit debris and duly notified the local police of their grim discovery. Police Constable William Stevenson was despatched from Market Drayton to attend what was undoubtedly one of the strangest calls of his career, dealing with a wartime RAF casualty.

At the crash site, Stevenson was confronted with a twenty-five-foot diameter pit which had already filled with water up to four feet from the top. Alongside was a trailer load of debris which he was told had once been an aircraft in which Donald Matthews told him he had found human remains. The remains, and associated clothing, were taken by Stevenson for HM Coroner and were ultimately delivered to the senior medical officer at RAF Shawbury on 21 November for examination by police officers and a civilian medical specialist in aviation pathology, Mr Underwood-Ground. It was found that the remains were those of a male, aged around his early 20s, and that the trousers and tunic were those of an airman but bore no name, number or any indication as to rank. However, a diary was found in which a pencilled note was still legible: 'My birthday 4th July'.

This information certainly tallied with the date of birth for John Carr which RAF records showed to be 4 July 1921. This, coupled with the aircraft number T8827, was sufficient enough evidence to allow Mr M T Gwynne TD, coroner for the East Shropshire District, to confirm the identity of the deceased pilot and convene an inquest at Wellington, Telford, on 13 February 1979. Here, at the formal hearing, Mr Gwynne pronounced a verdict of accidental death and released the remains for eventual burial with full military honours at Brookwood Military Cemetery in Surrey.

Unfortunately, John's parents had long since died and the trail ended at their last known address in Motcombe Lane, Eastbourne. The author, then living in the town, also tried to unearth clues that might lead to relatives or friends of the Carr's. Those who might have been comforted by his discovery and burial, had mostly gone and it was only later that his sister was traced. Nevertheless, the pledge to honour men like John Carr in perpetuity by the CWGC had been fulfilled.

In 1941, John Carr was deemed to be beyond reach and was one of those in the post-war years who were ignored in the much wider European searches by the MREU teams. Very often, and as we have seen in Chapter 4, the MREU teams chanced upon airmen of foreign air forces who served with the RAF, including Poles and Czechs. The latter, unusually, are commemorated at Runnymede and include the name of Wt Off Jindrich Landsmann of 310 Squadron, recorded as lost on 15 June 1945 in a mid-air collision with another Spitfire from his squadron.

The grave of nineteen-year-old LAC J T Carr is now at Brookwood Military Cemetery, Surrey, where he was buried in 1979 – another name that could be removed from the long Runnymede list. By 1979 only John Carr's sister, Mrs Mary Seagrief of South Africa, was left behind to grieve her long-lost brother.

The circumstances of his loss are that twelve aircraft of 310 Squadron (Czech), detached from RAF Manston, took off from RAF Wattisham at 14:00 hrs for a fighter affiliation exercise with a Mustang squadron. Flying Officer Viktor Popelka in Spitfire MH330 (NN*U) led Blue Section. At approx. 14:30 hours the Mustangs duly 'attacked' the Spitfires. The Spitfire leader commenced a climbing turn to port and despatched Blue Section to attack. They disappeared beneath and to starboard of the main formation. Blue Leader (Popelka) and Red 4, Warrant Officer Jindrich Landsmann flying Spitfire MH323 (NN*L), collided at 14:35 hours over Potters Bridge, South Cove, near Southwold.

Spitfire MH323 was seen to disintegrate and MH330 went into a spin from which F/O Popelka was able to bale out. He came down in the sea and was picked up after an hour by the Royal Navy trawler HMS *Florio*. His aircraft crashed on heath land overlooking the reed beds by Potters Bridge. No trace was ever found of Landsmann despite an extensive search. The Court of Inquiry found no evidence to show how the collision had occurred, although it was shown that pilots had been warned during briefing, and once again after take-off, of the possibility of mid-air collision.

Potters Bridge is situated about two miles north of Southwold and is less than one mile from the sea. Between the bridge and the sea lies marsh and reed beds and a local researcher and experienced aviation archaeologist, Geoff Carless, was told by witnesses that Landsmann's Spitfire had vanished in the reed beds although this has never been corroborated. If true, then these reed beds hold the remains of the last Czech airman to lose his life whilst flying with the RAF. If Spitfire and pilot are not hidden underground at Potters Bridge then the only alternative is that Landsmann also fell into the sea after abandoning his aircraft and his body was never found. Either way, he can surely be considered 'out of reach' although maybe someday and somehow that situation might change if a Spitfire wreck at Potters Bridge is ever recovered.

That possibility, however, is most likely rather slim although we need to bear in mind that

Left: Whilst the Runnymede Memorial records the names of RAF and Commonwealth air force personnel who are missing with no known grave, an exception is made for the non-Commonwealth Czech airmen who are missing. With no memorial in post-war communist Czechoslovakia it was deemed appropriate to remember Czech airmen this way, the Poles having their own memorial at Northolt. This is Spitfire pilot Wt Off Jindrich Landsmann who is missing with no known grave after a mid-air collision over the east coast of England on 15 June 1945.

Right: Landsmann collided with another Spitfire flown by fellow Czech, Fg Off Viktor Popelka, who baled out and was rescued from the North Sea.

John Carr, along with many other RAF casualties, were ere-long considered to be beyond reach. As the years roll by perhaps it is increasingly a case of applying that old adage "never say never". Sheer determination, and the availability of plant and equipment not dreamt of in the 1940s, has increasingly made such long-abandoned recoveries possible in the twenty-first century. Whilst Landsmann might not fall into this category, it is certain that there are yet missing RAF casualties on land within the British Isles who could be recovered, identified and honourably buried.

Had he completed his training and gained his 'wings', John Carr would have doubtless been posted, eventually, to an operational squadron. Perhaps he would not have survived a career as an operational pilot in any event. The odds would certainly be stacked against him. However, here was one young man who never got beyond the stage of his flying training before being reported as missing, presumed dead. Along with the Lancaster crews covered at the start of this chapter, John Carr was one of the many thousands lost during their training. On the other hand, Flt Sgt Reginald Thursby, lost over Normandy on 9 August 1944, had followed exactly the same tentative training course as John Carr; through initial training wings and thence to an elementary flying training school before he was posted to an operational squadron. It was here, as a Typhoon pilot with 198 Squadron, that his life was cut short.

CHAPTER 11

The Last Time He Was Seen…

I N *FINDING THE FEW* I told how an RAF maintenance unit had examined the crash site of a Spitfire at Sittingbourne, Kent, in September 1940 and discovered the serial number P9364 amongst the wreckage there. From this information it ought to have been easily possible to identify this as the aircraft in which Sgt Ernest Scott was lost on 27 September 1940 and thereby to have solved the mystery of his disappearance. Instead, that vital clue was overlooked or ignored and Ernest Scott remained missing until the winter of 1990, long after his still grieving mother had passed away still anxious for news of her son. A similar set of circumstances surrounded the loss of Reginald Thursby. They were circumstances that ultimately led to his name being recorded at Runnymede on Panel 222 and his status remaining as 'missing' until 1985. The story began on 10 August 1944 with the report of the French commanding officer of 198 Squadron, Sqn Ldr Ezanno:

Sgt Reginald Thursby.

"10 August 1944

Sir
Circumstantial Report – 1321893 Flt Sgt THURSBY R A
Reported Missing 9 August 1944
    I have the honour to refer to 123 Wing Headquarters signal T.201 dated 9 August 1944 and to submit the following circumstantial report on the above-named airman reported missing from operations.
    2) Eight Typhoon IBs of 198 Squadron, led by Sqn Ldr Y P E H Ezanno C de G, took off from B7 A.L.G, Martragny, France at 18.15 hours on 9 August 1944 on an armed recce south of Falaise. Flt Sgt Thursby was flying in Green section made up of four aircraft, led by Flt Lt Sweeting DFC and Flt Sgt Thursby was flying as Green 4.

3) At about 18.30 hrs this section attacked gun positions at Fourches and afterwards made an attack on the Bois de Feuillet in which movements of troops and tanks had been suspected. After this attack Green 4 (Flt Sgt Thursby) called up on the R/T to say that he had been hit by flak and was on fire but that he would try to put the fire out and make for our lines. The last time he was seen he was climbing with a slight stream of smoke pouring from his aircraft.

4) He asked for a homing and two minutes later informed Operations on the R/T that he was going to bale out. It is uncertain whether he landed in our own lines or the enemy lines. Nothing further has been heard of Flt Sgt Thursby and he has been reported as 'Missing'.

I have the honour to be,
Sir,
Your obedient servant,
Y Ezanno
Squadron Leader Commanding
198 Squadron RAF."

Although nothing further was heard from Thursby, villagers on the ground at Sainte-Marguerite-de-Viette, just to the east of Saint-Pierre-sur-Dives, saw an aircraft low over the village being engaged by German anti-aircraft fire. The aircraft suffered repeated hits, but climbed slightly before the canopy opened making it look as though the pilot were preparing to bale out. Suddenly, the aircraft rolled over onto its back and then dived vertically into the edge of a wood at Bois de Quevrue before the pilot had got out. When locals finally got to the scene they discovered the aircraft had buried

Bombing-up a Typhoon prior to yet another raid.

itself in soft ground on the site of a natural spring. Only the outer wings and tail remained above ground; the latter marked with the serial number JR256.

As the German forces were ejected from this part of France, so the invading allied forces came across unburied casualties and crashed aircraft of all combatant nations and it was clear that the tidying-up operation would be long and arduous. In the cases of sites like the one at Bois de Quevrue, these were added to the list of locations due for investigation by the RAF missing research and enquiry teams and in February 1945 the crash site was examined.

It was noted that the aircraft was JR256 and that the pilot (Thursby) could be identified by squadron records. However, the crater caused by the crash was full of water and when the MREU re-visited in June 1945 the wet and boggy nature of the ground still prevented further investigation. Consequently, the site must have been put on a back-list by the MREU and doubtless they intended, one day, to return to the scene. After all, they had a work load of some 40,000 potential cases and thus cannot be criticised for not having dealt with the Thursby case before the MREUs were wound-up in 1949.

Unfortunately, Reginald's mother and his fiancé Doreen were never told that the location where he had crashed had been found and the case was just one of some 20,000 that ultimately went unresolved and forgotten when the British government considered that it had discharged its responsibility to Reginald Thursby by the recording of his name at Runnymede.

It was a responsibility that the mayor of Sainte-Marguerite-de-Viette, M Michel Bonnissent, considered had been far from discharged when he became aware of the site and its circumstances in 1984 during preparations for D-Day commemorative celebrations. At once, he contacted the British Embassy in Paris about the plight of this missing pilot. He was perplexed and shocked to be told that the British MOD would not act in the matter of the recovery of this pilot's body, and that the policy of the MOD was that all crash sites known or believed to contain human remains should be left undisturbed. "In that case," said M Bonnissent, "if they do not want him I will have him buried in the village cemetery." The British response had unintentionally been the very catalyst for ensuring that Reginald Thursby would no longer remain on the missing list; the commune had now taken on that responsibility through its incumbent mayor.

Through a team associated with the Second World War Memorial Museum at Bayeux, M Bonnissent engaged a party led by M Jacques Brehin and the museum's curator, M Jean-Pierre Benamou, to dig out the wreckage and hopefully locate and identify the pilot's body. Of course, it is worth remembering that sensitivities in relation to the finding of human remains from the casualties of both world wars in France are much less heightened than might they be in the UK where such finds are relatively rare. In France, of course, it is almost a weekly occurrence – so many casualties having been lost on its soil. In any event, this was a quasi-official operation that had been sanctioned by the Mairie and on 10 September 1985 digging operations commenced at the site and began with the laborious task of pumping out the still-flooded crater. Scattered around were fragments identifiable as Typhoon wreckage and sticking out of the ground nearby was one of the Typhoon's under-wing rocket launch rails, thus far the only marker of Reginald Thursby's resting place.

By 13 September the team had extricated the wreckage, including the Napier Sabre engine, from a deep and muddy pit and working waist-deep in water they had to work blind with their hands to carry out the grim task of recovering what was left of the pilot. When they had finished their work they had found some 75% of the pilot's mortal remains and discovered a piece of wreckage with the serial number JR256 – a direct link to Reginald Thursby. With the British Embassy informed on 14 September Wg Cdr A P Bell RAF, the British air attaché in Paris, subsequently visited to view the wreckage and remains and he was shown the serial number and a piece of paper that had been found with the radio and marked '123 Wing'. Before any official pronouncements were made, however, the former CO Paul Ezanno was contacted in France and told about the discovery and the serial number JR256. Without any hesitation, Ezanno was able to say straightaway: "That was Reginald!"

Ultimately, Ezanno's pronouncements were officially confirmed by the Ministry of Defence who took over all responsibility for tracing relatives and organising a funeral in a

Embedded deep underground, the huge Napier Sabre engine was hauled to the surface after the remains of Reg Thursby had been carefully recovered. Here, the private recovery team pose with the engine after their rewarding task which would ultimately see another missing pilot appropriately buried.

CWGC plot – Mayor Bonnissent's original plans to 'claim' him and have him buried in the village now being set aside. In the event, it turned out that Reginald had no siblings and that his father had died in 1929. After all attempts to see if his mother was still living it was an announcement in *The Daily Mail* that finally led to the only relative coming forward, a distant cousin. He was able to confirm that Reginald's mother had since passed away, never knowing what had happened to her precious only son. As with the case of Ernest Scott in 1940, the opportunity to put at rest the mind of a grief-stricken mother had been carelessly passed over. No living family members could be traced, thus underlining how the conflict that was World War Two had often effectively eliminated family lines.

Whilst family and kin could not be present to see Reginald laid to rest by the Royal Air Force with full military honours at Saint-Charles-de-Percy British Military Cemetery on 5 November 1985, survivors of the 'family' that had been Reginald's 198 Squadron were there to say farewell. Of the party from 198 Squadron, Sheppard and Sweeting had flown on that fateful sortie of 9 August 1944, the latter having been leading Green Section that day. All of them were now old men who could only reflect on how fate had spared them to live full and fruitful lives whilst taking that of Reginald at just twenty-two. Who can imagine their private thoughts as the British Legion exhortation "At the going down of the sun" and "Age shall not weary them" was read at the graveside? Now, however, they finally knew exactly what had happened to one of their own.

Forty-one years after he had disappeared, Reg Thursby was laid to rest with full military honours at Saint-Charles-de-Percy military cemetery, France, in the presence of his former CO, Paul Ezanno, and other squadron pilots. They are, from left to right: Ken Kneen, 'Tatters' Tatham, Alex Sibbald, Dennis Sweeting, 'Titch' Hallett, George Sheppard, and Jos Reynolds. Also there was Paul Ezanno, Reginald's former CO, and Doreen Young his former fiancé.

CHAPTER 12 The Missing Air Gunners

I N *FINDING THE FEW* and *Finding The Foe* I examined several cases where the mysteries of individual disappearances had, to an extent, been solved except insofar as actually *locating* the bodies of the missing aircrew concerned. Thus it seems appropriate to look at some similar cases in this book; one British, one German.

Once again, the British case is one involving an accident on a training flight that needlessly claimed the lives of nine airmen on 17 January 1942. It was a tragic accident over the Cambridgeshire Fens that resulted in no trace of two of the nine men ever being found. Consequently, Sgt James McCarley and Sgt Walter James Mankelow's names are amongst those to found at Runnymede although one has to ask; should it not be possible to rectify that position?

High above Earith, Hurricane V6865 of 56 OTU wheeled and dived in a series of mock attacks on Stirling W7467 of 7 Squadron out of nearby RAF Oakington but in the late afternoon haze the pilot of the Hurricane, Plt Off D M Browne, misjudged one of his attacks and sliced violently into the bomber. It was a terminal blow for both aircraft, and Browne's Hurricane plunged away to crash outside the village, taking its pilot to his death. Stirling W7467, meanwhile, dived into the ground at Sutton Fen, one and a half miles north of Earith Fen, straddling a drainage ditch and taking its combat-experienced

By any standards, the Short Stirling was a huge aeroplane and its size is emphasised here in this truly classic photograph. Its weight and size caused Stirling W7467 to literally disappear beneath the soft fenland soil after a collision with a Hurricane above Earith, Cambridgeshire.

crew of eight with it. Nobody had any chance to abandon either aircraft, and in an instant nine lives had been extinguished.

The crash site of the Stirling was, as one might expect, very soft fenland terrain that simply yielded to the horrendous impact of many tons of machinery travelling at probably 200mph plus. Such was the force of impact that engines, fuselage and crew were driven deep into the ground by the crash although somehow the salvage gangs from an RAF maintenance unit retrieved the mangled bodies of six of the men from the wreckage. They were: Flt Sgt R W Taylor DFM (pilot), Sqn Ldr J N Mahler DFC, Sgt E Blacklaw, Sgt F J Lloyd, Plt Off A J Low and Plt Off J D Waddell. Of McCarley and Mankelow there was no sign. However, and although the facts are a little vague, it would appear that Walter Mankelow's wife travelled up to Cambridge Cemetery fully expecting to be attending her

One of the missing men was Sgt Walter Mankelow.

husband's funeral only to find that he was not amongst those accounted for. Instead, she placed her floral tributes on the graves of some of the others being buried there and later was sent a photograph of a cross bearing his name that had been erected at the crash site.

By 1987 all trace of the marker cross had gone, and just a slight depression either side of a small brook marked the crash scene. Incredibly, and notwithstanding the fact that two crew members were still missing, the Ministry of Defence gave permission to a private individual to excavate at the crash site on the basis that only the engines would be recovered and the impact area of the fuselage (believed to be in the ditch) would not be disturbed. In the event, that is essentially what occurred with massive sections of airframe, engines and undercarriage being hauled out of the ground. A number of non-engine-related items came to light but of the fuselage and missing men there was absolutely no sign during what amounted to a partial recovery.

Possibly, and had the recovery focussed carefully on the fuselage area (or been allowed to), maybe the cases of McCarley and Mankelow could have been closed. For the son of Walter Mankelow, also called Walter, that would have been a satisfactory outcome and he was prompted to write and ask the recovery team, post-excavation: "Did you find any part of the mid-upper turret or of the rear turret?" The reason for his questioning was clear; both missing men had been air gunners. Sadly, the answer he was given had to be negative. Quite possibly, the answer he sought lies buried deeper still at Sutton Fen. Most likely, that is where the answer will remain for at least the foreseeable future.

Perhaps rather less care was taken in the UK with German casualties than might have been the case with allied aircrew. In many ways, that is entirely understandable. However, in the case of a Junkers 88 shot down into Portsmouth harbour there was precious little that anyone could have done to retrieve the body of one of the unfortunate crew members who

In 1987 the MOD granted a licence to recover the Stirling wreck to a then-serving RAF serviceman, Peter Stanley. It is understood that this licence was granted on the basis that the fuselage impact area (and by definition where the two missing airmen ought to be) was not disturbed. Huge amounts of wreckage were recovered including engines and propellers, although it seems a great shame that an opportunity to recover two missing aircrew had evidently been vetoed. It is hard to imagine that the relatives of Sgts Mankelow and McCarley would have been anything other than delighted. Here, excavations are underway at the site with a propeller assembly and Bristol Hercules engine visible in the foreground.

had been taken down into the mud of the harbour not far from Portchester Castle. That said, French sailors from the battleship *Courbet* which had been moored in the harbour are known to have visited the wreck site and ugly and grisly rumours have abounded for many-a-year suggesting that the French matelots 'disposed' of the remains in one of the ship's boilers. Whilst there is no evidence that this actually occurred (and it certainly seems unlikely), French sailors from the battleship were photographed with part of a Luftwaffe-style knitted jumper, part of a German flying blouse and an Iron Cross First Class. The existence of these 'trophies' in French hands certainly suggests that it really ought to beggar belief that

The French battleship *Courbet* was anchored in Portsmouth harbour on 12 August 1940 and it has long been rumoured that French sailors played a part in the 'disappearance' of one of the crew from a Junkers 88 shot down into the harbour that day; Uffz Konrad Rösch still being missing with no known grave.

they had found no trace of the unfortunate owner of these items. That man was Uffz Konrad Rösch, a twenty-five-year-old man from Erlangen. Like Walter Mankelow, he was also an air gunner.

Alexander McKee was a teenager living near Portsmouth during 1940 and was an avid observer of the multitude of wartime events unfolding around him. He was also a keen photographer, painter and diarist – keeping meticulous records of all that he had seen and thus displaying a great sense of the history that was unfolding in front of him. Later, a career as a historian and writer (it was Alexander who came to discover the Tudor warship *Mary Rose*) seemed a natural progression from his recording of wartime events, albeit that some of his diarised remarks display more than a little of an excited youth rather caught up in the jingoistic atmosphere that generally pervaded news reports from that era. For example, on 11 August 1940 he noted in his journal: "Dover had a smashing attack a few days ago but one cannot visualise it here, although we know it will come." Alexander did not have long to wait. On the very next day the Luftwaffe came a-calling at Portsmouth and Alexander wrote: "We were about to get a Dover dose." He went on:

French sailors from the *Courbet* poring over recovered 'trophies' from the wreck.

Alexander McKee's rather naive representation of what he had seen on 12 August 1940.

"We heard AA fire and saw many shrapnel bursts over Pompey, so doubled back on our tracks to get to the top of the hill. We got as far as the small bridge and then it became apparent that this was more serious than usual. Countless clouds of smoke hung high over Portsmouth. Little specks were flying around, diving down almost vertically, and then zooming up in a hail of fire and through the balloons. A Junkers plunged headlong, twisting and jerking, in a vertical falling leaf. Like a dead thing it dropped out of sight. I had seen my first German plane shot down."

McKee goes on to describe the ongoing action; the bombs, anti-aircraft fire, columns of smoke and fire, roaring aero engines and raining shrapnel. He also saw another German plane going down "in a long flat slant over the Isle of Wight". Alexander had had his 'Dover dose', and he wrote about it enthusiastically, later capturing the scene in a rather naive and boyish watercolour painting showing 'his' Junkers 88 plunging towards the harbour with its entire tail section shot away by a direct AA fire hit. As Alexander had watched, the drama in the cockpit of this Junkers 88 was equally intense. Oblt Eberhard Wildermuth was the twenty-three-year-old pilot who suddenly found, as he had dropped his bomb load into the harbour, that he had lost all control of his aircraft and it was literally falling out of the sky. Little wonder that Alexander McKee had described the Junkers as a "dead thing". Wildermuth later described the last frantic moments in the cockpit:

"I had dropped the bombs and pulled back the plane to about 1,500 metres when suddenly I lost all feeling in the stick. The controls had gone and the plane went into a dreaded spin from which normally there is no escape. Through the throat-mic I yelled 'I can't hold the plane! Get out!' I threw off the cockpit roof and unclipped the seatbelt. The navigator, sitting by my side, did the same. Then the centrifugal force created by the spin pressed me into the glass dome of the front of the cockpit. The force was so strong that I was unable to move my arms. From where I was I could see the altimeter and follow the drop in altitude; 1400m…. 1300m…. 1200m…. I looked at the navigator who was pressed into the cockpit next to me and I was sure that now 'the stove had gone out'.

"Then, suddenly, a rush of air dragged us both out of the cockpit. After the roar of engines racing at super speed everything went deathly quiet. I saw the left wing whizzing past my head and shortly afterwards heard the air hissing in my parachute. I had released the

Oblt Eberhard Wildermuth (left) was the pilot of the Junkers 88 shot down into Portsmouth harbour on 12 August 1940. This is the aircraft seen in the background of this photograph; 9K+BS, werke nummer 4078. Here, Wildermuth talks to Uffz Dröse, another of the crew members that day. Wildermuth, Dröse and Oblt Stärk were all taken prisoner of war.

chute quite automatically and was now gradually floating down towards the waters of the harbour. Looking up, I noticed that my navigator, dangling above me on his parachute, was taking photos of me. He was a real photo fan and never went on a flight without his camera hanging around his neck."

When Wildermuth landed in the harbour, he noticed the third crew member in the water about fifty yards away from him. Of the fourth man, Rösch, there was no sign. Either he had been killed or incapacitated in the AA barrage or, more likely, he had simply been pinned further back in the cockpit by the overwhelming centrifugal force and been unable to get out. Either way, he was still in the cockpit when the Junkers 88 slammed into the harbour bed and, ultimately, the Luftwaffe would mark 'Gefallen – vermisst' (Fallen – missing) against his name.

Surprisingly, and again like the Earith Stirling site, an MOD licence to excavate the site under the Protection of Military Remains Act 1986 was granted to a team led by inveterate aviation archaeologist Steve Hall during 1987 despite the fact that one crew member, Rösch, was known to be un-accounted for and presumed to still be in the wreckage which was submerged on tidal mud flats. With no tangible evidence that the body of the missing airman was still in the wreckage having been discovered during numerous visits to the site by enthusiasts since the 1970s, the operation mounted on 11 June 1987 was of a different nature. This was not to be any half-hearted probing of the site using spades wielded by enthusiasts waist-deep in mud but, instead, a major recovery using a mechanical excavator on board a flat-bottomed barge positioned directly over the site. The potential for discovering the remains of Konrad Rösch was not insignificant.

Over the years since the 1970s the crash site of the Portsmouth harbour Ju 88 had been visited by many enthusiasts and amateur investigators and one of the many items retrieved from the harbour mud was this pair of binoculars and their leather case. It provides a tangible link to the human element of the episode.

In the event, however, Steve Hall's ambitious recovery operation recovered both engines and significant portions of airframe, propeller hub, a crew member's folding seat and a whole array of other artefacts – but discovered no trace of the missing air gunner. Maybe, after all, whatever pitiful remains might have existed on the site had already been removed or disturbed by the French sailors in 1940 or had later drifted away on subsequent tides. Certainly, no evidence could be found that his remains were trapped in the wreckage although, to be absolutely fair, this was not a forensic examination – a proper sifting of the foul and glutinous harbour mud may yet have concealed fragmentary remains. The possibility that his remains were simply missed cannot be excluded, and had the operation perhaps been conducted along the lines of the American CILHI recoveries then maybe a different outcome would have followed. However, that is speculation and not a criticism of the recovery operation *per se* which was conducted in accord with the relevant Protection of Military Remains Act licence and was a project that had set out to recover items from the Junkers 88 and not search for remains which, in any event, the recovery team were not licensed or authorised to do.

One day in the long distant future maybe other archaeologists will look at the site again in more scientific detail. If they do, then maybe some trace of this long-missing German flier will come to light although the time will then have long passed when such a discovery would have had any significance or importance to any living descendants of Konrad Rösch. For now, we can only state with certainty the exact place that he died on 12 August 1940, on board the Junkers 88 W.Nr 4078, 9K+BS, of 8/KG 51. Sometimes, even extensive recovery and salvage operations at crash sites like these have failed to reveal any trace of missing airmen on board the recovered aircraft.

CHAPTER 13 Unequal Combat Against Odds....

WHEN THE WEHRMACHT AND Luftwaffe unleashed their *Blitzkrieg* across France and the Low Countries on 10 May 1940 it signalled the start of an intensive period of fighting concentrated into just five or six weeks that would see a staggering number of losses suffered by the British, French and German air forces. Up until 24 June the total losses were as follows:

BRITISH
Aircraft: 1,924   Personnel: 2,018
FRENCH
Aircraft: 2,263   Personnel: 1,523
GERMAN
Aircraft: 3,290   Personnel: 6,047
NB – Not included are the Dutch, Belgian and Italian losses for this period.

Given that these casualties were sustained in such a short space of time, and an overwhelming percentage of them in a relatively narrow 'corridor' stretching from the Ardennes up to the Pas de Calais, the totals are both remarkable and shocking. Not only that, but given that the Germans were the victors of the campaign their losses were, perhaps, surprisingly heavy. The point of all this, however, is to illustrate not only the scale of losses sustained by the combatant nations but the inevitability that there would be a considerable percentage from amongst these losses who would be missing believed killed and would have no known grave. That is certainly the case.

However, the speed and scale of the enemy advance perhaps compounded the problem of finding and identifying the casualties – including their burial. Indeed, by the time the RAF, for example, had worked out where a certain aircraft had crashed it may well have been that its location had fallen into German hands and was out of reach. Not only that, but this was an army and an air force on the run – fighting a rearguard action whilst retreating on an almost hourly basis further back towards the Channel coast. Quite simply, fighting for survival and trying to keep abreast of a fast moving situation rather precluded any meaningful search for those killed in action. Or to put it another way, the British forces had more pressing things to do. Caring for the dead would have to wait for another day.

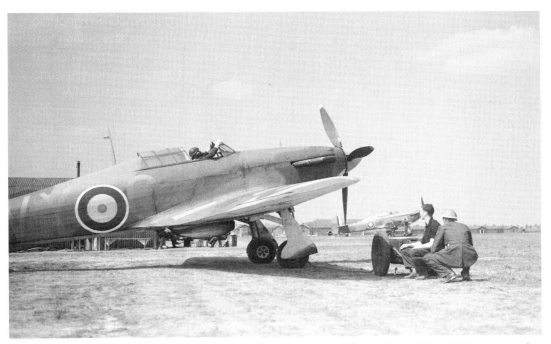

A pilot of 85 Squadron readies his Hurricane for take-off at Lille-Seclin in May 1940 as ground crew stand-by with the trolley accumulator for starting the aircraft. This was a scene that would have been all too familiar to Fg Off Derek Allen, one of the squadron pilots at this time.

Armourers belt up .303 ammunition for the Browning machine guns of 85 Squadron Hurricanes during the May of 1940. Primitive conditions like these were the norm for ground crew, and living conditions for pilots were often basic or primitive.

One of those squadrons caught in the frenetic activity and fighting from 10 May was the Hurricane-equipped 85 Squadron based, initially, at Lille/Seclin where the squadron operations record book very much sets the scene for the pace of the action:

"…Intermittently throughout the day, as each section and flight landed, the pilots and aircraft were on the ground only long enough to allow re-arming and re-fuelling and so it went on from dawn to dusk; by the end of the day the squadron had a total bag of seventeen aircraft to their credit with the loss of two of our aircraft."

Caught up in one of the actions that day was twenty-one-year-old Fg Off Derek Allen from Leicester, who experienced his first taste of battle six miles north-west of Armand at 20.50hrs and claimed one-third of a victory over a Junkers 88. The other two pilots were Plt Off P Woods-Scawen and Flt Lt R H A 'Dickie' Lee. Their combat report records:

"Section of three attacked in line-astern. After first aircraft attacked [Lee] starboard engine caught fire and one member of crew successfully jumped by parachute. Second and third aircraft [Woods-Scawen and Allen] set enemy aircraft completely on fire and it crashed in flames. First aircraft shot off 50 rounds per gun, the second aircraft 100 rounds per gun and the third aircraft 30 rounds per gun."

Twenty-one-year-old Fg Off Derek Allen, Hurricane pilot of 85 Squadron.

For Allen, blooded in combat, it was the start of a brief career flying on Lee's wing. In fact, it was a career lasting just one week and one day but during which Allen rose to 'ace' status and earned himself a DFC. However, his hard-fought war was shortly to be over although not before escaping with his life during a patrol on 15 May, with the squadron operations record book simply noting: "Fg Off Allen, Fg Off Pace and Plt Off Ashton failed to return from a patrol over Belgium." In fact, they had been engaged n an offensive patrol in the region between Ath and Namur when, as the squadron records later described: "Fg Off Allen had to bale out due to his machine being set on fire as a result of unequal combat against odds." In fact, Allen had landed ten miles north-west of Gembloux and did not make it back to his squadron until the next day. Exhaustion, mental and physical, was now taking its toll of the squadron's pilots and on 16 May, after only an hour and a half of sleep, Sgt 'Sammy' Allard took off for the first of four combat sorties that day.

Bombs were exploding on the aerodrome as he left on his second patrol, and on the third he fell asleep three times whilst flying over German territory. After landing from his fourth patrol he fell asleep as he taxied in and the ground crew had to lift him bodily out of the cockpit. He slept soundly until it was time to wake him for the dawn patrol, but when he could not be properly woken he was sent off to recuperate in England where he slept for thirty hours.

This apparently happy and relaxed group of 85 Squadron pilots are doubtless photographed just as the *Blitzkrieg* began on 10 May 1940. Their faces show little sign of the strain and exhaustion that almost immediately set in once the shooting war had begun. Pictured left to right (back row): Flt Lt J R M Boothby, Fg Off T G Pace, Sqn Ldr J O W 'Doggy' Oliver DSO DFC, Plt Off J H Ashton, Plt Off J W Lecky, Fg Off S P Stephenson, Sgt G 'Sammy' Allard, Sgt L A Crozier, Wt Off Newton. Front (left to right) Fg Off K H Blair and Sgt J McG Little.

It was the same for the others, too, and on the evening of 17 May, a shattered Derek Allen and his fellow officer 'Piney' Lepine were taken out to dinner by American war correspondent William H Stoneman in the Lion d'Or at Lille where Stoneman noted that "…both boys were red-eyed from lack of sleep and dozed over their meal that night." Meanwhile, Plt Off Lecky and Flt Lt Boothby were involved in a road traffic accident coming back from forty-eight hours leave in Le Touquet, with Lecky being killed and Boothby injured. Again, tiredness was the enemy. So tired were Allen and Lepine, however, that neither man made it far beyond breakfast next morning before they were both shot down. The lucky ones, though, were Flt Lt Lee, Fg Off Blair, Plt Off Ashton and Sgt Allard who had been sent off to England on 17 May to recover from their sheer exhaustion, although it had meant that for the first time Derek Allen would not be going into action on Lee's wing when the remnants of the squadron took off around 6am on the morning of 18 May to patrol between Le Cateau and Cambrai.

Exactly what happened on Derek Allen's last patrol is uncertain, and we can only speculate on how tiredness might have possibly affected what happened that day. What we do know, however, is that Allen and Lepine were both shot down at around 06.30hrs with Fg Off W N Lepine baling out safely but being taken prisoner of war by the rapidly advancing Germans. Of Allen, however, there was simply no trace and he failed to return from the patrol and nothing further was heard from him. Ultimately, when no word had been received six months after the date of his disappearance and he did not turn up on POW lists, for official purposes his death was presumed. Save for the telegram notifying his parents that he had failed to return there was no further news.

This is the fateful telegram that told the Allen family that Derek was missing, although it would subsequently add to confusion and yet more heartache for the Allens due to misunderstandings that would later arise.

Post-war, however, his was one of the thousands of cases looked into by the RAF missing research and enquiry units and a likely trail relating to his disappearance was picked up in the region of Cambrai, close to the town of Neuvilly, where local information had described the crash on 18 May 1940 of an RAF fighter on remote farmland at les Fonds de Solesmes. Both the date and the location of the crash fitted quite neatly with the loss of Allen, and when the RAF checked further they discovered that the locals were adamant that the pilot had been killed in the crash and not recovered.

If they were right about the date, then when one examines the CWGC casualty lists extant *today* there would seem to be only one 'missing' candidate; that is, Fg Off Derek Hurlstone Allen 39840. His name, as a casualty who has no known grave, is recorded on Panel 5 of the Runnymede Memorial. Strangely, and just adding to the mystery of his loss, he is recorded by the CWGC as having lost his life on _15_ May 1940 although it is clear from other surviving records that the date of his loss was certainly three days later.

Intrigued by this mystery, the author set about further investigating the loss of Derek Allen and in 2006 had established contact with his brother and his sister-in-law. Both were amazed that anyone would be interested in Derek almost seventy years after the event, and were most intrigued to learn about clues pointing to a crash location that *may* have been linked to the spot where their brother fell. All of the known facts were presented to them, but with the strong rider that there was no *absolute* evidence that the crash site of the Hurricane located at les Fonds de Solesmes really was Derek's. Only that it had certainly fallen in that immediate locality.

Even if it was his Hurricane, and even if the wreckage was ultimately recovered, there could be no certainty that Derek would be found there or that a positive identification of any remains would be achievable. At best there was a certainty that Derek had fallen in the immediate area and the recovery team were entirely confident that Derek had lost his life at or very near to Neuvilly. Additionally, some of the locals still living at Neuvilly knew exactly the location of the crash site and had always believed the pilot to still be there. However, once they had weighed up all the facts (such as they were) the family were adamant; a search for Derek in the Neuvilly area should go ahead. But what, exactly, was the evidence pointing to the les Fonds de Solesmes site as being the location where Allen had lost his life?

Principally, the most significant pointer was that when local residents were interviewed by MREU officers in 1946 or 1947 they were adamant about the date of the crash; it had been on 18 May 1940. However, further investigations at the site muddied the waters rather than cleared them. In fact, RAF investigators had found a makers plate amongst the wreckage and although it did not directly indicate a specific RAF serial number, the matter was referred to Hawker Aircraft Ltd at Kingston-on-Thames. The response was seemingly positive in that Hawkers were able to confirm that the plate came from a Hurricane built by Gloster's and had been the 263rd one built by them. However, this apparently helpful information does anything but help us tie down the *actual* serial number of the les Fonds de Solesmes crash at Neuvilly and, thereby, its related casualty.

From the first batch built by Gloster's, the 263rd aircraft would have been P2922 and this is an aeroplane we know to have been lost in the English

The crash at Neuvilly was witnessed by villagers who saw the stricken aircraft plummeting down and were mesmerised by the spinning Hurricane as it alternately displayed first its camouflaged top and then the black/white undersides in a surreally flickering and terminal display whilst it gyrated earthwards.

Channel off Calais on 13 July 1940, during the Battle of Britain, with 56 Squadron. Its pilot Sgt J J Whitfield, was posted missing believed killed. We can absolutely rule out that the Neuvilly crash is in any way associated with the loss of Sgt Whitfield, it being far too far inland from Calais to be connected. Thus, we can only conclude that the P2922 connection was somehow mistaken – a conclusion that was ultimately proven during eventual excavations at the Neuvilly crash site in 2007.

However, further confusion is also thrown into the mix when, in 1946, the MREU speculated that the aircraft might well be the Hurricane flown by Plt Off R C Whittaker of 17 Squadron. Richard Whittaker was also missing, but quite what it was that made MREU think the Neuvilly crash was his is unclear. Not only is the recorded serial for Whittaker's Hurricane (P2905) apparently adrift from the "263rd Gloster-built Hurricane" (P2922) by a factor of seventeen, but also the date of his loss in early June 1940 is at variance with the stated crash date at les Fonds de Solesmes.

That said, and as is the case with Allen, there also exists some confusion over the *actual* date of death for Whittaker. Again, we have the CWGC giving one date and the squadron operations record book another; according to the CWGC he was lost on 6 June although the 17 Squadron ORB shows 7 June. This is just another anomaly in the confused picture of archival material relating to air-fighting during the Battle of France, and an illustration of how tricky it can often be to nail these issues down with any certainty. There was, however, one likely way to resolve issues once and for all; excavation of the Neuvilly site in accord with the Allen family wishes.

Working with the mayor of Neuvilly, M. Hubert Lefevre, the local Gendarmerie, landowners and a representative of the Commonwealth War Graves Commission, a full-scale excavation of the site was carried out on 13 November 2007 when a mechanical excavator followed a buried trail of small pieces of wreckage down to a depth of eighteen feet. Before commencing work, the team assembled around the impact point and observed a two-minute silence as a mark of respect for the unknown pilot. Surprisingly, virtually nothing of the aircraft remained in the ground although there was sufficient to identify this as once having been a Hurricane. Save for a distorted Rolls-Royce Merlin piston at around eighteen feet, very little else was extant on site, although a pitifully small quantity of human remains were located and taken charge of by the CWGC field officer.

At first, there seemed to be little by way of identification of either the remains or the serial number of the Hurricane – by which means it might be possible to identify the unfortunate pilot. The results were both surprising and disappointing for the recovery team and the officials in attendance. They were a mystery, too, for the local farmers who were confident in their belief that this site had never been previously investigated. However, the evidence proved otherwise and it was concluded that the site must have been fully excavated during the late 1940s by the MREU teams but that this information had been unknown to the landowners of 2007.

The question was, if MREU *had* excavated here then who was the pilot and what had become of him? The fact remained that it could seemingly not have been either Allen or Whittaker since both men were still listed as missing. On the other hand, the possibility could not be excluded that if remains were recovered in the 1940s they had either been identified and buried in a CWGC plot or else had not been identified and been buried as 'unknown'. During the site clear-up in November 2007, however, a significant piece of evidence emerged that might yet unlock the mystery.

Team member Emmanuel Bril, field-walking the area to look for any missed clues, made an interesting discovery in a plough furrow just a few metres from the impact point. This was one of the ejector chutes for bullet cases and belt links from one of the wing-mounted Browning .303 machine guns. On it was stencilled P3533 in black paint. It was clearly a Hurricane serial number. Certainly it was the case that these particular components were always stencilled with the aircraft serial number and so here, at least at face value, was evidence to identify the aircraft and potentially its squadron along with its date of loss and its pilot.

Unfortunately, it wasn't that easy and despite the aircraft movement card for P3533 (the AM Form 78) being traced at the RAF Museum, Hendon, it didn't add anything to our sum of knowledge. All that is recorded here is the fact that P3533 had been built by Hawkers and taken on charge by 10 MU on 26 April 1940. From here, on 17 May 1940, it had been allocated to HQ Combined Forces France as part of a replacement 'pool' of aircraft. If the reported date of the les Fonds de Solesmes crash was accurate (18 May 1940) then P3533

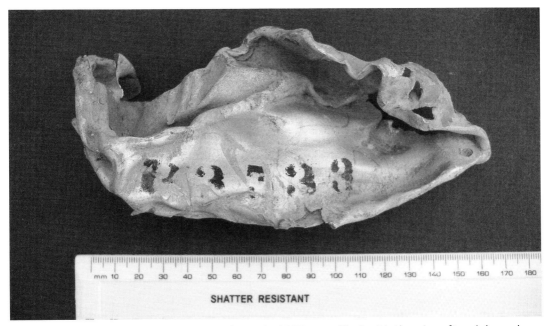

SHATTER RESISTANT

The gun ejector chute found at the crash site in 2007, stencilled with the aircraft serial number; P3533. No link could be made with this serial number to Derek Allen, or for that matter with 85 Squadron. Human remains found during the recovery are due to be buried as an unknown airman in a Commonwealth War Graves Commission plot as this book goes to print.

had almost immediately been transferred to an operational squadron from HQ CFF. Unfortunately, the AM Form 78 failed to record which particular squadron it had been issued to, merely stating 'Struck off charge May 1940'. However, work by another French researcher, Arnaud Gillet, has subsequently unearthed yet another piece of information in a local French archive containing a contemporary report relating to the Neuvilly crash. It reads:

> "Neuvilly: Aircraft shot down on May 18th 1940. One engine. Light grey colour. No trace of any crew member. No documents. Written on part of aircraft 'DANGER COMPRESSED...' and P3533.'

Whilst it adds nothing, specifically, to our knowledge of the Neuvilly crash it at least offers corroboration of the date and of the serial number, P3533, found again in 2007.

And so the mystery endured. The pilot of P3533 remained unknown and Fg Off Derek Allen continued to be listed as missing in action. However, the MOD's Service Personnel and Veterans Agency, Innsworth, requested a full report on the recovery from the author, together with all known and relevant details, the precise crash location etc. Shortly afterwards a detailed report was duly submitted to the agency. Subsequently, this was passed to the RAF Air Historical Branch for further investigation and possible identification of the Neuvilly remains.

In May 2011, and during the production process of this book, the Service Personnel and Veterans Agency contacted the author to say that investigations into the Neuvilly casualty had been completed, reporting as follows:

Authority	Reason for Allotment	Special Fitments, etc.	Write off or Strike off Details: Date	Extent of Damage	Source of Informat'n
1713	Reserves for fighter command				

Date
Authority
Unit
Total Flying Hours
Remarks :-

A.M. Form 78.

AIRCRAFT

Contract No. 962371/38

Type HURRICANE I R.A.F. No. P2555 Contractor Glosters.
Type of Engine Merlin III Engine Nos. 118918

Taken on Charge of: 27 MU, 4 S of T, 1 ASP, 85 Sqdn, P.S.O. Spec
Date taken on Charge: 12.12.39, 25.1.40, 26.1.40, 25.6.40
Authority: 1632, 1623.A, 1623 A, 1623

Taken on Charge of
Date taken on Charge
Authority

Date	Unit to whom allotted	Authority	Date	Unit to whom allotted	Authority
6.12.39	27. MU	1713.			

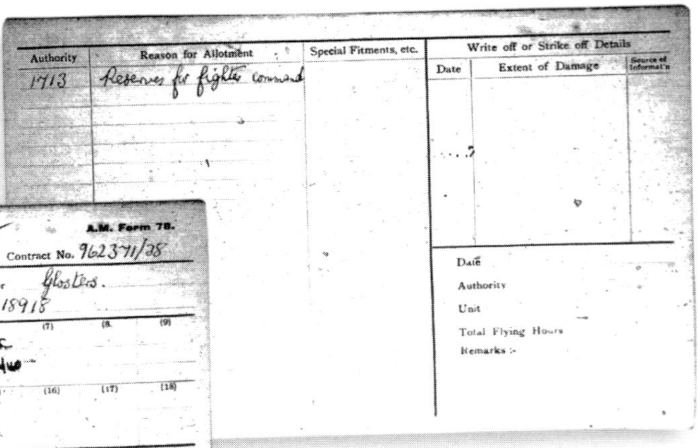

The Air Ministry Form 78 record card for Hurricane P2555. It will be seen that the recorded detail is sparse, highlighting the difficulties often encountered when trying to unravel the historical background to RAF losses during the Battle of France period.

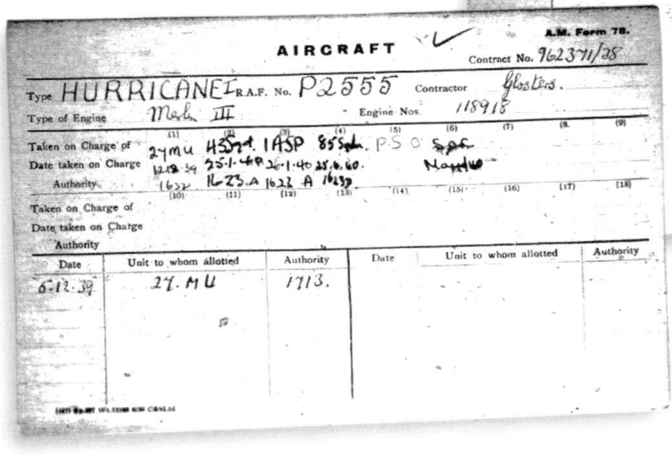

"After investigation it has been decided that there is insufficient evidence to identify the aircraft which crashed at Neuvilly or name any casualty linked to this site, therefore we have taken the stance that these are not the remains of Fg Off D H Allen."

The letter went on, however, to make a further surprising and most welcome disclosure, stating:

"However, upon further investigation it appears that the current unknown soldier [*sic*] interred at Poix-du-Nord Communal Cemetery and Extension came from a crash site between 0630 and 0700 hrs on 18 May 1940 of a Hurricane with the serial number P2555. It has therefore been decided that this is the resting place of Fg Off D H Allen."

It was indeed welcome news for the family and for the recovery and investigation team, whose view that Derek Allen had been lost in the Neuvilly area had been fully vindicated with the Poix-du-Nord 'discovery' – this town being next door to Neuvilly and only a few short kilometres distant. The headstone in the Poix-du-Nord cemetery stands just in front of the CWGC Cross of Sacrifice and it is inscribed as follows:

AN AIRMAN OF THE
1939 – 1945 WAR
AN OFFICER
ROYAL AIR FORCE
18 MAY 1940

Quite what evidence the Air Historical Branch were able to draw upon to link Derek Allen with P2555 and the Poix-du-Nord burial is unclear, since the 85 Squadron Operations Record Book does not record the serial number of the Hurricane in which he was lost. However, we do know that the mayor of Poix-du-Nord in May 1940 had recorded the crash of Hurricane P2555 in his commune on 18 May and that its pilot had been buried in the CWGC plot. The AM Form 78 for P2555, however, certainly confirms that P2555 was issued to 85 Squadron on 25 April 1940 and that it was eventually struck off charge with that same squadron during May 1940. Quite possibly, 85 Squadron had sent a signal from the field on 18 May 1940 to the Air Ministry Casualty Branch confirming that this pilot had failed to return that day whilst flying P2555*. Either way, the MOD were satisfied in 2011 that the Poix-du-Nord burial was certainly that of Derek Allen and having notified the family, the agency duly instructed the Commonwealth War Graves Commission to replace the headstone currently marked to an unknown airman of the 1939-45 war with a personal one bearing the name of Fg Off D H Allen DFC.

*Note: In February 2008 the Ministry of Defence confirmed that within a couple of years of that date all RAF casualty records would be transferred to The National Archives at Kew where they have already been allocated a listing under AIR 81 documents. In view of 'personal service sensitivities' the MOD stated that these records would need to be individually reviewed prior to transfer. When no transfer had been effected by June 2011 the MOD were pressed as to progress in the matter. It was stated that: "Work on the transfer of the RAF Casualty Reports did commence in 2008. This has now been suspended, however, following the identification of some material within the reports which may contain residual sensitivity. To resolve this issue we currently plan, subject to the necessary approvals, to conduct a limited public consultation in the autumn of 2011. Assuming this led to a decision to proceed with transfer then those files that have already been prepared for transfer would be transferred to Kew shortly thereafter."

Clearly, this is a frustrating situation for researchers, historians and family members who are all currently denied access to this important resource. It is difficult to see what "residual sensitivity" has been uncovered that the MOD had not already acknowledged was present in 2008. The significance of these records in the case of missing aircrew is huge. For example, it is highly likely that the matter of Allen might well have been resolved by researchers long ago if the pertinent records had been in the public domain. There can be little or no justification for the continued withholding of these important records more than seventy years on – especially where identical records and reports relating to Commonwealth air force casualties are readily available from their respective governmental agencies and very often accessible online.

In order to understand properly the lack of any meaningful data contained within the 85 Squadron operations record book, it is only necessary to look at one specific entry in that particular ORB, dated 20 May 1940, and just two days after the loss of Derek Allen. It reads:

"At 1530 hrs the Adjutant received orders from Sqn Ldr Peacock to destroy all squadron files, records and ciphers etc – jettison all kit belonging to officers and airmen and move off in thirty minutes by road to Boulogne."

Sometimes finding minutiae such as aircraft serial numbers can be vital in establishing the identity of a missing airman, as we have seen in this chapter. Whilst it is now established that P2555 was lost on 18 May 1940 with Fg Off Allen as the pilot, published sources indicate that it was crash landed by Sgt H N Howes of 85 Squadron near Abbeville on 20 May 1940. Clearly, that cannot have been the case. Sgt H N Howes is photographed with another squadron Hurricane.

Herein must lie the root of much confusion surrounding what amounted to the ten-day war of 85 Squadron in France and the paucity of detail relating to operations and aircraft flown and the very considerable uncertainty about what became of specific pilots and when. As it currently exists at the National Archives, Kew, one must conclude that the relevant ORB entries for the period 85 Squadron were in France were filled in at a later date *after* the unit had returned to England. How this was done is unclear, but it may have been an amalgam of collected and collated memories or notes and scraps of detail retold by squadron personnel or perhaps from data previously transmitted to the Air Ministry from France.

However, it is a fact that the RAF and Air Ministry were themselves in a muddle over what was going on with specific casualties. In the case of Allen, for instance, the family were in receipt of a telegram on 18 May 1940 (the date on which Allen is now recorded as having died) stating that Derek was reported missing as a result of air operations on *17* May. It can only be concluded that this was a telegram sent to notify the family of Allen's 'disappearance' on 15 May after being shot down for the first time. For a while, on the 15th and at least until the next day, nobody knew where he was or if he was safe and this doubtless gave rise to the telegram in which the incorrect date of 17 May was given. Coincidentally, and with almost tragic irony, the telegram arrived with the family on 18 May – the date on which he was ultimately shot down and killed. This is just a further illustration of the monumental confusion that reigned at this time in respect of accurate recording of casualties.

At last, however, the seventy-one-year mystery of Derek Allen's disappearance has been solved and the sad tale of this twenty-two-year-old pilot from Leicester can be told. And it is certainly an incredible and previously unknown story which began with Derek's short service commission on 5 July 1937 when he trained at 5FTS, RAF Sealand, before joining 85 Squadron in February 1938 and being promoted to Fg Off on 10 December 1939.

As we have seen, Derek was first caught up in the fighting of 10 May 1940 when the German forces launched their attack in the west and it was on that very first day that he claimed his first aerial victory. The pace of activity for 85 Squadron over the next few days was frantic and frenetic and Derek was in the thick of it, flying as wing man to the B Flight commander Flt Lt R H A 'Dickie' Lee. Whilst individual combat reports for Derek Allen have not been traced (other than the combined report for 10 May – see page 108) it is recorded that Fg Off Allen scored the following confirmed victories:

1 x Hs 126	10 May 1940	⅓ x Do 17	11 May 1940
⅓ x Ju 88	10 May 1940	2 x He 111	13 May 1940
⅓ x Do 17	11 May 1940	1 x Ju 87	15 May 1940

Thus, and inside the period of just one week, Derek had gone from being an inexperienced combat pilot to an ace with at least five victories to his credit. Indeed, one of the third-share Dornier 17s claimed on 11 May could well have been an aircraft shot down in the combat where Lee had himself been shot down whilst pursuing a Dornier at 8,000ft over Belgium in the Tongres/Maastricht sector. Lee baled out safely although slightly wounded and did not return to the squadron until the next day. Still in action every day, Allen himself followed Lee in being shot down four days later on 15 May to the north-west of Gembloux, Belgium, in a fight that was described as being "against unequal odds".

Whilst the circumstances of this combat are unclear, we do know that a huge land battle was taking place that day around Gembloux and the Hurricanes of 85 Squadron apparently engaged the Junkers 87 Stukas of StG 2 who were attacking armour in the region of Gentinnes at around 14.00hrs. It would appear that Allen's aircraft was hit by anti-aircraft fire during this action, forcing him to bale out. Whilst we cannot be certain, it seems very likely that the Ju 87 he claimed to have shot down in this action may well have been the 9./StG 2 aircraft which plunged, burning, into a wood alongside the Rue du Sart, just to the south of the village of Ernage.

The pilot, Uffz Fritz Urban, and his crew-man Ogefr Arno Brandt were both killed, with Urban still listed as missing in action and having no known grave. Initially, Allen too was listed as missing that day and it was not until the following morning that he re-appeared back at his squadron. The next evening we know that he dined with the American war correspondent, William H Stoneman. Before breakfast the next day he had been shot down and killed.

Not long after Derek's disappearance on 18 May the *London Gazette* announced the award of his Distinguished Flying Cross, the citation (published in *The Leicester Mercury* of 31 May 1940) stating as follows:

'Flying Officer Allen has taken part in all combats with Flight Lieutenant R H A Lee, following his section leader with great loyalty. He took part in shooting down a

On 13 May 1940 Fg Off Derek Allen was credited with destroying two He 111s. Pictured here is another He 111 shot down by Hurricane pilots of 85 and 607 Squadrons on 10 May near Albert.

Junkers, and the next day another aircraft of the same type. After his aircraft had been severely damaged by anti-aircraft fire he did not hesitate to attack a Junkers 87 over enemy territory and shoot it down.'

News of the 'discovery' of Derek's grave was met with delight by his brother, Richard, and sister-in-law Marjorie. Said Richard:

"As a family it is comforting to know, at last, where Derek is buried. After all these years, just finding out is wonderful and we are so grateful to the work done by Andy Saunders and his team that has ultimately led to this marvellous result by triggering the MOD to look anew at their records. We are now looking forward to the dedication of his new named headstone in a ceremony that will be attended by his family, a British embassy official and a padre. A truly wonderful result."

Derek Allen was a popular young man and a keen motorist and rugby player. He is seen here with his pride and joy, a 1936 Standard Avon, with a group of friends and contemporaries. This was the very epitome of a fighter pilot's car!

The agony of waiting for news, in the very early days at least, had been compounded by a telephone call to the Allen family from one of Derek's colleagues saying that if they heard he was missing then not to worry as he had now turned up. Clearly, this was referring to the episode when he had baled out on 15 May and subsequently returned and the telephone call most likely came from Flt Lt Lee who had returned to England on leave on 17 May. By the cruel stroke of fate mentioned earlier, of course, Derek must have been shot down and killed within a day of that telephone call, if not on that day itself, and thus when he was finally reported missing the family took no notice, quite believing him to be safe. It was only when the squadron adjutant visited the family some time after 85 Squadron had returned from France that the awful truth dawned on them. It was a truth compounded by the return of presents

This is the headstone to an unknown RAF officer who died on 18 May 1940 which was identified in 2011 as being the grave of Fg Off Derek Allen DFC.

mailed out to Derek from his family for his 23rd birthday which would have been on 19 May, the day after his death.

Whilst recent researches had given comforting finality and closure to the Allen family who had waited for over seventy years for news of Derek there is some irony in the fact that the remains discovered at Neuvilly in 2007 are still unidentified and that a mystery still surrounds the history of Hurricane P3533. Bizarrely, unlocking and solving one puzzle had inadvertently created another.

Note: As this book went to print the Commonwealth War Graves Commission were preparing to replace the headstone at Poix-du-Nord with one named to Derek Allen. Preparations were also underway to bury the remains of the unknown pilot in a nearby CWGC cemetery.

14 Not Always Missing

A S WE HAVE SEEN in the previous chapter, the cases of missing airmen are not always solved by archaeology and recovery. Sometimes, it is a case of looking at existing records to solve what happened to a particular flier and although unlocking the mystery of Fg Off Derek Allen's un-named grave *did* require an excavation of an aircraft crash site it is not always so. Indeed, sometimes the graves of missing fliers have simply been lost in dusty archives and official records. Such is the case of Fg Off George Bernard Penman.

Fg Off George Penman's aircraft (AL983) was identical to those illustrated here, although these Mustangs are actually from 2 Squadron. (Coincidentally, the Mustang nearest to the camera was lost just a few days after AL983.)

On 15 August 1942 an RAF Mustang was seen diving to earth, out of control and on fire before crashing at East Marden in West Sussex. The RAF accident report relating to the incident makes for harrowing reading when one realises that the pilot had been struggling to abandon his aircraft:

"Aircraft dived into ground and exploded due to an accumulation of explosive gas in the wing which ignited due to causes unknown. Fire was set up by the explosion around the air vent, and flames were seen issuing from the undercarriage doors. The pilot attempted to jettison the hood but was only partly successful and his attempts to abandon the aircraft account for it being out of control."

The unfortunate pilot was Fg Off George Penman of 169 Squadron who stood no chance of survival when his Mustang I, AL983, impacted with the chalk of the South Downs. His shattered body was extracted from the wreckage by the authorities and passed to Littlehampton undertakers Messrs Hollands & Co who held the contract with RAF Tangmere to deal with the burial of RAF and Luftwaffe casualties in the district. By great good fortune, the records of Hollands & Co still survived with the company during the early 1970s when they were made available to the author for research purposes. Each and every casualty dealt with was listed, including details of the disposal and burial of the body. Among those listed was an entry for Fg Off Penman. It read:

'Entry 179 (War Burials) – Fg Off G Penman died 15 August 1942. Aged 28. Body to Mrs Penman via Waverley Station, Edinburgh.'

Whilst the exact location of Penman's grave was not at that time investigated any further by the author, it was certainly clear that he had been returned home for burial by his family. However, it was not until the 1990s that the case of George Penman surfaced once more when enthusiast Ian Hutton applied for an MOD licence under the Protection of Military Remains Act 1986 to excavate the crash site of his Mustang. Almost at once the MOD responded stating that a licence could not be granted due to the fact that George Penman was still regarded as missing with no known grave, the presumption being that he was buried with the wreckage of his Mustang at the crash site.

Nothing could have been further from the truth, but the basis for that premise by the MOD was apparently that his name was recorded on the RAF memorial to the missing at Runnymede. And indeed it was. Panel 289 of the memorial clearly recorded the name of Flg Off George Bernard Penman, 44656, who died on 15 August 1942, these details leaving no doubt at all that this was the very same man who had died in his Mustang at East Marden. Given the clear and yet seemingly contradictory record of the return of his body to Waverley Station, it was certain that he must have a known grave, and presumably somewhere not too far from Waverley Station or Edinburgh. So, how was it that his name was recorded at Runnymede? And if he *had* been buried, then where on earth was his grave? It didn't take the author too long to find out.

Using Edinburgh as a starting point the reports of his death and subsequent funeral were quite quickly tracked down via local newspaper archives and this in turn indicated his grave location to be Camelon Cemetery, Falkirk. To be precise; section 3, grave 407. Very clearly his commemoration at Runnymede was in error, and in November 2007 the issue was raised with the Commonwealth War Graves Commission who undertook to look into the matter further. By May 2008 the commission were able to report that they had indeed tracked down and confirmed the grave location of George Penman, his last resting place being marked by a three-metre-high, grey-granite headstone that had been erected by his family. As a result, the CWGC records were duly amended and, in time, George Penman's name will be removed from the Runnymede Memorial.

Here was a case of simple confusion that had recorded Penman as a missing RAF casualty of World War Two when, in actual fact, he had long been returned home to his family. Quite how this error occurred is unclear, but given the huge number of RAF casualties sustained between 1939-45 it is hardly surprising that a few errors, omissions and anomalies will have crept into the records. This case, and that of Derek Allen in the previous chapter, serves to illustrate that sometimes things are not always as they seem to be in official archives. However, it is always pleasing to be able to put things right and to have a line drawn under such cases – howsoever they might have arisen or been discovered. And sometimes, like the matter of Penman, such discoveries can be purely accidental. Take also the case of a thirty-seven-year-old WAAF, Phyllis Duffield.

Surprisingly, there are no fewer than fourteen WAAF and two female ATA personnel commemorated on the Runnymede Memorial. Surprising, perhaps, because the natural perception is that all of those commemorated there were lost in action or on military service that resulted from combat operations. Put simply, the likelihood of women being involved in such activity during World War Two (aside from ATA aircrew) might not always occur to the average observer, although the story behind some of the women remembered here is more than remarkable to say the very least.

Take, for example, the cases of agents Yolande Unterhahrer, Cicely LeFort, Noor Inyat-Khan and Lilian Rolfe. All of them were brutally murdered in concentration camps and their remains disposed of in various camp crematoria. These four are amongst those listed at Runnymede, and understandably so. Certainly there could be no more fitting names to be inscribed there with honour. Of the ATA girls, one is famed aviatrix Amy Johnson, a first officer with the ATA, who was lost when her Airspeed Oxford plunged into the icy Thames estuary on 5 January 1941. Others amongst them were passengers on board RAF aircraft lost at sea, but Phyllis Duffield is an unusual case amongst them and one which also has echoes of the George Penman saga.

Unlike the agents lost at Ravensbrück, Dachau and Natzweiler camps, the death of Aircraft Woman 2nd Class (ACW2) Phyllis Mary Duffield 2006225 on 2 March 1942 was far more ordinary when she succumbed to pneumonia in the sick bay of RAF Kirkham. However, recorded on her death certificate as a spinster and music mistress, this unassuming casualty of World War Two (albeit dying of natural causes), because she was on military service, is as entitled to Commonwealth War Graves commemoration on a basis equal to those WAAF personnel who died in concentration camps. Indeed, her name is remembered at Runnymede no less grandly than those unfortunate agents.

But like George Penman it should not be there, and why it is there is baffling since the record is clear; Phyllis Mary Duffield was buried on 7 March 1942 in the churchyard of St

Mary The Virgin, Brancaster, Norfolk. Unlike George Penman, though, her grave is unmarked and so at least her commemoration at Runnymede currently fulfils the obligation placed on the CWGC for the commemoration of casualties by name. That said, the Runnymede inscription is clearly in error and as this book was in preparation a case had been submitted to the CWGC by the author for the possible erection of a named headstone at Brancaster, the correction of corresponding CWGC records and the eventual removal of her name from Runnymede.

If the cases of Penman and Duffield are just straightforward instances where there has existed confusion as to burial locations there is another case of a RAF fighter pilot, still listed as missing over France, where the outcome has thus far not had such a satisfactory conclusion as that of Derek Allen. In a sense, it is almost a counter-point to the Allen case and is an instance where a quantity of powerful and circumstantial evidence exists to link a positively identified Spitfire crash site with the grave of an unknown aviator. Unfortunately, it is a case where it has so far proved impossible for the authorities to be satisfied that a particular war grave marked as an unknown RAF airman is indeed that of the most likely candidate; Fg Off Ernest Russell Lyon.

Fg Off Ernest Russell Lyon lost in the post-D-Day air fighting over Normandy.

Ernest Russell Lyon was born on 19 December 1922 and was a flying officer in 234 Squadron RAF. Volunteering to join the RAFVR just three months after his 18th birthday he undertook pilot training in the USA, after which he became a pilot instructor in the USA and Canada. He later asked to join an operational squadron and was posted to 234 Squadron, joining them during the autumn of 1943 where he acquired the nickname 'Ben' after the American film star Ben Lyon. At the time of D-Day the Squadron was based at RAF Deanland, East Sussex, but soon afterwards was moved to RAF Predannack on the Lizard Peninsula in Cornwall from where they flew further missions over northern and western France. At 19.00hrs on the evening of Thursday 27 July 1944, Russell took off in Spitfire Vb AR343, flying with seven other Spitfires, on a mission over Lorient in southern Brittany to attack Kerlin-Bastard airfield. At around 19.54hrs his Spitfire was observed to be hit by flak when flying at 6000 ft in the target area and was seen to crash in flames near Ploemeur.

His father Ernest Lyon (his mother had died in 1935) received the inevitable telegram at his home in Balerno, Midlothian, notifying him that his son was missing as a result of air operations. No doubt he endured an agonising wait for news in the not-unreasonable hope that he had survived, been picked up by the French Resistance and was in hiding or on his way back to England. However, and as the German forces were swept away across France by the overwhelming tide of allied forces, it very soon became apparent that Russell must have lost his life in the absence of any trace of him – albeit that no confirmatory evidence had yet come to light. Ultimately, however, his death was presumed for official purposes. On the ground, however, we can now be sure of certain events around 27 July 1944 that prove his death, the exact place of his death and almost certainly his burial as an unidentified airman by the Germans.

In 2001 local enthusiasts were alerted to the crash site of an aircraft in woods at Kercaves, near Ploemeur, where objects like pipes had been seen sticking out of the ground. Upon investigation the 'pipes' were found to be a pair of 20mm aircraft cannon that had speared into the ground on impact with associated wreckage buried between the two guns, including a few shattered fragments of Rolls-Royce Merlin engine and propeller hub. The wreckage was easily identifiable as a Spitfire, but there was a question that needed to be answered. Which Spitfire and who was the pilot?

The answer, or at least a very strong clue that pointed towards an answer, rested with a local farmer who recalled the crash and remembered seeing the shattered body of its pilot lying nearby. Hustled away by the Germans, the French farmer did not see them remove the airman but on a visit to nearby Guidel a few kilometres away and just two days later, he was told by a gravedigger of a fresh grave being dug which was for a British pilot. Not unnaturally the French farmer assumed that this was for the burial of the casualty from the crash he had seen. Here, then, was perhaps the starting point for the local French researchers to establish the identity of the pilot and it did not take very long to link the grave of an unknown RAF pilot at Guidel with the crash near Ploemeur. Not only that, but relatively unusually for graves of unidentified airmen the CWGC headstone was marked with the date – 29 July 1944. Corresponding to this date was an entry in the burial register for Guidel which recorded the interment of an 'Aviator Anglais – inconnu' on 29 July.

The loss of Russell Lyon seemed to be the only RAF fighter pilot casualty in the region who was *missing* around the relevant date, although the evidence linking him to the 'inconnu' at Guidel was only circumstantial. There needed to be something far more substantial to provide some linking evidence to this grave and to the loss of Fg Off Lyon and the team who recovered the Spitfire

The Lyon family believe that this is Russell's grave in the CWGC plot at Guidel, France, and have been campaigning for some years to have the MOD accept that it is where he is buried. As with the case of Major 'Mick' Mannock the MOD are seeking evidence that proves beyond reasonable doubt that the grave is that of the specific casualty. Clearly, the term 'beyond reasonable doubt' might be subjective in these cases since some would surely argue that there really cannot be much 'reasonable doubt' that these are their graves when one examines all of the available evidence, notwithstanding the fact that such evidence is often circumstantial in its basis.

wreckage could not find it. What they could not find, either, was any other grave of an allied flier in the district that might reasonably be associated with the Ploemeur crash, and the evidence of witnesses certainly pointed to the pilot in that incident being killed.

Coincidentally, and not long after the recovery of the Spitfire wreckage, a family member created an internet memorial page to Russell Lyon and this was promptly picked up by the French enthusiasts. Apprised as to the discovery of the wreckage thought to be Russell's Spitfire, and of the nearby grave marked to an airman 'Known unto God', the family took up the case with the Ministry of Defence and Commonwealth War Graves Commission in order to seek a review of the facts relating to the loss of Russell.

By March 2008 the Air Historical Branch was able to confirm that the crash site discovered by the enthusiasts near Ploemeur was *definitely* Spitfire AR343, the aeroplane in which Lyon had been lost. With the absence of any human remains being found at that crash site by the team of enthusiasts, and the eye-witness account of the body of the pilot being taken away for burial by the Germans in 1944, it was clear that Fg Off Lyon's body *had* been found and buried somewhere – albeit that he must have been laid to rest as unidentified given his continuing status as missing. Indeed, he is recorded as such on Panel 207 of the Runnymede Memorial. Given all of the facts and circumstances the link with the Guidel burial seemed highly likely. That said, the overwhelming majority of unidentified burials in occupied and enemy Europe had been subject to scrutiny by the missing research and enquiry units during the immediate post-war years. Of course, clues could have been missed as they were with the case of Derek Allen but we do know that the Guidel burial did come under examination by one of the MREU teams.

In fact, we know that a MREU team had exhumed the grave of the 29 July 1944 burial on 12 July 1946, but had found no clues leading to the identification of the unknown casualty buried there. Had enquiries then led to the linking of this burial to the Kercaves crash then, quite possibly, a positive identification might have been made. Unfortunately, any linking clues were either missed or simply not found with the inevitable result that the casualty remains unidentified to this day. Of course, the family remained keen and anxious to know what had become of Russell and wrote to the Air Ministry on 31 October 1949 asking if there was any news. There wasn't, and in fact the Air Ministry replied stating that whilst four unknown airmen were buried in Lorient (Kerentech) cemetery, all investigations by the missing research teams had concluded that the deaths of these men had taken place in 1941 and 1942.

Naturally, Russell's father wanted to know if there were any 1944 dated unknown RAF casualties buried in the district but the Air Ministry told him that "...a careful check of cemetery lists in the Lorient area has disclosed no burial of an 'unknown' in 1944."

In fact, this was patently not the case as the Guidel burial of an unknown RAF casualty was certainly already known to them by virtue of the MREU's exhumation of that grave three years earlier. Had the family known of the Guidel grave, and had they become aware of the date marked on its headstone, it is surely likely that they would have made their own detailed enquiries locally. Since this was only a few years after the event, it is not beyond the realms of possibility that they might well have turned up vital 'fresh' clues; clues that have now been lost in the passage of time.

In considering the various aspects of this case, and indeed others of a similar ilk, it is worth reflecting upon one element of the standing instructions issued to MREU units and the requirements for the completion of forms issued to them. A report on the RAF and Dominions Air Forces Missing Research and Enquiry Service for the period 1944-49 (contained in AIR 20/9305 at The National Archives, Kew) provides much detail on the search methods to be used and of the various best practice that would assist in the identification of missing aircrew. From this report the following (verbatim) notes are significant:

> "Search officers, when conducting enquiries and interrogations of local inhabitants and officials, must recognise the ring of truth and ignore garrulous gossip, but, on the other hand, not to omit to question any individual who may be able to contribute information."

This statement, in a way, strikes at the heart of this case in that the Air Historical Branch have indicated that witness statements are not acceptable as evidence and contain 'hearsay'. On the other hand, the witness statements certainly contain that 'ring of truth' to which the Air Ministry had referred in its instructions to MREU officers, albeit that the accounts are almost seventy years after the event.

Ultimately, and after careful consideration by the Air Historical Branch, it was decided that insufficient evidence existed formally to link Russell Lyon to the burial at Guidel. The date inscription, whilst close to the date Russell was killed, was not the date of death of the casualty buried there and apparently just reflected the date of interment. It is also appropriate to point out here that the CWGC are always opposed to the exhumation of existing graves within their care for identification purposes unless it is absolutely necessary to do so. It is a perfectly understandable stance, designed to protect the sanctity of the burial and so as not to set a precedent for other families who might wish to see other graves exhumed for possible identification of the casualty buried there. Perhaps not unreasonably, too, the MOD concluded that whilst this might well be Russell Lyon it might equally be that of a casualty washed ashore on the nearby coast*.

Identification 'beyond reasonable doubt' was required to formally name the headstone, and the circumstantial evidence in this case could not be regarded as meeting such an exacting test. However, perhaps the parameters for a different set of test criteria *have* already been met in this case, and that is a test that enables the Commonwealth War Graves Commission to name a headstone but to prefix that name with the inscription 'Believed To Be' (See Chapter One and the case of Major Mannock). The precedent for this inscription has long been made, and there are a number in France for example, marking the burial of World War One casualties. The criteria for such an inscription is set out by the CWGC to be "…where identification may be considered reasonable but not absolute".

It is difficult not to conclude that identification of the Guidel grave is 'reasonable but not absolute', especially given the established facts. After all, we have the crash site of Russell Lyon's Spitfire officially confirmed by the MOD's Air Historical Branch. We have the burial of an unknown airman just two days after Russell's death at a cemetery only a few kilometres from that crash site. We also know that the Germans buried Russell's body, although there are no other graves of unidentified airmen anywhere in the area. And we have no other RAF pilots shot down in the area between 27 and 29 July 1944 who are not otherwise accounted for.

Reasonable but not absolute is surely a fair assessment of how 'identification' of the Guidel grave might be described, although it is apparently the case that in the absence of any further evidence Fg Off Russell Lyon's name will remain on Panel 207 at Runnymede. However, at the time of going to press with this book the matter of Russell Lyon was still being pressed by family members who yet remain hopeful of a more positive outcome and the possibility that the 'beyond reasonable doubt' criteria might yet be relaxed in this and possibly other similar cases.

Up until 2000 the responsibility for the naming of previously unidentified casualties already within the care of the Commonwealth War Graves Commission rested with the commission alone, the Ministry of Defence being solely responsible for the identification and naming of newly discovered casualties from WW1 and WW2. From 2000 that specific remit of the CWGC was transferred to the Ministry of Defence following controversy surrounding the identification in 1992 of an unknown soldier of the First World War named by the commission as Lt John Kipling of The Irish Guards, son of Rudyard Kipling. Doubt has since been thrown on the validity of that positive identification, thus highlighting the sensitivity of such decisions and transferring responsibility from the CWGC to MOD as a consequence of that controversy.

CHAPTER 15

Yet Another Sacrifice…

I N THE IMMEDIATE AFTERMATH of the D-Day invasion of Europe on 6 June 1944, the formidable and overwhelming allied air power had achieved total air superiority over the Luftwaffe. That is not to say, however, that the Luftwaffe were not present nor that the outnumbered German aircrew fought anything other than bravely and tenaciously against the might that had been thrown against them. Of course, one of the problems facing the German defenders was the desperate need to be kept appraised as to the rapidly changing situation on the ground as the allies struck deeper into Normandy. Where the allied forces were deployed, when and where they were moving and what equipment was being moved across the channel and inland from the beaches was absolutely vital knowledge for the Germans if they were to be able to understand the invader's moves and to plan where to counter them.

Another post-D-Day casualty of the air fighting over Normandy, and described by his commanding officer as "…yet another sacrifice", this is Messerschmitt 109 pilot Uffz Herbert Blochberger.

Hptm Heinz Feilmayer was Herbert's commanding officer who had the sad duty of writing to Frau Blochberger to tell her that her beloved son had failed to return from an operational flight.

Flying with Blochberger on his final mission was Oblt Werner Kohla who later wrote to Frau Blochberger telling her what had happened on that last flight.

In this respect, aerial photo reconnaissance was a vital tool but like all other resources available to the Germans at this time, there was a reduced availability of men and machines to carry out this important task. One unit, however, which stepped into the breach was the Me 109G-5-equipped Fernaufklarangsgruppe 123 which performed valuable work for the beleaguered defenders in this dangerous role. A cadre of experienced pilots went into action day after day over the beachheads and battlefields during the weeks and months post-invasion, gathering crucial aerial photos and visual reports of what was unfolding hour by hour on the ground below. It was not without cost, however.

On 24 June 1944 two aircraft of the 4th Staffel, F.Aufkl.Gr 123, took off from their St Andre base to fly a high altitude reconnaissance flight to the Seine Bay region after a detailed briefing of their allotted tasks by their Staffelkapitän, Hauptmann Heinz Feilmayer. The pair were led by Oblt Werner Kohla, with Uffz Herbert Blochberger flying as his rottenflieger (wingman). Unfortunately, the pair ran into the inevitable fighter umbrella that the allies had in almost permanent place over the invasion area and were 'bounced' by P-38 Lightning aircraft of the USAAF. It was a swift thrust and parry action that saw the P-38 sweep in, attack the 109s and peel away leaving one of the Messerschmitts critically hit and diving away vertically towards the French countryside far below. Herbert Blochberger had flown his last sortie. Inevitably, it fell to Herbert's commanding officer, Heinz Feilmayer, to write a letter home on 26 June to Blochberger's mother, Hedwig:

"Dear Mrs Blochberger,

"Again there is yet another sacrifice and I have the responsibility to give you the sad news that on 24 June 1944 your son Herbert failed to return from his mission. I know that this news must be very hard for you and I offer condolences on behalf of myself and the whole of the Staffel in your tragic loss.

"Since your son has been with the Staffel he proved himself, with his youthful ways, as a talented pilot. It was not long before he reached a very senior position within the Staffel. He was well respected by all of his comrades and sadly he has now given his country the greatest sacrifice.

"As to the incident, I can tell you the following: your son, together with Oblt Kohla, was flying a reconnaissance mission in the invasion area. At a great height they were intercepted by four enemy fighters which attacked them. Herbert dived straight away to try and shake off his attackers but they followed him down. Oblt Kohla then pursued the enemy fighters in an attempt to help his comrade. Eventually after a very steep dive Oblt Kohla's cockpit cabin iced-up and at this point he lost sight of your son and the enemy. After the attack we had no further radio contact with Herbert and at this time we have no further news. When Oblt Kohla landed I immediately notified all the relevant authorities and asked that they should start investigations but until now we have had no positive results.

"It is awful that you are completely in the dark regarding the fate of your son and I am sorry that I cannot offer you any more possibilities to bring to light the facts of this tragedy. I can only presume that your son did not recover from his steep dive and hit the ground. Or he could have been shot down by the enemy fighters. In both instances, you can be sure that his death was quick and painless. If I get any further new information on the tragedy of your son I will of course pass it on to you straight away.

Yours,
Heinz Feilmayer"

A grief-stricken Hedwig Blochberger, desperate for news of her son, wrote directly back to the man who was with Herbert when he disappeared, Werner Kohla. On 11 August 1944, Kohla replied:

"Dear Mrs Blochberger,

"Thank you very much for your letter which I received today. Of course I will answer you straight away.

   "I wanted your son as my comrade because I liked him personally very much indeed. We have flown a few difficult missions together during the first few days of the invasion, but we also knew each other before this time. On our last day together we were flying at a height of 8,000m and as we approached the area of Le Havre we were suddenly attacked by four enemy fighters. Your son immediately contacted me on the radio 'Achtung! Enemy fighters from the left'. At the same moment he turned his aircraft on its side and went into a steep dive almost vertically, to escape the attacking fighters. I saw the enemy fighters and dived after them and I followed the enemy machines to try and help my comrade but unfortunately I was flying so fast and so steep that my cabin began to ice-up. I had great difficulty in pulling out of my dive and it was not until I reached a height of 2,000m that I managed to pull out. I lost sight of the enemy and of your son.

   "I then flew back to our airfield at St Andre in the hope that my comrade had already landed before me. Sadly this was not the case. I can only presume that he did not survive the enemy attack or else he could not recover his aircraft from his dive and suffered an airman's death. Your son, as far as I can see, has crashed approximately 20 km N.E of Le Havre. His aircraft should be found by German soldiers in the area and maybe he has already been buried as an unknown airman. All enquires made on behalf of the Staffel are without any result and I don't think that your son could be a P.O.W. in England because we were flying over our own lines.

   "As soon as I receive any information about your missing son I will pass it on to you straight away but please allow me a few words of comfort. Dear Mrs Blochberger, only time can heal your pain and sadness. Maybe, however, a relief for you is the knowledge that after endless missions against the enemy he gave his young life for us all and for Germany.

Dearest regards,
Werner Kohla"

Herbert Blochberger taxies out in a Messerschmitt 109G. It is thought that this is the actual aircraft (Blue 1, W.Nr 27107) in which Herbert was lost on 24 June 1944.

Unfortunately, Kohla's hope that Herbert's aeroplane would be found by German forces in the area was a forlorn one. So, too, was the belief that he may have already been found and buried as an unknown airman and no further news was received by the Blochberger family for another fifty-two years.

The initial research regarding the presumed crash of a German aircraft at Ecretteville-les-Baons, France, was initiated by French researcher Laurent d' Hondt who had spent much spare time during the 1990s researching and investigating crash sites in the Seine-Maritime region. During his investigations in the Yvetot area he discovered an eyewitness who clearly remembered witnessing an air battle between a German fighter and a 'twin-tailed allied fighter' [sic] high in the sky over the little village of Ecretteville-les-Baons on 24 June 1944, approximately 50 miles south west of the port of Dieppe.

By June 1994 Laurent had already established the field where the aircraft crashed thanks to the help and co-operation of the landowner, Monsieur Leon Racine. Armed with his unusual detection kit of two small aluminium divining rods, Laurent and his eyewitness discovered the approximate area where the aircraft had crashed to earth and eventually pin-pointed the precise spot. Subsequently, and during the July of 1996 members of the UK-based Aircrew Remembrance Society were invited to travel to Ecretteville and help Laurent establish the identity of the aircraft and the fate of its pilot.

The team were very willing to get involved in the hope of establishing the identity of what was then just a mystery German fighter who had been lost there some time after D-Day in June 1944. Although there were indications as to the precise date of the crash the testimony of eye-witnesses so long after the event must always be accepted with a degree of caution. However, on the date that had been suggested (24 June 1944) there was a name that fitted; Herbert Blochberger. As to the specifics of his loss, German records showed that he had been lost in Messerschmitt 109G-6 'Blue 1', with the Werke Nummer 27106 (sic). His service number was recorded as 58225/66 with his date of birth being given as 7 May 1915 in Radefeld. Team member Melvin Brownless provides us with an account of his team's work on the crash site:

"We initially carried out a preliminary hand dig after discovering a very large 100% reading with our deep-seeking metal detectors. The area was marked off and we proceeded to dig through the sun-baked soil in the hope of finding evidence to establish the type of aircraft. After a few hours of hard toil we discovered substantial corroded aircraft remains two feet below the surface. Due to the abundance of metal and the hard soil only minor progress could be made. However, a few fragments were recovered and one piece was clearly marked '109'. This part and its numbering sequence were identified as coming from the tail-plane of a German Messerschmitt 109 aircraft – whilst we were still unaware of its sub-type we presumed it must be a Messerschmitt 109G. Small corroded parts from the ailerons were also found. After this discovery plans were drawn up to undertake a major recovery operation using heavy digging equipment. This was put in place, the equipment arranged and the date was finally set for the excavation to take place on 23 November 1996.

"After an overnight crossing from Newhaven we arrived early in the morning but locating the exact crash site in the pitch dark with the vegetation totally different from when we were there in the previous July, proved to be a considerable challenge. Just to add to the difficulties, and predictably in northern France during winter, the rain began with a vengeance. However, the challenge of what would probably be a difficult recovery overcame all despondency – to hell with the weather!

"Dawn was breaking as we approached the crash site area, which we soon identified from the disturbed patch of ground, the evidence from our previous initial investigation in July. With the mechanical digger not due to arrive until 9.00 a.m., it was decided to start an initial hand dig until then. The group split into pairs, and armed with spades we removed two feet of soil from a circular hole approximately eight feet in diameter. At this depth we discovered some corroded tail-plane wreckage, and for the next hour of digging we collected several bags of partially corroded airframe aluminium.

Following investigations by French and English researchers a crash site at Ecretteville-les-Baons was located which according to local information was thought to be that of a German aircraft shot down there on 24 June 1944. Over fifty years later, a team of investigators carried out a major excavation at the site.

"At this point, with everyone sweating profusely, the rain subsided and the digger was sighted coming up the lane in the distance, much to everyone's relief. Once the machine had started its work it was immediately apparent that our attempt to dig by hand to the depth of three feet over the previous couple of hours could be achieved in minutes using this mechanical advantage and with Laurent using appropriate instructions to the driver an area was soon cleared of top soil and the serious work of the recovery operation was under way.

"The first recognisable items to be unearthed were corroded airframe sections of both tail-plane and port wing, followed at a depth of five feet by a rusty propeller boss and one of the broad propeller blades in reasonable condition. The next item to emerge was the port undercarriage oleo leg minus the wheel and tyre, the leg itself being in good condition. Also a section of rear fuselage still with some surviving paint and stencil markings was uncovered. We had now reached a depth of around eight feet when suddenly parachute shroud lines had caught on the teeth of the digger bucket and our thoughts then turned to the fate of the unfortunate pilot. Was he lying just beneath our feet?

"The digger was immediately stopped so we could assess the situation. The parachute shroud lines were embedded in the soil below at this stage and we had to work very carefully to remove the soil around the lines and the parachute silk. We were successful in releasing the parachute in one piece, followed by the parachute pack and its harness together with the D ring (parachute rip-cord handle) and parachute pack release box. We realised, of course, that we must now be on the verge of finding a missing German pilot.

"After the discovery of the parachute, we carefully searched emerging remains of flying clothing and uniform fragments for any clues that might lead us to the identity of the pilot. Searching these uniform items and other fragments was a necessary task we had to carry out as we were hoping to find the pilot's erkennungsmarke (identity disc) but unfortunately this was not discovered. It is amazing that after over fifty years buried in the soil the textile material had survived incredibly well. Every effort was made to find and collect the remains of the airman and in doing this we discovered other clues as to his identity. At this time all of our thoughts were of this young man who paid the ultimate sacrifice in war and we were comforted in our task with the knowledge that after the recovery this young pilot of the German air force would no longer lie in an unmarked

Items buried deeply underground at such crash sites are frequently in a remarkable state of preservation since they are cut off from oxygen and are often preserved in aviation fuel and oil. If there has been no major fire or explosion on impact then finds like this amazingly preserved parachute with its pack and harness are not always unusual. The state of preservation with artefacts such as these is very often the key to quickly unravelling the identity of missing aircrew. They are also poignant and tangible reminders of young lives lost.

grave in a French field. He would now have a grave amongst his fallen comrades.

"The dig carefully continued and more cockpit and airframe parts emerged together with some remains of blue service Luftwaffe trousers. In one of the pockets we discovered the pilot's fliegerkappmesser (gravity knife), and on the wooden grip we found the initials H.B. and these same initials were found embroidered on a handkerchief. Other uniform fragments included the collar tabs showing the rank of unteroffizier. The digging machine had now stopped as we carefully searched in the cockpit area where we found the remains of a wallet containing one locker key together with some French bank notes and lose coins. All around the site were different piles of aircraft wreckage which consisted of a huge variety of airframe parts, hydraulic fittings, fuel tank rubber structure and assorted components. Many of the airframe structural parts were in good condition with no sign of any fire damage whatsoever.

"We also found the dinghy with its Walther signal pistol and flares. An extremely interesting find was the glass lens from the Rb 50/30 photographic camera, together with long strips of photographic film. This positively identified this Messerschmitt 109 as a photo-reconnaissance version rather than the fighter variant of the type. Then came a most incredible find – there lying on the ground was a strip of aluminium measuring approximately six inches by two inches which I immediately picked up and turned over in my hand to examine. Here in front of my eyes was the aircraft manufacturer's data card for a Me 109G, factory coded DQ+GA, with the aircraft werke nummer 27107. [Note: Luftwaffe records incorrectly recorded the number as 27106.] We now had the most important piece of evidence, stating the type and construction serial number of this particular Me 109 G-5 R/2 to which the loss of the pilot, and his name, could doubtless be tied.

"The excavation was at a depth of approximately twelve feet when suddenly there was a heavy thud as the digger struck something big. Within a few seconds the Daimler Benz 605 inverted V12 was lifted from its resting place in the jaws of the mechanical digger. On inspection, the Daimler Benz had suffered severe impact damage to the front of the engine and the crankcase had split down the centre with the crankshaft itself holding the two cylinder heads together. The last major recognisable relic to come out of the deepening crater was the tail-wheel oleo and tyre which was found, incredibly, under the engine.

"The excavation had finally revealed all of its secrets including the mortal remains of the long-lost pilot, Herbert Blochberger. After the last remains of the pilot had been found, a really strange thing happened. All morning the weather had been appalling with strong wind and heavy if not torrential rain. It hadn't stopped. Just when we had finished placing the remains of the pilot into a casket, and had placed a wreath as a tribute into the box and closed the lid, the dark clouds parted and rays of sunlight pointed down like golden fingers onto the site. This was just a very moving moment, with all the team's thoughts now concentrated on the memory of the missing German airman.

"On return to England we set about the task of identifying the pilot and his unit and urgently made contact with fellow aviation historians in Germany and America

Top left: Another poignant reminder during the recovery of Herbert Blochberger's Messerschmitt was this discovery of his wallet with coins, banknotes and a locker key. His pilot's badge was also recovered from the wreckage of the cockpit.

Top centre: A highly unusual find was this Deutsche Kreuz (German Cross) in gold which was a decoration awarded to acknowledge repeated and remarkable deeds of bravery or leadership. When discovered, it was found still pinned to a portion of Blochberger's tunic.

Top right: Here is Herbert Blochberger wearing that very same badge.

Middle left: A portion of a Luftwaffe flying map was also found in the cockpit wreckage.

Middle right: This interesting discovery was the engine manufacturer's badge from the Daimler Benz engine and is a symbol that will be familiar to car enthusiasts and owners!

Bottom: This data card was still clearly legible with its handwritten inscription and gave the aircraft type and werke nummer, albeit that it was out by just one digit from the number actually noted in Luftwaffe records.

and within a week we had the confirmation of the pilot's identity which we so desperately needed. At the time of writing this report it is not known what the *exact* cause of the loss of this aircraft was, but we do have the information written in the personal diary of an eyewitness. The entry for 24 June 1944 stated that he saw two aircraft very high up engaged in combat. The German aircraft was attacked by a 'twin-tailed allied aircraft'. During our 'dig' we did actually find bullet strikes in the first-aid access panel from the port side of the rear fuselage, the projectile having come through from the starboard side. The calibre was possibly .303, or maybe .50. The time of the crash was reported as being around seven o'clock, but we are not sure if this was am or pm."

After duly confirming, officially, the identity of Herbert Blochberger the German war graves service (VDK) organised his burial in the German military cemetery at Champigny St Andre, France, in Grave 285, Row 5, Block 13 and with the date of his funeral being on 6 June 1998. It was a ceremony attended by family members, including his younger brother and sister. At the graveside his sister, Ursula Strauss, made a poignant address. Whilst lengthy, it tells us the human story of this young German pilot and of the grief suffered by his family. It also demonstrates, once again, the overwhelming importance of the recovery, identification and burial of long-missing airmen to the relatives left behind.

At rest. Finally, in 1998 Herbert Blochberger was afforded a named grave in the German military cemetery at Champigny St Andre.

"It seems hardly possible to take on board that we are standing today, here in France, in a German war cemetery by the grave of our dear brother Herbert Blochberger. One and a half years ago nobody would have even remotely guessed at this possibility. During this ensuing period so much has happened which has touched us deeply. Painful but also happy memories emerged, happy that you dear Herbert existed, and that, despite the great difference in age we were allowed to share in part of your journey through life. We are remembering good events and time spent with you. Very sad though is the memory of all your pointless battles in France – the despair and sorrow when Mutti received the news that you were missing. There was great sorrow and uncertainty as to what should have befallen you, dear Herbert, but we are standing today, your brother Horst and his dear wife Moni, I your sister Ursula, and my dear husband Werner to say goodbye to you. This only became possible due to our English and French friends and especially Melvin with his group.

"So many memories tumble through our heads, of the month of June fifty-four

Er gab fein Lețtes, wir unfer Beftes!

Hart und fchwer traf uns die fchmerzliche Nachricht, daß mein lieber,
hoffnungsvoller Sohn, unfer lieber, guter Bruder, Neffe, Enkel und Coufin,
der Uffz. und Flugzeugführer

Herbert Blochberger
geb. 7. 5. 1919   geft. 24. 6. 1944

von einem Aufklärungsflug über dem Invafionsraum nicht zurückgekehrt ift.
Er folgte feinem lieben Papa nach 3 Jahren in die Ewigkeit nach.

In tiefer Trauer:

Hedwig Blochberger, geb. Sander
Horft und Urfula Blochberger
Familien Paul Sander und Krutzfch
und alle, die ihn lieb hatten.

Z. Z. Radefeld über Delitzfch, im Juli 1944.

It is hard to imagine the pain of Frau Blochberger as she sent out these memorial cards to record the loss of her much loved and eldest child. Whatever the cause for which he had fought and died he was still a mother's son.

years ago – when Mutti received what must have been your last letter, we could feel between the lines the hopeless, serious situation in which you found yourselves. This madness of war demanded from you to the last, and from us, the best. Mutti was full of worry and anxiety – in her thoughts she was always with you. She once said to me that she was begging with all her heart that the Lord may take you away from all the horrors. She had not meant it to happen this way. At the end of June 1944 we received from Hauptmann Feilmayer the message that you were missing, that you, dear Herbert, did not return from an enemy mission – three years after father's death.

"For Mutti, the world collapsed. You were in every way her great support, we all were missing you so much. After all, you were not only a big brother to us but also a father! The post-war days were a bad time for us. How should Mutti pay the rent on our large apartment? We were always hungry and there was very little to eat. Therefore we moved to Radefeld, to grandma's, where you were born and where you always felt at home.

"Many a childhood memory of you is still alive in my heart. We were always looking forward to your parcels from the front – your laundry, but from your flyer's 'special rations' always a tin of chocolate. For us, always a reason to celebrate. When Mutti's parcels did not reach you because you had been moved, I still remember with relish the dried-out crumbly cake as it always tasted wonderfully good. I also remember with pleasure, how you, when on leave, used to play the piano, even during the night, for your own enjoyment and relaxation. Remember before we had to go to bed, you carried us on your shoulders quickly and flew along our long corridor with crash landings onto our beds? Horst and I always made sure that neither was able to enjoy one go more than the other. Mutti often talked about the long cycle tours that you went on – from Berlin to Radefeld. In those days, unusually long distances for such tours.

"When we talk to people in Radefeld about their memories so many of them still remember you. Some are even able to recall how when flying across Radefeld you flew very low three times and made it obvious that you were paying us a visit. Your flying skills certainly impressed the Radefelders as many recall. Dear Herbert, our Mutti tried all her life to find out about your fate. At first she hoped that you were taken prisoner, German engineers were always sought after. Searches by the German Red Cross were without result. She very much regretted that by father's strict upbringing, and by your own dedication to fulfil what was expected of you, you missed out on the more enjoyable pursuits in your young life.

"Music played a great part in enhancing your life – you loved it so. During difficult missions, your trust in God gave you the strength which you needed and we felt this in your letters home. Dear Herbert, what you could not experience any more, we have been given in our lives. Horst and I have wonderful families, we have healthy children, who are happily married and we are both proud grandparents. Our children know of you, they know you, and your pictures hang on our walls in our houses. They are interested in your fate, and they supported us during the last months in our correspondence with the authorities and our friends in England and France. They gave us moral support and their thoughts are with us all today. Our dear Mutti had hoped right to the end of her life by some miracle to hear news of your fate. Our father's death hit her hard, but she wanted to live to see what had happened to you. Werner nursed her during the last years of her life. She died peacefully in April 1995 in her 97th year. Dear Herbert, that your fate was determined and that we are standing here by your last resting place to say goodbye to you is only possible because of the young people of the Aircrew Remembrance Society and the Maurice Choron Association, who endeavour responsibly to determine the unknown fate of war casualties. With all our hearts we thank these young people; Melvin Brownless, Steven Hall, David King, Laurent d'Hondt and Mike Croft.

"During the excavations on 23 November 1996 near Ecretteville-les-Baons they found your Messerschmitt 109 and were able to recover your remains with dignity and respect. It was meant to be, because even after all these years you wanted to be found. Through the great personal and self-financed dedication of the recovery team, and consequent tireless and meticulous work, the group uncovered your fate. In February 1997 they found our address and we were overwhelmed and deeply touched by your recovery. We followed their exhausting work with great interest. These wonderful young people deserve our greatest respect. We are feeling so very grateful for what they have done for us and a deep friendship has formed between us.

"In June 1997 Melvin, Udo and Steven were in Radefeld. It was such a joy for us and anything which concerned you, dear Herbert, was for us of great interest. They looked up where you were born at grandma's, and all of your favourite spots in the beautiful garden. They also visited Mutti's grave and we all wished so very

Music played an important part in Herbert's life and he gained great solace from playing the piano, especially when home on leave from the front. This pre-war Christmas family photograph shows Herbert at the piano while his father, his adoring mother Hedwig and brother Horst and his sister Ursula look on. One can almost hear the melody of 'Stille nacht, heilige nacht' when looking at this image.

much to be able to take you home and lay you to rest in Mutti's grave. Despite all our efforts it was not possible. It simply could not be done. Our hearts grieve that you, dear Herbert, have been resting with your plane in foreign soil for fifty-two years. We are so grateful – with all our hearts – that you now have a worthy place amongst thousands of German soldiers in Champigny/St Andre. And here, quite nearby, lies your Staffel commander Hauptmann Heinz Feilmayer.

"Our English and French friends are also present to say 'Good Bye' to you and we know that you are now together with Mutti. We your siblings and our marriage partners, as well as your English and French friends, bow to you. Rest in peace with your comrades and here is a token from grandma's garden, where you loved to be. Some homeland earth in a foreign country. This will keep you as you rest here. I say thank you from our family, and with overflowing hearts, that we were given the chance to be here."

In its deeply touching way, Ursula Strauss's address mirrors almost exactly the sentiments expressed by another sister bereaved through the loss of her much-loved brother in another and much later war. Colleen Ijuin also lost her beloved fighter-pilot brother, 'Skip' Foulks, many years after Herbert went missing. It was a different war and they were fighting for vastly different ideologies, but the aching pain of loss suffered by two sisters was identical. And so was the bitter-sweet joy at their respective brother's return (see Chapter 17).

CHAPTER 16
Thunderjet Down!

TO AN EXTENT, THE cases like those of Russell Lyon and Herbert Blochberger from the 1939-45 period in north-west Europe are relatively commonplace and usually quite straightforward in respect of dealing with the host governments concerned. Culturally, politically and ideologically it is what might be termed a 'level playing field' and even though some of Britain's European partners were former enemies there is clearly a degree of understanding and common accord when it comes to bringing home casualties of respective European and fellow NATO countries. However, in March 2009 the North Korean ambassador to the United Kingdom, His Excellency Ja Song-nam, made a speech at the House of Commons which tantalisingly made reference to the discovery of a set of remains of a British pilot in North Korea who had been lost during the Korean war. It proved to be the opening, at least in any official sense, of a case that had been pursued, unofficially, by the brother of the pilot concerned since at least 2004.

According to the official history of the Korean War by Anthony Farrar-Hockley, some 1,078 British service personnel died in the war including twenty-seven members of the RAF (another source tends to suggest that number to be twenty-eight), comprising twelve officers and fifteen other ranks. Farrar-Hockley refers to how RAF officers became attached to the USAF in order to achieve "manpower savings which could be passed to the US Fifth Air Force in Korea". The book goes on to tell us that "...by the end of the war, twenty-one RAF pilots had served with the 4th and 51st Fighter Interceptions Wings". However, as we shall see, these were not exclusively the only USAF units to which RAF pilots were assigned. Additionally, some thirty-two other

Flt Lt Desmond Hinton DFC (right) plans another mission over North Korea with American pilot colleagues of the USAF. Hinton was a decorated RAF World War Two pilot.

RAF pilots were attached to 77 Squadron, Royal Australian Air Force, for the duration of hostilities in Korea.

In respect of the RAF attachments to the USAF, each tour was for a period of approximately four months and as one group went home another was in training in the USA, usually at the Nellis Air Force Base, Nevada. Sixteen RAF officers in total completed active air operations with the USAF in Korea flying F-86 Sabres and all of these pilots damaged one or more Mig-15 during combat and with some of them officially credited with 'kills'. At least one other pilot (the subject of this chapter) flew the F-84 on ground-attack missions.

By comparison to the quite-recent world war the number of personnel committed to action was insignificant, and yet the percentage of losses (especially within the RAF flying contingent) was relatively high. For example, of the thirty-two pilots attached to the RAAF six of them were killed. Of those, only one has a known grave. Of the forty-one attached to the USAF, four were killed and none of those four has a known grave. It is this latter group of pilots who are of interest in the context of this chapter. Those pilots were:

Wg Cdr J R Baldwin DSO & bar, DFC & bar, AFC – missing 15 March 1952
Sqn Ldr G S Hulse DFC – missing 13 March 1953
Flt Lt D F W Hinton DFC – missing 2 January 1952
Flt Lt J E Y King – missing 4 June 1953

Of specific interest from that group is Flt Lt Desmond F W Hinton attached to the 49th Fighter-Bomber Group, 9 Fighter-Bomber Squadron, and flying F-84 E Thunderjets out of Taegu air base, Korea. The circumstances of his loss were set out in a letter to Hinton's wife from Colonel William L Mitchell, the group's commanding officer, on 21 January 1952, just two weeks after Desmond's disappearance:

"He was leading his squadron in a strafing run on some trucks a few miles north-east of Pyongyang. He called that his plane was hit and he would have to bale out. He jettisoned his canopy and two other pilots saw the seat was empty which makes me believe that Des got clear of the seat. His parachute was not seen, however he was wearing a white parachute and the ground was completely covered with snow. This would have made it difficult to see the opened parachute. The other pilots circled the area for some time and they could not locate Des. I personally feel that he made it OK, and I feel that he will be held until the cease-fire becomes a reality.

"Des has made many close friends here and we feel his loss greatly. All join me in expressing our deepest sympathy during these difficult days and pray that it will not be too long until we know that Des is alive and well.

"Des is one of the most courageous and skilful pilots I have ever known. He helped in many ways and I think of him as one of my closest friends."

Sadly, Mitchell was wrong when he optimistically suggested that Des was alive and would be released after any cease-fire. After the shooting war had finished there was no word whatsoever about him, his fate or of his whereabouts. All that was known were the brief circumstances as set out by Mitchell, and that he had been flying F-84 E, number 51-664,

A F-84 E Thunderjet of 49th Fighter-Bomber Group, 9th Fighter-Bomber Squadon, in Korea at around the time of Hinton's loss. Note the under-slung bomb beneath the port wing signifying that this aircraft is preparing for another ground-attack mission.

when he had been lost in the Pyongyang region of North Korea.

In 2004 Desmond Hinton's brother, David, made a formal request to the North Korean government in efforts to trace what had happened to his brother and on 2 July of that year the official North Korean news agency (KCNA) reported as follows:

> "Some days ago, British citizen David Hinton requested that the Democratic People's Republic of Korea should correctly ascertain the fate of his elder brother Frederick William Hinton, former lieutenant of the British Royal Air Force, who participated in the Korean war as an airman. From a humanitarian point of view the DPRK side confirmed with much effort that his elder brother died in the Korean war and informed him of the correct crash site and the grave site. Recently he paid a visit to the DPRK [North Korea] during which he went round these sites. He expressed his thanks to the DPRK government and the Korean People's Army for helping him realise his hope."

David Hinton, himself a former RAF pilot, indeed visited what he was told was the grave site of his sibling on 28 June 2004 in what was certainly an emotional trip for the younger brother who had never given up hope of finding Desmond. (According to subsequent British press reports the grave site was "located" in 2002.) The crash site and grave site were situated near the village of Kus-ri and close to what is now Pyongyang International Airport located at Sunan, north of the capital. It was here that David found what was quite literally a field grave, surrounded by a white picket fence. One of the villagers poignantly gave David a piece of Desmond's flying suit during his visit, prompting David to say: "I was very close to my brother who was very much my role model. I never stopped missing him in every one of the fifty-seven years since he was lost."

However, the visit of David Hinton to North Korea was perhaps the catalyst for events which culminated on 5 May 2011 with the handing-over of what were believed to be Flt Lt Hinton's remains to the British authorities when Colonel Pak Gi Yong of the Korean People's Army turned over two caskets to the British ambassador to North Korea, Mr Peter Hughes. Of course, this is

The remains of Desmond Hinton being handed over by the authorities in North Korea.

not quite the end of the story as the remains now need to be subject to physical and scientific analysis to establish that they do, indeed, belong to Desmond. In order to facilitate this process the remains have been transported to the CILHI laboratory, Hawaii, for DNA testing against samples collected from close family members. At the time of going to print with this book the results of those tests are still awaited.

Whilst there certainly seems to be a reasonable degree of optimism that these are, indeed, the mortal remains of Flt Lt D F W Hinton DFC it is of course essential that an absolute confirmation of this fact is established. In the past, the methodology of the North Koreans in repatriating remains of United Nations allied troops has sometimes hindered rather than helped, with the returned remains not always being the person they have purported to have been, or else having been returned with several sets of remains co-mingled along with intermingled or non-associated personal effects.

However, in the case of Desmond Hinton it would appear that the remains have been collected from a single site which, say the North Koreans, was emphatically the resting place of Hinton. So far as can be ascertained, however, the remains are not associated with any known or identified adjacent crash site of an aircraft, although clearly the establishment of such a crash site nearby, and the identification of the aircraft by type and serial number, would doubtless aid and assist the identification process. However, the question of searches for and repatriation of missing casualties from Korea is one that has recently engaged writer and researcher Michael Rank who writes as follows of those ongoing efforts;

"As regards to the process of searching for personnel missing in action in North Korea, Admiral Robert F. Willard, the head of U.S. Pacific Command, said on 27 January 2010:

'We're going to enter into discussions with North Korea about MIAs. That is what we know right now. They are willing to talk about it and we're willing to address the particulars with them. It's a complex problem. We've been in (North Korea for recovery missions) before, and it appears that we're being invited to consider going back again,' Willard told reporters at Camp Smith, Hawaii.

According to the *Honolulu Advertiser* he went on to say. 'It's something that we'll take seriously and we'll enter into dialogue with them and find out where it will lead.'

"No date has been agreed on restarting the search for the remains. More than 8,100 Americans remain unaccounted for from the Korean War, according to the Department of Defense.

"During Operation Glory in 1954, North Korea returned the remains of over 2,000 Americans, the Department of Defense says.

" 'Between 1954 and 1990, the US was not successful in convincing North Korea to search for and return additional US remains,' the Defense Prisoner of War/Missing Personnel Office states on its website.

" 'However, from 1990 to 1994, North Korea exhumed and returned what they claimed were 208 sets of remains. Unfortunately, their records and recovery methods have hampered US efforts to identify most of these. The North Koreans co-mingled the remains and the associated personal effects. These difficulties underscored clearly the need for joint field activities in which US expertise would guide the recovery process and improve the identification results.'

"Larry Greer, director of public affairs of the DPMO in Arlington, VA, confirmed that the North Korean army 'informed the United Nations that they were willing to talk about remains recovery operations. That was at a Panmunjom meeting on the 26 Jan. The US has not yet responded.'

"The US military newspaper *Stars and Stripes* last year quoted a US Defense Department anthropologist who had taken part in the hunt for MIA remains in the North as saying he was frustrated that the operation north of the border had been suspended.

" 'I am always disappointed when politics interfere with human rights and bringing closure to families whose relatives died in Korea so long ago,' said Jay Silverstein during a search for remains in South Korea close to the border with the North. He said he hoped some day to return to North Korea to continue to search for the remains of US service personnel. 'I found the North Koreans very pleasant to work with,' said Silverstein, who was overseeing the excavations in Hwacheon county about eight miles from the border with North Korea.

" 'My experience was very positive. It gave me a lot of hope for the future … that relations between the North and the South and the West and the rest of Asia will someday be improved.

" 'I found the North Koreans to be very reasonable people. Very friendly. We could sit down and have a beer, or smoke a cigar, and talk. It was quite pleasant,' he added.

"Apart from the suspended agreement with North Korea, the United States reached an agreement with China in 2008 'to formalize research in Chinese archives on Korean War POW/MIA matters.'

"The Chinese side seems to have been reluctant to share much information with the Americans so far, but the Chinese news agency Xinhua reported last October that 'Chinese military archivists have identified more than 100 documents that could lead to the repatriation of the remains of the United States personnel who disappeared during and after the Korean War.'

"It added that 'China's People's Liberation Army (PLA) Archives Department has been combing more than 1.5 million archives of the then People's Volunteer Army (PVA), the Central Military Commission (CMC) and the PLA headquarters during the Korean War.

" 'Archivists have given at least four valuable archives found in the first 10 percent to the Defense Prisoner of War/Missing Personnel Office (DPMO) of the US Department of Defense.'

"The Chinese report mentioned how archivists had located the site where a US bomber crashed in 1950 in the southern province of Guangdong. 'After visiting the site and interviewing 19 witnesses who helped them identify the burial site of US crew, they believe the possibility of finding the remains is high,' it added. The DPMO's Greer said that 'We are making slow steady progress' in the joint archive project.

"He said that in September 2009 the US hosted six PLA archivists for annual discussions and to review arrangements, and that the archivists provided additional information on the Guangdong crash site which was part of their annual report in June 2009.

"In October 2009, General Xu Caihou, vice-chairman of the PLA's Central Military Commission, presented four Chinese-language documents to Defense Secretary Robert Gates during a visit to Washington.

" 'The documents concerned the Guangdong site and a F-86 Korean War crash site in China about which we were already aware. We have requested permission to investigate the Guangdong Province crash site in April this year,' Greer has said.

" 'At the September 2009 meeting we also discussed amending our arrangement to facilitate the transfer of actual documents from the PLA archives to us and to permit joint PLA archives-DOD accounting community remains recovery work in China. The amendment process is underway now, but not final,' he added.

"The South Koreans, who lost tens of thousands of soldiers in the war, would also like to hunt for their remains in the North. President Lee Myung-bak said in a New Year's address this would be an appropriate way to mark the 60th anniversary of the start of the Korean War."

The foregoing, then, is an interesting assessment of the missing allied service personnel in North Korea – albeit that it affects primarily American servicemen there are some British airmen involved as we have seen. In the event that the remains from Sunan, North Korea, are identified as the twenty-nine-year-old pilot from New Malden in Surrey, they will probably be buried in the United Nations Cemetery at Pusan. However, a British embassy official is also quoted as stating that an option for the repatriation of the remains is also possible. That being the case, and notwithstanding the more recent repatriation of British casualties from the Falklands, Iraq and Afghanistan, the repatriation of remains to the UK from the Korean conflict would be a first. Certainly, this is also a 'first' in terms of the location and probable identification (yet to be confirmed) of an RAF victim of the Korean war. Either way, it stands likely that Flt Lt Desmond Hinton will shortly be declared as no longer missing. Of course, another Asian war not many years later claimed yet many more missing aircrew, although none of them British. However, the quest for missing US aircrew from Vietnam is active and ongoing as this is being written.

CHAPTER 17

Old Salt 303

THE CONFLICT IN VIETNAM was one that resulted in a total of 2,583 US servicemen being lost in action who remained unaccounted for at the cessation of hostilities, although reports received by the US government after the withdrawal in 1975 built a strong case for very many of those unaccounted for being actually being alive and still held as prisoners of war. Inevitably, a strong lobby began to build in America championing the cause of the so-called POW/MIA cases. In effect, many of those missing personnel who had been previously presumed dead by the US military were having their cases raised by families and by pressure groups who sought answers as to what had happened to their loved ones. For the most part, at least initially, there were no answers to questions being raised by families and next-of-kin and

Lt Ralph Foulks, USN.

even dialogue with Vietnam, let alone any access to the country, was not an option. Consequently, any detailed investigations by CILHI were out of the question. However, for some of the MIA/POW organisations the not-unreasonable view was taken that the words "unaccounted for" was something that should refer to numbers and not to men. Unfortunately, for many years and for many families, "unaccounted for" was the status that remained for a considerable percentage of missing Vietnam casualties.

By December 1988, however, a sufficient thaw in relations between Vietnam and the USA had resulted in thirty-eight boxes containing remains alleged to be those of American missing servicemen being handed over by the Socialist Republic of Vietnam. One of them was marked with the name Foulks, the date of death given as 5 January 1968 and the death stated as having taken place at Gia Vien, Ha Nam Ninh province.

The details certainly made some sense to CILHI, whose laboratory had been charged with the responsibility of identifying the various sets of repatriated remains. However, there needed to be an absolutely positive identification of any remains before they could be turned over to respective families. And in the case of the casket marked Foulks there was a problem; the box contained no skull. This would have normally been a route to enable a name to be applied to the remains. However, from the scant information supplied by the Vietnamese and attached to the set of remains subsequently described by CILHI as Case # 0252-88, an early conclusion was drawn. The conclusion was that these were probably the remains of Lt Ralph Foulks of VA163, US Navy, who had been lost on 5 January 1968 in his A-4E Skyhawk jet over North Vietnam. The problem was that it had to be proven beyond any doubt.

On the night of 4/5 January 1968, a section of two A-4E aircraft of VA163 (Attack Squadron 163) were launched from the USS *Oriskany* for an armed reconnaissance over the North Vietnamese road system south of Nam Dinh. Their briefed area of operation included the densely populated and fertile coastal plain which was laced with numerous rivers, canals, waterways and rice fields to the north east of Thanh Hoa. Eventually, a truck convoy was located eleven miles east of the coastline and the flight leader directed an attack and went in first with Foulks following on his wing. As he pulled up off target his wingman, Lt Foulks in aircraft number 150131 with the tail number AH303 (call-sign 'Old Salt 303'), acknowledged that he had the bomb bursts of his leader in his sight. The time was 22.10hrs on the night of 5 January, and after Foulks had reported his leader's strikes nothing further was heard from him and although the section had received anti-aircraft fire it was impossible to know if Foulks had been hit, or if he had simply flown into

Lt Ralph Foulks, US Navy, poses with his A-4E Skyhawk of VA163 aboard the USS *Oriskany* during the Vietnam War.

the ground. This was always a potential hazard during night dive-bombing attacks.

However, no crash or fire was seen on the ground and there had been no sign of any ejection or of a parachute. No further radio contact could be made with Foulks, and no emergency beacon transmission was picked up. He had simply disappeared, somewhere in the region of Phar Diem city. Under the circumstances, it was thought there was a good chance that Lt Foulks could have experienced radio failure along with possible battle damage and chosen to divert to an alternative airfield rather then attempt to return, damaged and possibly wounded, to the USS *Oriskany* at night.

The closest alternate airfields capable of handling jet aircraft were located at DaNang and Chu Lai, South Vietnam. The squadron duty officer contacted both airfields. After his inquiries netted no information about the whereabouts of Ralph Foulks, he was immediately listed missing in action. However, in early 1973, 591 American prisoners of war

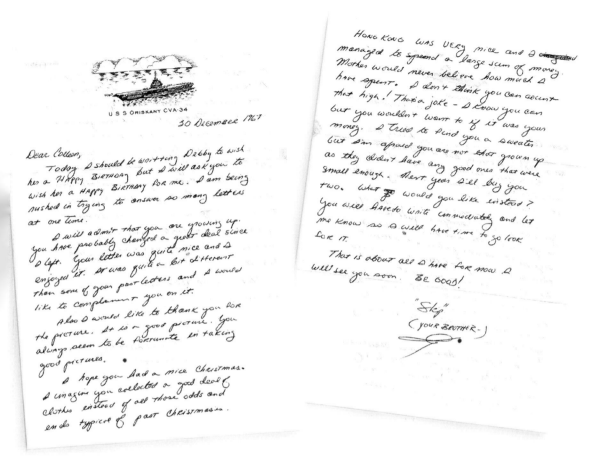

This last letter home from her big brother Ralph (or 'Skip' as he was known) remains a treasured keepsake for Colleen Ijuin.

were released by the communists during Operation Homecoming but Foulks was not among them. All returnees were debriefed by US intelligence officers to discover any information each possessed about other Americans who were known or believed to be prisoners and who had not been released from captivity.

According to an air force pilot released from one of the camps in Hanoi, he believed Ralph Foulks was possibly a POW in the same camp he was in. Further, the Defense Intelligence Agency (DIA) correlated intelligence data they believed supported the probability that Lt Foulks's aircraft sustained severe battle damage and that he was forced to eject his Skyhawk and was subsequently captured by the North Vietnamese. Unfortunately, the returned casket marked with his name and date of death clearly indicated that this was most probably an incorrect assumption.

However, when the various sets of remains were turned over by the Vietnamese, the timing of that transfer happened to coincide with the very recent introduction of mitochondrial deoxyribonucleic acid (DNA) sequencing, a technology now being applied to the identification of human remains, both civilian and military, on a routine and worldwide basis. Naturally, it was a new technique embraced by CILHI but it wasn't until Ralph Foulks's mother attended a meeting of the National League of Families of American Prisoners and

Campaigns across the United States to remember those classified as missing in action, and possibly held as prisoners of war, gathered momentum in the post-Vietnam war years. To keep the names of those classified MIA/POW in public mind, relatives and pressure groups distributed numerous bracelets bearing the names of those who were unaccounted for. Thus, there were many people who had worn bracelets wearing Ralph Foulks name and although they hadn't known him they kept his name alive in this rather special manner. When Ralph was eventually found, many of those who had worn bracelets in his memory sent them back to the Foulks family with touching notes and letters.

Missing in South East Asia, where she learned about DNA, that events started to take another turn.

At once, Ralph's mother provided a blood sample at that meeting for it to be compared with DNA recovered from the casket marked Foulks. By December 1992, CILHI had contacted the family to say they had a match, thus making this the first identification of a previously missing American serviceman made possible through the DNA route. At last, Ralph Foulks had come home and on 21 January 1993 it was formally announced that the remains were his and they were duly buried in Site 376, Section 38, Barrancas National Cemetery, at the Pensacola Naval Air Station. The pledge given by President Reagan had been honoured by a nation that has adopted a simple ethos towards its military; you may be wounded doing your duty, you may even be killed, but you won't be left behind on the battlefield.

In its efforts to ensure that nobody is left behind, CILHI teams have now accessed Vietnam and Laos on the ground investigating crash sites including F-4 Phantoms, B-52 bombers and even Huey helicopters looking for remains of the missing. On each occasion, and adopting techniques identical to the World War Two A-20 case in Chapter Five, the crash sites have been excavated and examined archaeologically in the utmost forensic detail. Where remains are located they are returned to the CILHI laboratories. Almost invariably, and however pulverised and degraded, the recovered bone or dental material is DNA matched to the families of suspected casualties. Case by case, casualty by casualty, the list of the missing is slowly but surely being worked through for an eventual full accounting of the men brought back from what has often been called "the land of the lost".

Ralph Foulks's sister, Debra Campbell, was selected as one of the first US Navy Reserved Officer Training Corps women in 1972 who were 'experimentally' engaged to see if women could make it through the four vigorous college years and pass out an officer. She excelled and retired a commander twenty-five years later with one of her last assignments to stand duty as the plane arrived in Pensacola for Ralph's funeral. She escorted her brother's casket off the plane with full colours prior to his burial at Barracas National Cemetery.

Ralph Foulks's mother pictured with Ralph as a young boy. Unlike Frau Blochberger, Mrs Foulks thankfully lived to see her son found and brought home.

151

CHAPTER 18

The Blackest Day

WHILST VIETNAM MAY WELL be the land of the lost to the Americans it could well be said that the whole of Western Europe might be considered exactly as such for many aircrew members of all the combatant nations who fought in European skies during two world wars. The numbers of missing runs into literally countless thousands of men as we have already seen. We have also already seen how many of those men have been found and are still being found even as this book is being written. However, searches for these casualties do not always have the hoped-for or expected result. One such case is the search for a Dutch pilot, Flt Lt Jan Plesman, who disappeared over northern France in 1944. He was a Spitfire pilot flying with 322 Squadron on what its operations record book described as the blackest of days for the squadron.

Dutchman Flt Lt Jan Plesman, like many escapees from occupied Europe who had fled to Britain in order to continue the fight, went to extraordinary lengths to come and join the RAF.

Jan Leendert Plesman was the son of Albert Plesman, a Dutch aviator who founded the KLM airline on 7 October 1919 (the oldest commercial airline in the world) and it would be true to say that flying was certainly in the young Jan's blood. Consequently, it was just about inevitable that he would join the Dutch air force to train as a pilot and on 16 August 1938 he entered the training school at Soesterberg and embarked upon a path that would ultimately see him prepare to become a fighter pilot in anticipation of flying the Dutch air force's standard fighter, the Fokker D-21. Unfortunately, however, fate took a hand in Jan's plans and on 10 May 1940 the Germans launched their devastating attack on Holland which resulted in the rapid and inevitable capitulation of his country. It also resulted in the virtual annihilation of his father's beloved KLM at its Schipol base.

Viewing the destruction there had filled the young Jan with hatred for the invading

This group shot of 322 Squadron with one of their Spitfire Mk IXs is probably taken at RAF Deanland, in East Sussex. It was from here that Jan Plesman flew his last sortie, and also from here that he racked up a healthy score of twelve V1 flying bombs confirmed destroyed.

Germans, and with a determination that he would somehow continue the fight. As a result, and like so many determined young men around occupied Europe, Jan and his friend Geert Overgauw hatched an escape plan which would ultimately see them setting out at the end of December 1940 and making their way down across Holland, Belgium and France in an extremely hazardous journey to the Spanish border. From here they managed to make it to Madrid and thence to Lisbon where Jan found his father's KLM airline still operating commercial flights to England. On 23 May 1941 he and Geert boarded a DC-3 to Bristol. They had made it. It was now just a case of getting into the RAF and eagerly taking the fight back to the enemy.

After the usual process of de-briefing and interrogation, Jan progressed through flying training and an operational training unit before eventually being posted to an operational squadron, 322 Squadron, at the end of the year. By 28 March 1942 he had flown his first operational sortie, a convoy patrol in the English Channel, and when a Dutch fighter squadron (322 Squadron) was formed in June 1943 it was natural that Jan should be posted there. Whilst this chapter does not set out to tell the operational detail of Jan's career it would be invidious not to mention some brief detail of his time with 322 Squadron, although a fully detailed account is given in Albert Plesman's (jr) book *A Flying Dutchman*. Variously, Jan flew Spitfire VB and VCs and later Mk XIVs followed by Mk IXs.

From 20 June 1944 the squadron was based at RAF West Malling but moving to RAF Deanland, near Hailsham in East Sussex, on 21 July 1944 when it reverted from Mk XIV Spitfires to Mk IXs. During the period of the flying-bomb attacks against south-east England in the summer of 1944, Jan became a 'doodlebug ace', destroying no less than twelve of these missiles. However, the squadron regularly carried out operational flights deep into occupied Europe in support of the ongoing allied assault through France following D-Day and it was on one such flight on 1 September 1944 that Jan failed to return to his Deanland base. The operations record book for 322 Squadron tells the story:

> "Today is doubtless the blackest day the squadron has ever experienced. At 07.12 hours the squadron took off on an armed reconnaissance in the Calais-Ghent-Aulnoye [*sic*] area during which four M.E.T and one light A.F.V were destroyed and one heavy A.F.V. and one M.E.T. were damaged. Whilst going down to shoot up something he had seen the C.O, Major Kuhlmann DFC was apparently hit by flak and he baled out. His number two, however, saw him land and wave his hand. He landed five miles inland from Cap Gris-Nez. This is a terrible blow to the squadron and we can only hope that he will find a way of evading capture and eventually make his way back to take charge of the squadron he has led so admirably.
>
> "This was not the end of the bad news today for at 10.27 the squadron took off on an armed reconnaissance in the same area during which a gun post was attacked and two M.E.T. were damaged. This time, however, two aircraft were hit by flak with the result that the 'A' Flight commander, Flt Lt van Eendenburg, made a belly landing south-east of Lille. The aircraft was seen to tip up and break off a wing but he was not seen to get out of the aircraft. The 'B' Flight commander, Flt Lt Plesman, was seen to have had his tail-plane shot off and he spun in north east of St Omer and he was not seen to leave his aircraft. Thus it is that we have lost in one day the CO and both flight commanders. Mere words could not possibly express the feeling of the squadron at this moment and we shall wait anxiously until further news."

This was not long in coming in respect of Flt Lt L C M van Eendenburg who had managed to evade capture and return to the squadron by 11 September that year. For Major K C Kuhlmann (the CO) there was, however, to be no joyous reunion with his pilots. Instead, he had drifted down on his parachute into enemy held territory and unfortunately became a prisoner of war. In his place, van Eendenburg was appointed CO upon his return to the squadron just over a week later, there still being no news of Jan Plesman. Indeed, the circumstances of Plesman's loss and the fact that he was not seen to escape from the stricken Spitfire had already led the squadron to conclude without any doubt that he must be dead.

Quite when the first news of Jan's disappearance reached his mother and father in Holland is unclear, although messages were regularly being sent to and from the family during Jan's time in Britain (often via a KLM route) and so it is entirely possible that they were notified not long after he had failed to return. Either way, and unlike Kuhlmann and van Eendenburg, it was clear that Jan was not coming home and in the immediate post-war period there was some effort made to locate Jan's crash site and his body. Most likely, this would have been via the offices of the MREU teams although Albert Plesman, in *The Flying Dutchman*, had his own version of the investigations after the war:

"When St Omer was liberated in late 1944 by the Allied Forces, 322 Squadron officials tried to locate the spot where Jan's Spitfire had crashed into the ground, but in the short time available they were unable to find a clue.

"After the war, no Dutch government ever showed any gratitude by trying to locate the place where Jan Plesman had disappeared so that he might have an honourable funeral. A sickening ingratitude and disgrace after he had served his country and Queen with devotion and loyalty!

"Jan's dynamic father also made an effort to have the disaster spot located. He strongly desired to give his son a decent resting place. He had mentioned in a letter to Jan; 'We will have to pay a tribute to those who died to make it all possible.'

"No one so far has been able to find the wreckage of Jan Plesman's Spitfire nor his remains.

No funeral was ever held for Jan Plesman,!"

These strident words strongly reflect the Plesman family's ongoing desire to find Jan and to bring him home. That desire still burns strongly in the heart and mind of Jan Plesman Jr (Jan's nephew) who was born just after his uncle's death and was named after him as a mark of familial respect. In July 2011 Jan was still active in trying to discover what had become of his uncle. However, the clues are minimal with the starting point and only tangible clue being the 322 Squadron operations record book which states Jan's loss to have taken place 'north east of St Omer'. This is the vaguest of clues and covers an awfully large expanse of countryside. In essence, this is another example of a small needle in a very large haystack. However, given that van Eendenburg had made a forced-landing on that same operation, and having been hit by the very same flak bursts, might it not be reasonable to assume that Jan's aeroplane may have crashed at least somewhere nearby or in the same vicinity? It is at least a starting point, but at once it throws up an immediate problem.

Again, and according to the squadron's operations record book, van Eendenburg was *seen* to make a belly-landing to the south east of Lille. However, we know that the place he made his forced-landing was actually near the village of Mametz, some fifty kilometres due *west* of Lille. So, nowhere near Lille by a long way and directionally out by almost 180 degrees! It must therefore throw into question the accuracy of Jan's crash site as being described to the north east of St Omer. Possibly, this might well be an accurate description anyway, although we have no way of knowing and no real clues and an absence of hard evidence to guide us. The only measure of the operations record book accuracy is the description of van Eendenberg's crash place, and we now know that to be flawed. Beyond the vague 'clue' in the 322 Squadron record book the trail has long gone cold. Or has it?

In 2006 a French research team didn't think that it had, and firmly believed they had located the crash site of Jan Plesman's Spitfire at Wallon Cappel about ten kilometres due east of St Omer. Whilst not exactly north east, it was getting generally towards the area indicated by 322 Squadron. However, the clue was tenuous to say the very least and was based upon an eye witness who claimed to have seen a Spitfire have its tail shot off by flak and dive vertically into the ground before the pilot could escape. Those facts, at least, could be said to 'fit' the known circumstances of Jan's loss and maybe were cause enough to investigate further.

They were not, though, any cause to proceed with excavating the crash site based on that information alone. To take at face value the eye-witness statement that it was a Spitfire was at best misguided and at worst foolish. Had some basic site investigations been carried out before a major recovery was undertaken it would have been a very simple matter indeed for a team of experienced aviation archaeologists to determine that this was in fact a German aeroplane!

The operation involved the Musée de la Coupole and a team led by M Yves Le Maner from that museum, although according to press reports in the local newspaper, *La Voix du Nord*, the whole operation was set up by Air France on behalf of KLM, acting for the Plesman family – KLM now being a subsidiary of Air France. The major excavation at the crash site on Tuesday 5 April 2006 certainly revealed a mass of buried wreckage down to a depth of some six metres, although long before that depth was reached it became clearly apparent that this was a Messerschmitt 109 and not a Spitfire at all. By coincidence, however, the wreck *did* contain the remains of its pilot who could only be identified by his identity tag marked 68454/173.

Unlike British or American identity tags, those worn by German servicemen did not record their name and were only inscribed with their service number. However, it did not take long for the German authorities to identify the pilot as Uffz Horst Seeman of 9./JG 1 who had been lost on 4 September 1943 during air combat near St Omer. (The date of the crash, interestingly, is out by almost *exactly* one year as compared to Plesman's loss.) Horst Seeman had been flying a Messerschmitt 109 G-6, Werke Nummer 20021, that had been marked with the fuselage code, yellow 2.

It was a bitter blow to the Plesman family who had been assured that this was Jan's aeroplane, although as a by-product of that failed search yet another missing airman could now be identified and laid to rest in the German military cemetery at Meurthe-et-Moselle. Jan, meanwhile, is still missing but the search for him goes on. There are, however, some other possible explanations that might yet lead to Jan and these are being actively pursued by the author, in conjunction with the present 322 Squadron of the Royal Netherlands Air Force and the Plesman family. As this book goes into production further leads are being followed and investigated. Some possibilities amongst the scenarios for Jan's disappearance are quite simple, but one has not previously been considered.

First, there are a number of *known* Spitfire crash sites not too far from the site of the excavated Messerschmitt 109. What if the eye witness who pointed out the Me 109 crash site had simply got confused in the intervening sixty-plus years? Maybe he had remembered a Spitfire being shot down by flak and losing its tail with the pilot not escaping – just that perhaps he had got muddled as to where it had crashed? That would tend to be the easy answer, although it is still the case that researchers are really grasping in the dark when it comes even to approximately identifying the crash location. If the crash site is out by the same factor as that recorded for van Eendenburg's crash, then one could almost draw a radius of fifty kilometres out from either St Omer or Lille and assume that Jan Plesman crashed somewhere within those radii. That, of course, is an awful lot of countryside. On the ground there are no real clues, and there are no contemporary French archives that help us with dates and locations of such incidents. Additionally, at the time of writing the identity of the supposed French eye witness has not been revealed and thus any chance of quizzing him about what he saw, and where, is impossible. But what of the other likely scenarios?

First, we know that MREU teams scoured this part of France as best they could. Certainly, we know that many such casualties were missed or overlooked but what if Jan *had* been found but simply not been identified and had thus been buried as an unknown. This is not an impossible scenario. First, it is certainly possible that there was simply insufficient by way of remains or personal effects to identify him and it was sometimes the case, anyway, that airmen from occupied countries flying with the RAF over Europe were very careful as regards to their identity in case it should compromise the safety of their families if they were captured. Indeed, we know that Jan's father, Albert, had been imprisoned in Holland by the Germans and thus Jan would have wanted to protect his father from any unfortunate and further repercussions. So, if Jan was flying with little or no identification on his person then this could easily explain why he was not identified. Indeed, he might have been buried as unknown in September 1944 if either the Germans or local French folk could find no means by which to name him.

This scenario cannot by any means be ruled out, and a visit to the Commonwealth War Graves Cemetery at Longuenesse (St Omer) Souvenir Cemetery where many of the casualty burials from this region are concentrated will reveal an astonishing number of World War Two graves, many of

322 Squadron, a Dutch air force squadron operating under RAF control, had a grey parrot on its squadron badge. Inevitably, the squadron acquired its own grey parrot mascot, 'Sgt Polly Grey'. Here, Jan plays with Polly Grey in the pilot's briefing room not long before he was shot down.

them being airmen. Amongst these 1939-45 burials there are a number of unknowns, many of whom again are airmen. It is surely possible that one of these could be Jan Plesman.

The importance of identifying Jan's grave for his family, and indeed for any family with a missing relative, was perhaps highlighted for the author during a visit to Longuenesse cemetery in 2007. Here, on a CWGC headstone to an unknown pilot, a newly made bronze plaque had been fitted bearing the name of Zdzisław Brózda of 308 Squadron who had been lost in Spitfire P8573 on 7 August 1941. The plaque had been professionally made

The possibility cannot be excluded that Jan Plesman is already buried, but as an unknown airman. Indeed, there are many such 'unidentified' RAF aircrew burials in the CWGC cemetery at St Omer (Longuenesse) including one that is dated 7 August 1941. In 2007 this headstone had had a privately made bronze plaque inscribed to Zdzisław Brøzda unofficially screwed to it.

and then drilled out and screwed onto the headstone, clearly without any reference to the CWGC and strictly at odds with the stringent rules for altering or defacing headstones. On the face of it, there appears to be absolutely no evidence to say that the man in this grave *was* Brózda, albeit that the headstone (relatively unusually) bore the date of this casualty's death as 7 August 1941.

However, there are other casualty candidates for this date who also died in this area, and so whoever made this addition and alteration to the headstone should have presented any evidence they might have for it to be changed to the Ministry of Defence and Commonwealth War Graves Commission*. Nonetheless, this episode points up two things; the ongoing importance to families and next of kin properly to mark and name such graves and it also supports the possibility that Jan Plesman may *already* be buried but as unknown, possibly even here at Longuenesse. If the currently 'closed' RAF casualty files were available, however, there may be some more clues if not the answers hidden away there – just as they were in the case of Derek Allen as detailed in Chapter 13. Meanwhile, the search goes on for Jan Plesman and his Spitfire, MK905 (3W-P), but it is a search that may yet reach no satisfactory conclusion.

*(*This unauthorised and unofficial name plaque has subsequently been removed by the CWGC after the matter of this irregularity was raised with them by the author.)*

CHAPTER 19
First Casualty – Last Home

WHEN THE FIRST GULF War, Operation Desert Storm, got under way on 17 January 1991 it was inevitable, of course, that losses would be suffered by the coalition forces and whilst Saddam Hussein's promise of "the mother of all battles" was perhaps an over-exaggeration, the allied commanders were nevertheless braced for significant casualties. The very first of these combat casualties was thirty-three-year-old US Navy pilot Lt Cdr Michael Scott Speicher (known as Scott) flying an F/A-18 Hornet fighter of VFA-81 'The Sunliners' operating from the USS *Saratoga*. Whilst his story has been told extensively in the world's media, on the internet and through Amy Waters Yarsinske's excellent book *No One Left Behind* it is the case that a work of this nature, and covering the subject matter that it does, would be incomplete without at least a summary of the extraordinary Speicher case.

Whilst the precise circumstances of his actual loss are uncertain, the initial cause was stated by the US Navy in 1997 to have been a surface-to-air missile hit although an unclassified summary of a 2001 CIA report suggested that Speicher was shot down by a missile fired by an Iraqi Mig-25 flown by Lt Zuhair Dawood of the 84th Sqn, IQAF. At the time of his shoot-down, Speicher was flying at 28,000ft and moving just under the speed of sound at 0.92 Mach when the front portion of his aircraft suffered a catastrophic event which caused the stricken Hornet and its unfortunate pilot to plunge earthwards.

Out of control, the aircraft crashed into a remote uninhabited wasteland some 100 miles west of Baghdad at Tulul ad Dulaym. Initially, there was absolutely no indication as to whether Speicher was dead or alive but the following day the US Navy gave his status as missing in action. This, of course, is standard procedure when an airman has failed to return from operations and his exact status remains uncertain. However, such a description is certainly how Scott Speicher's status might be accurately described for the next eighteen years.

Lt Cdr Michael Scott Speicher became the first coalition casualty of the war but whose fate remained uncertain for eighteen years.

On 22 May 1991, after the end of the Gulf War, Speicher's status was changed to killed in action/body not recovered (KIA/BNR) and in the July of 1992 Scott's widow, Joanne, married a friend of her late husband who was also a fellow aviator, Commander 'Buddy' Harris of the US Navy. With two young children of four and two years old, Joanne had accepted that Scott was not coming home and ultimately made the decision to move on with her life albeit that her husband's body had not yet been found. Clearly, the official US

Scott Speicher was flying a F/A-18 Hornet much like this one (also from VFA-81 'The Sunliners') when he was brought down over Iraq. Much has changed in aerial warfare since the loss of Major 'Mick' Mannock over seventy years before. What hadn't changed was the importance to family and friends of bring home the missing casualties of war.

Navy status of KIA/BNR gave her the confirmation that Scott was dead and she was now a widow although her new husband, Harris, became an outspoken advocate for a proper search for Scott to be undertaken. How that search developed, and all of the twists and turns along that route, resulted in the most excruciating emotional roller coaster for Joanne and 'Buddy'.

By the December of 1993 a military official from Qatar had discovered the wreckage of an aircraft in the desert and this was subsequently identified as Speichers, although with its canopy found some distance away the first suggestions that Scott might have ejected began to emerge. Of course, this begged an important question; if he had ejected and perhaps survived then what had happened to him? Four months later, in April 1994, a US spy satellite photographed what were apparently man-made symbols on the desert floor near the wreck site prompting suggestions that these were his escape and evade 'come and get me' signals. All of these pointers caused suggestions to grow that he had survived the crash, but of course neither his body nor Scott as a live captive had been offered up by the Iraqi regime. Nevertheless, his status remained officially KIA/BNR but now with a background of ever-growing doubt.

Finally, in December 1995 the crash site was accessed through the International Red Cross and investigators from CILHI conducted an excavation and although they found no trace of Speicher either in or anywhere near the wreckage, it was concluded that he had most likely ejected and was not in the plane when it had hit the desert floor. Obviously, life would have certainly been extinct had Scott not ejected from the aircraft but even an ejection did not absolutely guarantee safety. After all, he could have ejected too low, suffered a parachute malfunction, died from injuries or dehydration in the desert or, worse, died at the hands of his Iraqi captors.

On the other hand, he could have been taken alive and might still be being held in captivity by the Iraqi government. However, and despite the apparent evidence that Speicher had exited the Hornet, the Secretary of the US Navy reaffirmed the presumptive finding of death in September 1996 and Scott was given a commemorative 'tomb' at Arlington National Cemetery. To an extent, and despite the questions that had been raised, a further line had been drawn under the case with another official confirmation of his death. And yet there was still no body. And there was evidence that he had ejected.

In January 2001 things changed once again when the Secretary of the US Navy altered Scott's status to missing in action, with a CIA report also being published that same year suggesting that Scott Speicher may have ejected and survived. So, from MIA at the time of his shoot-down, to KIA/BNR later, Speicher's status had again reverted back to simply missing. With the presumption of death now removed it must have placed the re-married Joanne in an emotional turmoil. All of the signals now coming out of the Department of Defense were that Scott could well be alive after all. It was very much like the aftermath of the Vietnam war where the missing were often believed to be prisoner and where the National Alliance of Families clamoured, pressed, lobbied and campaigned for a full accounting of those who were missing in action or, potentially, prisoners of war.

Speculation continued to be rife that Scott was still alive and being held captive in Iraq with theories abounding as to where he was and why he was being kept. Of course, if he was alive then he might ultimately become some kind of bargaining chip for the Iraqi regime who were certainly not beyond such behaviour and headed, at this time, towards further confrontation with the international community. But if he was alive then Joanne and Buddy were in a desperately difficult situation. Whilst the American nation wanted to know, Mr and Mrs Harris *needed* to know. The possibility that he was still alive was surely a bittersweet one for both of them.

On 11 October 2002, one day after the United Nations had sanctioned the use of force against Iraq, Scott's status was this time changed again. This time to missing/captured. This was a significant change, with the Secretary of the US Navy stating:

> "While the information available to me now does not prove definitively that Capt Speicher is alive and in Iraqi custody, I am personally convinced the Iraqis seized him sometime after his plane went down. Further, it is my firm belief that the government of Iraq knows what happened to Capt Speicher."

So, as the pressure mounted militarily on Iraq the likelihood of his survival, capture and the possibility he was still alive were very much back on the agenda.

With the invasion and occupation of Iraq from March 2003, it was now possible for the US military to begin conducting on-the-ground searches and investigations for Speicher which had now become an exceptionally high profile case. Indeed, his possible plight had even been mentioned by President Bush in a speech to the United Nations. Finding what had become of him was now politically important and efforts to take things forward were ratcheted up. However, clues were thin on the ground and there were no leads that offered any positive information although there was a surprising find in Baghdad's Hakmiyah prison where the initials MSS were located scratched on a cell wall. The possible connection to

Compare these photographs with that on page 16 depicting the searches for World War One field graves. All that has changed are that scientific and technological advances allow easier identification of remains. However, the hard physical labour and the search by eye for clues, as well as the detective-like assembly of evidence, have never significantly altered in all those years. Neither has the raison d'être for carrying out such extensive and detailed searches for the missing.

Michael Scott Speicher was obvious, but once again the clues dried up and human hair found in the cell's drain were DNA tested but found not to be Scott's. If he had been taken alive then all efforts to find him, to find witnesses of his capture or imprisonment or even to locate any paper trail, came to naught.

Six years later, on 5 January 2009, the US Navy Board met to consider closing the Speicher case since no new information or evidence had come to light in the intervening period. In the event, however, it was announced on 10 March 2009 that his status had reverted once more to missing in action. And so, for the Speicher family, the awful roller-coaster of emotion just continued on. And then, on 2 August 2009, came news that a search party had finally found evidence confirming his death with the US Navy issuing the following statement:

"The Armed Forces Institute of Pathology (AFIP) has positively identified remains recovered in Iraq as those of Captain Michael Scott Speicher. Captain Speicher was shot down flying a combat mission in an F/A-18 Hornet over west-central Iraq on January 17th, 1991 during Operation Desert Storm.

" 'Our thoughts and prayers are with Captain Speicher's family for the ultimate sacrifice he made for his country,' said Ray Mabus, Secretary of the Navy. 'I am also extremely grateful to all those who have worked so tirelessly over the last eighteen years to bring Captain Speicher home.'

" 'Our Navy will never give up looking for a shipmate, regardless of how long or how difficult that search may be,' said Admiral Gary Roughead, Chief of Naval Operations. 'We owe a tremendous debt of gratitude to Captain Speicher and his family for the sacrifice they have made for our nation and the example of strength they have set for all of us.'

"Acting on information provided by an Iraqi citizen in early July, US Marines stationed in Al Anbar Province went to a location in the desert which was believed to be the crash site of Captain Speicher's jet. The Iraqi citizen stated he knew of two Iraqi citizens who recalled an American jet impacting the desert and the remains of the pilot being buried in the desert. One of these Iraqi citizens stated that they were present when Captain Speicher was found dead at the crash site by Bedouins and his remains buried. The Iraqi citizens led US Marines to the site who searched the area. Remains were recovered over several days during the past week and flown to Dover Air Force Base for scientific identification by the AFIP's Office of the Armed Forces Medical Examiner.

"The recovered remains include bones and multiple skeletal fragments. Positive identification was made by comparing Captain Speicher's dental records with the jawbone recovered at the site. The teeth are a match, both visually and radiographically."

Within twenty-four hours DNA tests had confirmed the initial findings. Captain Speicher was no longer missing and on 13 August 2009 the first casualty of the first Gulf War, and the last man home, was laid to rest at Jacksonville Memory Garden after a funeral service at All Saints Chapel on the Jacksonville Naval Air Station, Florida.

In *Finding The Few* I told how the discovery of South African pilot George James Drake during the 1970s had enabled his family finally to deal with outstanding legal issues relating to his estate, as well as being able properly to mourn a long-lost brother. In *Finding The Foe* we saw how detailed research by the author had enabled a German family to find closure, and comfort, in the knowledge that their relative, Gefr Franz Becker, had died in the crash of his Junkers 88 over Britain. Even though his body could not be recovered, their sadness was assuaged in the certain knowledge that he had not died a slow agonising death in the English Channel as they had feared for so many years. In *Finding The Fallen* we can see that solving the losses of the distant past are often just as important to families left behind as it is for the families in more recent cases like Scott 'Spike' Speicher. Finding the fallen remains as important today as it was when battlefield searches first set out to find men like Major Mannock in the immediate aftermath of the First World War. With so many still unaccounted for, from every nation and from every war, the search goes on.

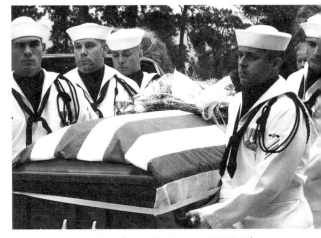

Homecoming. Dateline: 13 August 2009. The first Gulf War casualty becomes the last home as Scott Speicher is laid to rest with full military honours at Jacksonville Memory Garden, Florida, on 13 August 2009. Finally returned to the bosom of his family, his long-uncertain fate had become something of a cause célèbre in the USA.

Apart from his grave site, other memorials to Speicher (left) have been established elsewhere in the US including this memorial plaque (below) in a tree-lined avenue commemorating those who were lost during the Gulf War.

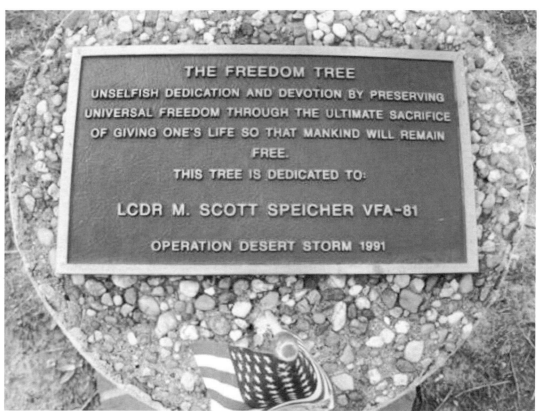

THE FREEDOM TREE
UNSELFISH DEDICATION AND DEVOTION BY PRESERVING UNIVERSAL FREEDOM THROUGH THE ULTIMATE SACRIFICE OF GIVING ONE'S LIFE SO THAT MANKIND WILL REMAIN FREE.
THIS TREE IS DEDICATED TO:

LCDR M. SCOTT SPEICHER VFA-81

OPERATION DESERT STORM 1991

The Ongoing Task

CHAPTER 20

I NDEED, THE SEARCH DOES go on!
Even as this book was in its final stages of preparation we learnt from the American newspaper *Stars and Stripes* on 1 July 2011 of an ongoing operation at St Vith, Belgium, to find and identify a missing P-47 Thunderbolt pilot of the USAAF. The author would like to thank *Stars and Stripes* and the journalist Kevin Dougherty for permission to use the article on this current search:

"Of all the digs archaeologist Dawn Johnson has surveyed over the years, a small site on a wooded hillside in south-eastern Belgium ranks as the most meaningful.

"For this, she believes, is the last patch of earth her long-lost, outdoor-loving uncle glimpsed before his P-47 fighter crashed while attacking a German convoy on Christmas Day 1944. Army investigators toured the area after the war, but found neither the remains of 2nd Lt Hilding Roy Johnson nor the wreckage, Dawn Johnson said.

"Now, more than six decades after his plane was shot down, a team of Americans from the Joint Prisoners of War, Missing in Action Accounting Command is at the site searching for 'Uncle Roy', as she refers to him.

2nd Lt Hilding Roy Johnson, photographed in front of his P-47 Thunderbolt.

" 'At least he's going to come home,' Dawn Johnson said as she stood a few feet from the impact crater.

"Based in Hawaii, JPAC devotes most of its time to repatriating the remains of Americans lost in South East Asia. However, the joint command does dispatch recovery teams to Europe at least once a year.

"Teams typically work multiple sites. 'The ten-member ensemble operating in

Belgium will head to a couple of sites in Germany later this month to help two other JPAC teams,' said Kelley Esh, who, as a forensic anthropologist, is the scientific leader for the Belgian excavation.

"There are approximately 74,000 Americans listed as missing from World War II, according to JPAC's 2010 annual report. About 35,000 service members are categorized as 'recoverable'. The rest of the missing are mainly individuals lost at sea, or who died in a direct artillery hit.

" 'There's a lot of work for JPAC out there, without a doubt,' said Army Maj Ramon Osorio, a spokesman for the organization.

"Second Lt Hilding Roy Johnson of Sacramento, Calif., was declared missing in action following the Battle of the Bulge, Germany's last major offensive of the war. In October 1945 he was listed as killed in action. JPAC officials got an unexpected break in the case when Dawn Johnson told them in 2008 that her uncle's crash site may have been located near the town of St.Vith by the Belgian-German border.

"Two years before, Manfred Klein, a local archaeologist who has handled similar cases, came across the shards of a plane on a hillside.

"Klein visited the site again and discovered more debris just as loggers began clearing part of the hillside. Among the items he found was a scrap of metal bearing the serial number of one of the aircraft's .50-caliber machine guns. That number helped lead him to Johnson. Klein eventually tracked down the pilot's niece. At the time, she was helping to unearth the remains of a Paleolithic mastodon near Monterey, Calif.

"She contacted Quentin Aanenson, a P-47 pilot featured in Ken Burns's documentary The War. As fate would have it, Aanenson 'loaned' his plane, nicknamed the 'Rebel Jack', to her uncle on Christmas Day 1944.

"In 2008, Dawn Johnson travelled to St. Vith. Using Klein's information and her archaeology skills, she located the impact crater and started shoveling. To her astonishment she found bone fragments, including a large bone, possibly a tibia.

"Standing on the hillside, holding a bone she thought might belong to her uncle, Dawn Johnson said, a flood of memories washed over her.

"She remembered the photo of Uncle Roy in his uniform on top of her grandmother's Steinway piano, with fresh cut flowers and a bowl of M&Ms beside it. It was as if grandma wanted sweets to be ready should Roy stroll into the house one day.

"The oldest of five children, Roy Johnson's life, death and absence had been part of family lore for decades.

" 'I just felt my grandparents' presence,' Dawn Johnson said. The moment of discovery 'was so bittersweet. He was still a member of the family.'

"As a rule, family members typically don't visit JPAC excavation sites. However, an exception was made, and Dawn Johnson was permitted to link up with Esh's team when it arrived in Belgium last month, but despite her background, only as an observer.

"All Esh is allowed to say until the investigation is complete is that her team 'has found possible osseous remains', meaning bone material.

" 'Multiple lines of evidence are what we really try to focus on,' Esh said.

"Between the bones, the old crash report and the machine-gun serial number, Dawn Johnson feels JPAC probably has enough evidence to say this is her uncle's crash site.

"Also discovered was part of a grip to a possible Colt 45, the type of gun Johnson was known to have owned. But it will be months, if not a year or more, Esh said, before JPAC can close the case.

" 'It all fits,' Esh said as a light rain fell.

"When the rain intensified, a couple of her colleagues briefly found shelter under some trees, surveying the surroundings where the biggest and bloodiest battle of the war for US forces was fought. Directly below them was the road the German convoy was using when Johnson and his fellow fliers in the 391st Fighter Squadron dove down on them.

" 'Kind of hard to imagine with all these trees,' Marine Sgt. Brandon Rodriguez said of the battle that claimed more than 19,000 American lives. 'It's pretty crazy.'

"Army Sgt Michael Carroll said getting to know Dawn Johnson, and thus 2nd Lt. Hilding Roy Johnson, personalizes this dig in ways others before it have not.

" 'I'm here to bring her uncle home,' Carroll said.

"Carroll, 26, is from Mahtomedi, Minn., while Rodriguez, 25, calls West Covina, Calif., home. Each has been deployed to war zones multiple times. Both called it an honor to help bring closure to families, no matter how many years have passed.

" 'I would want my fellow soldiers to keep looking for me,' Carroll said.

" 'It's part of our warrior ethos to never leave a fallen comrade behind,' Carroll added. Johnson 'has been missing for 66 years and we're still looking for him.' "

2nd Lt Hilding Roy Johnson was flying a P-47 of 366th Fighter Group, 391st Fighter Squadron, when he was shot down at Wallerode-Setz, St Vith. The aircraft number was 42-29324 and was named 'Rebel Jack'. As with all such USAAF losses the relevant missing aircrew report provides us with much useful information relating to Johnson's loss and it is reproduced overleaf. Unfortunately however, and as we have read earlier, corresponding RAF casualty reports remain closed to public access at the time of writing this book.

As work was drawing to a close at the as yet unconfirmed crash site of Johnson's 'Rebel Jack' in Belgium, further news came in from the other side of the world that a skull and possible parts of a Japanese aircraft had been dredged up from the bottom of Pearl Harbor, reminders of the losses to Japanese air crews during the attack of 7 December 1941. On the same day, too, came news from Italy of the discovery of the wreckage of a Boston V, BZ590, of 18 Squadron lost on 21 April 1945 with its four crew; Sgt D K Raikes, Flt Sgt D M Perkins, Flt Sgt A T Bostock and Wt Off J P Hunt. Perhaps by the time this book is published all of these men will have been officially accounted for.

THREE HUNDRED NINETY FIRST FIGHTER SQUADRON
Office of the Intelligence Officer
APO 595   US Army

26 December 1944.

Statement of 1st Lt., Harry H. Bristol concerning Missing
In Action report involving 2nd Lt., Hilding R. Johnson in
aircraft AC number 42-29324.

I was leading Blue flight on the morning of 25 December
1944. Lt., Johnson was flying my number four position.
We made a dive bombing run on some enemy motor transports
and then made a strafing pass. My wingman had a hung bomb
so I told him to come in last. However, he was slow in re-
joining formation and I had already started my strafing pass.
After I pulled off the target I looked back and saw my number
four man crash about fifty yards from the target and burst
into flames. I saw no parachute. It is my belief that Lt.,
Johnson was hit by flak and went in with his ship.

HARRY H. BRISTOL,
1st Lt., Air Corps.

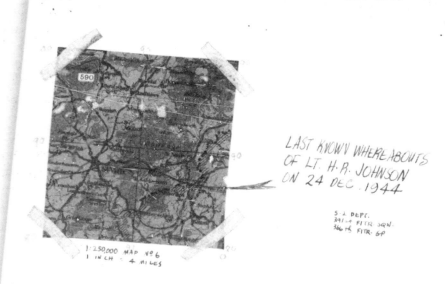

LAST KNOWN WHEREABOUTS
OF LT. H.R. JOHNSON
ON 24 DEC. 1944

S.2 DEPT.
391ST FTR SQN.
366TH FTR. GP.

1:250,000 MAP No 6
1 INCH - 4 MILES

590

The MOD Joint Casualty & Compassionate Centre

URING THE POST-WAR history of discoveries of RAF and Commonwealth servicemen on a worldwide basis there has been the integral involvement of the UK Ministry of Defence. Indeed, their involvement is dealt with or mentioned in many of the cases detailed in this book and as long ago as the 1970s this has been through various departments and branches of the RAF; The Air Force Board Secretariat, Departments S4c and S10r & s, and Department AR9. From 1994, the task was undertaken by the Command Secretariat (CS [Sec] 2a1), at HQ Personnel & Training Command, RAF Innsworth, Gloucestershire, but following an RAF internal reorganisation in 1998, licensing responsibility was transferred to the RAF Personnel Management Agency Casualty Section (PMA Casualty) also based at Innsworth. Subsequently, following the amalgamation of the three service casualty branches in April 2005 into a single organisation, the responsibility was taken on by the Historic Casework team within the new MoD Joint Casualty and Compassionate Centre (JCCC), part of what was then called the Armed Forces Personnel Administration Agency (AFPAA). This agency is now known as the Service Personnel and Veterans Agency (SPVA) and the historic casework team is referred to as Commemorations and Licensing to clarify the work they undertake from their office on the former RAF Innsworth site, now known as Imjin Barracks and home to the NATO Allied Rapid Reaction Corps as well as the JCCC.

Amongst its various roles, the JCCC is responsible for casualty reporting and the notification of relatives for current casualties in the British armed forces, repatriation of the bodies of recently deceased service personnel from overseas, arranging compassionate travel back to the UK for servicemen overseas in the event of a family crisis or illness at home, the marking of service-funded graves, arranging payments from the MoD to the deceased's estate, and arranging commemorative funeral services and answering enquiries on historic casualties. The JCCC also provides the MoD emergency response centre / public enquiry bureau in the event of a mass casualty incident involving service personnel, such as the loss of the RAF Nimrod n September 2006.

To perform the commemorative role, the JCCC has a small team that answers correspondence relating to individual military fatalities outside the recent past and co-ordinates investigations following the discovery of human remains of personnel killed in the First and Second World Wars. This fascinating and important work involves attempts to identify the casualty and trace his/her next of kin or descendants and the subsequent arrangements for an appropriate military funeral in the country concerned if that is the wish of the family.

The JCCC commemorations team works closely with staff at the CWGC and single services, advising the CWGC on the validity of claims from members of the public or specialist researchers suggesting identities for bodies buried as unknown soldiers, sailors or airmen as has already been illustrated in this book with the cases of Major Mannock and Fg Off Allen. However, identities will only be confirmed and the headstone on the grave changed where the identity can be "proved beyond all reasonable doubt" after careful consideration by the relevant service arm's historical branch.

The commemorations team is also responsible for the issuing of licenses (on behalf of the secretary of state) under the Protection of Military Remains Act 1986 to groups or individuals wishing to carry out archaeological investigations at aircraft (British, American or German) crash sites in the UK.

No Trace Ever Found

Plt Off Francis John Blackwood OBE was the pilot of a 140 Squadron photo-reconnaissance Spitfire, X4502, missing from an operational flight to Essen and Cologne. It was assumed that he was lost somewhere in the target area, although no trace of him has ever been found. He is photographed here with Blenheim L1417.

Left: Flt Sgt James Gerard Shandley of Coventry was an air gunner with 23 Squadron when he was lost on 27 February 1942. The aircraft in which he was flying, Boston BB900, crashed into the sea just north-east of Margate lifeboat station at 3.40 pm with Plt Off Offord at the controls. The other members of the crew, except Shandley, were rescued from the sea but no trace was ever found of the twenty-one-year-old air gunner.

Below: One of the RAF's most notable fighter pilot aces of World War Two was Flt Lt Eric Stanley Lock DSO DFC & Bar who was credited with twenty-six enemy aircraft 'confirmed destroyed' and a further eight 'probably destroyed'. On 3 August 1941 whilst flying Spitfire W3257 of 611 Squadron, he was observed strafing German troops near the coast at Calais. He was not seen or heard from again.

In relation to their involvement with the licensing of aviation archaeology and the identification and burial of historic casualties, however, the JCCC do not have a remit, nor the funding or resources, to pro-actively seek out missing casualties although they play a central role in dealing with the aftermath of all such recoveries and discoveries. In some instances, however, they have become involved in co-ordinating officially sanctioned efforts to recover wartime casualties but as regards to their position relating to the discovery of such casualties, the JCCC set out their official position thus:

"In the immediate aftermath of the major conflicts of the 20th Century, significant efforts were made by the government of the day to recover and identify the bodies of UK service personnel. It is no longer feasible or possible to methodically excavate all known crash sites/ battlefields using official resources. The MOD discourages the disturbance of crash sites and battlefields other than where necessary in respect of host government approved action, such as land reclamation, building work or health and safety grounds.

"Where human remains are found overseas, the MOD works closely with the Governments concerned and the Commonwealth War Graves Commission to identify the individuals involved and where positive identifications can be made, notify any surviving relatives of the discovery and ensure the casualty is given a burial in accordance with MOD policy at the time the casualty died. Funding is also provided for the next of kin and a companion to attend the burial."

Whilst it would certainly be accurate to state that the MOD discourages the disturbance and recovery of historic casualties, it is also the case that when called upon the staff of the JCCC work tirelessly, efficiently and sensitively in dealing with all issues surrounding such discoveries. Dedication to the task in hand is undoubtedly second to none, and gratitude for the work of the JCCC staff by those families affected is always assured. The final outcome of many cases detailed within this book would quite probably have been very different were it not for the input of JCCC staff.

Mannned twenty-four hours a day, seven days a week, the address and contact details for those having an interest in aviation archaeology or needing to get in touch on historic case matters are as follows:

Service Personnel and Veterans Agency
Joint Casualty & Compassionate Centre
Post Death Administration – Commemorations & Licensing
Innsworth House, Imjin Barracks
Gloucester GL3 1HW
Telephone 01452 712612 Ext 6303/7330

APPENDIX II

Joint POW/MIA Accounting Command

THROUGHOUT THIS BOOK WE have seen examples of the work of CILHI teams and that of the subsequently established JPAC organisation. This book would thus be incomplete without studying the JPAC organisation. For that purpose this appendix examines JPAC's work through the medium of publicity material issued directly by that command and it is used here in accord with the US government's policy for the free use of this material.

The Joint POW/MIA Accounting Command, located on the island of Oahu in Hawaii, was activated on 1 October 2003. Created from the merger of the thirty-year-old US Army Central Identification Laboratory, Hawaii, and the eleven-year-old Joint Task Force – Full Accounting, JPAC is commanded by a flag officer.

The mission of JPAC is to achieve the fullest possible accounting of all Americans missing as a result of the nation's past conflicts. The highest priority of the organisation is the return of any living Americans that remain prisoners of war.*

The command is made up of approximately 400 hand-picked soldiers, sailors, airmen, marines, department of the navy civilians and contractors. The laboratory portion of JPAC, referred to as the Central Identification Laboratory (CIL), is one of the largest and most scientifically diverse laboratories in the world, and is the only accredited Skeletal Identification Laboratory (ASCLD-LAB) in the United States.

The American government takes very seriously its declared intent to search tirelessly and ceaselessly for a full accounting of all its missing servicemen from every conflict and every continent. This poster advertising a recent POW/MIA day serves to illustrate the continuing importance of these issues to the American people.

*To date, the US Government has not found any evidence that there are still American POWs in captivity from past US conflicts.

Three permanent overseas detachments assist with command and control and in-country support during investigation and recovery operations: Detachment One located in Bangkok, Thailand; Detachment Two in Hanoi, Vietnam; and Detachment Three in Vientiane, Laos. A fourth detachment, Detachment Four, is located in Hawaii and is responsible for recovery team personnel when they are not deployed.

To date, the US Government has not found any evidence that there are still American POWs in captivity from past US conflicts.

About JPAC

The core of JPAC's day-to-day operations involves investigating leads, recovering, and identifying Americans who were killed in action but were never brought home. This process involves close coordination with other US agencies involved in the POW/MIA issue, including the Defense POW/Missing Personnel Office, US Pacific Command, Department of State, the Joint Staff, Defense Intelligence Agency, the Armed Forces DNA Identification Laboratory, and the US Air Force's Life Sciences Equipment Laboratory.

In order to ensure mission success and the return of all unaccounted-for Americans, JPAC routinely engages in technical negotiations and talks with representatives of foreign governments to promote and maintain positive in-country conditions wherever JPAC teams deploy.

On average, the CIL identifies an MIA about every four days. Since 2003, JPAC has identified more than 560 Americans, and more than 1,800 since the accounting effort began in the 1970s.

The search for unaccounted-for Americans starts with in-depth research. Historians and analysts gather information such as correspondence, medical and personnel records, maps, photographs, and unit histories from many sources. At any given time, there are approximately 700 active case files under investigation.

In most cases, the search for a missing person will involve outside researchers, the national archives, and record depositories maintained by the US and foreign governments. Veterans, outside historians, private citizens, families of missing Americans, and amateur researchers also routinely provide information about cases. All of this information is put together in what is called a 'loss incident case file' for each unaccounted-for person.

In addition to conducting research to support ongoing field activities, the research and intelligence section also provides historical analysis to help with the identification of remains.

Once research is completed to pinpoint the likely location of an unaccounted-for individual, an investigative team (commonly referred to as an 'IT') will be assigned to visit the site. Field ITs deploy to locations around the world for about thirty-five days at a time. Four to nine JPAC personnel with specialized skills make up an IT: a team leader, assistant team leader, analyst, linguist, communications specialists, and medic. Sometimes an anthropologist, explosive ordnance technician, or life-support investigator (for identifying aviation life support equipment) will augment the team if the need arises.

During a typical mission, teams interview potential witnesses, conduct on-site reconnaissance and survey terrain for safety and logistical concerns. In many cases, investigative teams turn up new information that may help with eventual identifications. Teams operating in countries with active media outlets or a strong community network often gain new, valuable information about additional sites simply by talking with people who reside in the area. The main goal of an investigation mission is to obtain enough information to correlate or connect a particular site with an unaccounted-for individual. If enough evidence is found, a site will be recommended for recovery.

Eighteen authorized recovery teams travel throughout the world to recover missing Americans from World War II, the Korean War, the Vietnam War, and the Cold War. Recovery missions can last from thirty to sixty days, depending on the location, terrain and nature of the recovery.

Reaching a site can be a challenge in itself. Team members routinely walk through jungles, traverse difficult terrain in 4x4 vehicles, rappel cliff sides, wade through swamps, and climb mountains. Transportation methods may include horseback, all terrain vehicles, boat, train or helicopter.

Adding to the difficulty, teams travel with up to 10,000 pounds of survival and excavation equipment. To date, teams have travelled to locations as diverse as rice paddies in South East Asia, cliff sides in Papua New Guinea and Indonesia, 16,000ft mountain tops in the Himalayas, and underwater sites off the coasts of Tunisia and England. At any given time, JPAC has a queue of more than 200 sites that have already been investigated and validated, and are *ready for recovery*.

In order to facilitate ready support to teams, JPAC maintains storage facilities in Hawaii, Thailand, Vietnam, Laos, Europe, and Papua New Guinea. This is an almost incredible commitment and requires great organisation. Moreover, having these facilities strategically placed around the world saves the cost of shipping, and more importantly, provides ready access to supplies for teams in remote locations. The equipment necessary to support a recovery mission ranges from generators, wet or dry-screening stations, tents, and medical supplies, to batteries, bottled water, and eating utensils.

The Joint POW/MIA Accounting
JPAC History

- *1973*: Central Identification Laboratory, Thailand (CIL-THAI) established; focused on the Americans still missing in South East Asia
- *1976*: Central Identification Laboratory, Hawaii (CIL-HI) established to search for, recover, and identify missing Americans from all previous conflicts
- *1992*: Joint Task Force – Full Accounting (JTF-FA) established to focus on achieving the fullest possible accounting of Americans missing as a result of the Vietnam War
- *2002*: Department of Defense (DoD) determined that POW/MIA accounting efforts would be best served by combining JTF-FA and CIL-HI
- *Oct. 1, 2003*: The two separate organisations joined together to form the Joint POW/MIA Accounting Command

Repatriation

In honour of the sacrifice made by those individuals whose remains were found during a recovery mission, JPAC holds an arrival ceremony with a joint service honour guard and senior officers from each service. Veterans, community members and local active-duty military attend the ceremonies to pay their respects as the remains are transported from a US military plane to JPAC's Central Identification Laboratory, where the identification process begins.

Site Selection

Factors such as weather, terrain, site accessibility, and various logistical concerns help determine how and when JPAC teams deploy to recover a site.

If a site is in jeopardy (due to urbanization, environmental concerns, political issues, etc.) a recovery may be launched quickly so the site is not lost.

Past and Future Missions

In Fiscal Year 2010, JPAC recovery and investigation teams searched in eighteen foreign countries while on seventy-five recovery and investigation missions. Sixty-seven individuals from World War I, World War II, the Korean War, and the Vietnam War were identified and returned home to their loved ones.

During Fiscal Year 2011 (October 1, 2010 through Sepember 30, 2011), JPAC will deploy about seventy-five investigation and recovery teams on thirty-three missions to fourteen countries worldwide. Of those, forty-three teams are deploying to support Vietnam War operations, twelve are supporting Korean War operations, and twenty-one are supporting World War II operations. In South Korea, four joint forensic reviews (sets of remains are evaluated to determine their racial affiliation) will be performed in-country, while the first two excavations in Vietnam will be done unilaterally with US and Vietnamese recovery personnel.

At the beginning of a recovery, the anthropologist sections the site into 4x4 metre grids with stakes and string and each section is excavated one at a time. This allows the team to track precisely what evidence is found and where it is recovered. To help with what can be a massive soil removal effort, JPAC may hire anywhere from a few to more than 100 local workers. Every ounce of soil dug from the site is sifted by hand through quarter-inch wire screens. The screens allow team members to catch even the smallest pieces of remains, artefacts or personal effects. Recovery sites range in size from a few square metres, such as individual burials, to areas larger than football fields for aircraft crashes. When dictated by the environment or soil conditions, wet-screening techniques, where all soil/mud is washed through wire mesh with high-pressure hoses, are used.

Once the recovery effort is completed, the team returns to Hawaii. All remains and artefacts found during the recovery operation are then transported from a US military plane to JPAC's Central Identification Laboratory.

Upon arrival at the laboratory, such materiel recovered from a site is signed over to the custody of the CIL and stored in a secure area. Only a small percentage of JPAC personnel have access to the remains to maintain the highest level of security.

Depending on the amount and condition of recovered remains, the CIL's staff of forensic anthropologists first produce a biological profile from recovered skeletal remains that includes sex, race, age at death, and height of the individual. Anthropologists may also analye trauma caused at or near the time of death and pathological conditions of bone such as arthritis or previous breaks.

Nothing could illustrate in a more graphic manner the US commitment to the finding and recovering of its war dead. Here, an official investigation team including forensic archaeologists, odontologists, anthropologists, ordnance experts and other specialists have excavated a deep pit, down to sterile soil, whilst digging out the wreckage of a USAF aircraft lost in jungle terrain during the Vietnam War to locate and recover its missing crew.

Lab scientists use a variety of techniques to establish the identification of missing Americans, including analysis of skeletal and dental remains, sampling mitochondrial DNA (mtDNA), and analyzing material evidence, personal effects and life-support equipment. The JPAC's scientific director evaluates these overlapping lines of evidence in an effort to identify the remains.

This anthropological procedure is carried out *in the blind*. The forensic anthropologist assigned the case in the laboratory is not the individual who completed the recovery in the field.

This anthropologist does not know the suspected identity or details of the loss incident. This prevents any bias from influencing the scientist's analysis.

Teeth are often the best way to identify remains because they are durable, unique to each person, and may contain surviving mtDNA. Ideally, JPAC's forensic odontologists (dentists) will have antemortem (before death) X-rays to use for comparison, but even handwritten charts and treatment notes can be critical to the identification process.

Scientists from JPAC use mtDNA in about three-quarters of their cases. All mtDNA samples taken at the CIL are analyzed at the Armed Forces DNA Identification Laboratory (AFDIL), in Rockville, Md. These genetic patterns are compared with genetic patterns from family reference samples provided by each unidentified individual's family. Unlike nuclear DNA, which is unique to that person, mtDNA is passed directly from a person's mother. Generally, all persons of the same maternal line have the same mtDNA sequences. Since these sequences are rare but not unique within the general population, they cannot stand alone as evidence for identification.

All items relating to an unresolved case, excluding skeletal or dental remains, are considered material evidence. Examples include aircraft data plates, ordnance, and pieces of issued items such as weapons, packs, mess kits, and uniforms. These artefacts are examined in the field. Items considered relevant to the identification are selected by the anthropologist or life-support technician and brought back to the laboratory for analysis. This material evidence often aids in identifications.

Personal effects are a special category of material evidence. Every effort is made to recover all personal items (rings, photos, watches, combs, etc.) from the excavation sites since these items aid in identification, but are also invaluable mementos for surviving family members. Once the identification process is complete, these items are returned to families and loved ones.

Life-support equipment includes any piece of gear associated with a pilot that would indicate his presence within a crashed aircraft. Items such as parachute parts or helmet pieces can be critical in determining if a pilot was in the aircraft at the time of impact and if the crash was survivable. Furthermore, multiple life support items may indicate the number of individuals associated with a crash site. JPAC utilize the US Air Force's Life Sciences Equipment Laboratory at Brooks City-Base, Texas, to help analyze items recovered in the field.

While JPAC's CIL identifies about seven Americans a month on average, the recovery and identification process may take years to complete. In addition to the factors previously mentioned, each separate line of evidence must be examined at the CIL (bones, teeth, and material evidence) and correlated with all historical evidence. All reports must also undergo a thorough peer review process that includes an external review by independent experts. Additionally, if mtDNA is part of the process, the search for family reference samples for mtDNA comparison can add a significant amount of time to the identification process.

Once identification has been completed, cases are forwarded to the appropriate service mortuary affairs office, whose members personally notify next-of-kin family members.

Forensic Science Academy

In 2008, the Central Identification Laboratory opened the Forensic Science Academy, an advanced and highly competitive forensic anthropology programme consisting of five courses. Students (Fellows) are accepted into the programme each autumn, and receive a one-time $12,000 stipend and up to fifteen semester hours of credit through their university.

In the lab, Fellows receive training in anthropology, archaeology, and odontology, and train in a variety of techniques and identification methods in a unique and technologically advanced laboratory. Fellows also receive specialized training in establishing a biological profile, cause and manner of death, remote sensing, soils, and more.

In the field, Fellows receive unique training during a thirty-five-day mission to the Lao People's Democratic Republic, assisting in an archaeological excavation. Fellows will also study at Khon Kaen University, Kingdom of Thailand, honing their skills in human variation, bone disease, and innovative identification methods. Students will also be provided training in land and underwater archaeological equipment and methods.

Details of the Command are as follows:
Joint POW/MIA Accounting Command Attn: Public Affairs Office
310 Worchester Ave., Bldg 45
JBPHH, HI 96853-5530
Phone: (808) 448-1934
Fax: (808) 448-1998
pao_mail@jpac.pacom.mil
www.jpac.pacom.mil

To put into context the scale of American commitment to the finding of its missing war dead, the following casualties have been notified as those just recently identified following recovery or identification operations. The list is only for those US personnel thus far identified during the production phase of this book in 2011:

- **Col. Leo S. Boston**, US Air Force, 14th Air Commando Wing, 602nd Fighter Squadron, was lost on April 29, 1966, while aboard an A-1E aircraft on a search and rescue mission over North Vietnam. His remains were identified on April 4, 2011.
- **Spc. 4 Robert B. Bayne**, US Army, B Company, 141st Infantry Regiment, 36th Infantry Division, was lost on March 28, 1945, while on a reconnaissance patrol near Schwegenheim, Germany. His remains were identified on March 14, 2011.
- **Sgt. Ralph W. Carlson**, US Army, 25th Reconnaissance Company, 25th Infantry Division, died on April 30, 1951, while captive at Suan Prisoner of War camp, North Korea. His remains were identified on Feb. 18, 2011.
- **Lt. Cmdr. William Patrick Egan**, US Navy, Attack Squadron 215 aboard the USS *Hancock*, was lost on April 29, 1966, while on a strike mission in an A-1H Skyraider aircraft over Laos. His remains were identified on Feb. 11, 2011.
- **Capt. Arnold E. Holm**, Jr., and **Spc. 4 Robin R. Yeakley**, US Army, 8th Cavalry, 11th Aviation Group, 1st Aviation Brigade, were lost on June 11, 1972, when the helicopter they were aboard crashed in Vietnam. Their remains were identified on Feb. 7, 2011.
- **Pfc. Wayne Bibbs**, US Army, Troop F, 8th Cavalry, 11th Aviation Group, 1st Aviation Brigade, was lost on June 11, 1972, when the OH-6A Cayuse helicopter he was aboard crashed after departing from Camp Eagle, South Vietnam. His remains were identified on Feb. 7, 2011.
- **Pfc. Peter Kubic**, US Army, K Company, 3rd Battalion, 9th Infantry Regiment, 2nd Infantry Division, was lost on Feb. 12, 1951, after enemy forces overran American positions near Chowon-ni, Republic of Korea. His remains were identified on Feb. 1, 2011.

- **Pfc. Floyd T. Coker**, US Army, K Company, 3rd Battalion, 38th Infantry Regiment, 2nd Infantry Division, was lost on April 15, 1951, while captive at Suan Prisoner of War camp, North Korea. His remains were identified on Jan. 31, 2011.
- **Pfc. Samuel K. Watkins**, US Army, 2nd Reconnaissance Company, L Company, 3rd Battalion, 9th Infantry Regiment, Infantry Division, was lost on Feb. 14, 1951, when his unit was attacked near Chuam-ni, South Korea. His remains were identified on Jan. 18, 2011.
- **Spc. 4 Randall D. Dalton**, US Army, 3rd Squadron, 17th Cavalry, 12th Aviation Group, 1st Aviation Brigade, was lost on July 24, 1971, when the aircraft he was aboard went down in Cambodia. His remains were identified on Jan. 18, 2011.
- **Sgt. Wyatt H. Belton**, US Army, C Company, 1st Battalion, 24th Infantry Regiment was lost on Nov. 28, 1950, while engaged in combat operations near Unsan, North Korea. His remains were identified on Jan. 13, 2011.
- **Sgt. 1st Class Donald M. Shue**, US Army, 5th Special Forces Group, was lost on Nov. 3, 1969, when he was attacked by enemy forces near the Laos-Vietnam border. His remains were identified on Jan. 6, 2011.
- **Capt. Darrell J. Spinler**, US Air Force, 1st Air Commando Squadron, was lost on June 21, 1967, after conducting an air strike mission in Lao. His remains were identified on Jan. 5, 2011.

 # Wall of Missing – Madingley American Cemetery

THE CAMBRIDGE AMERICAN CEMETERY, 30.5 acres in extent, is one of fourteen permanent American World War II military cemetery memorials erected on foreign soil by the American Battle Monuments Commission. It was established as a temporary military cemetery in 1943 on land donated by the University of Cambridge. The site was later selected as the only permanent American World War II military cemetery in the British Isles and was dedicated on 16 July 1956. About forty-two percent of those temporarily interred in England and Northern Ireland during the war were reinterred in this cemetery with the remainder being repatriated home for burial in the United States at the end of the war. (*Of course, the possibility of re-burial back in the UK has never been offered to British casualties from the First and Second World Wars, with such an option only being offered after the Falklands war and with the return of casualties from conflicts in Iraq and Afghanistan being a matter of course.*) A high proportion of the 3,812 American servicemen and women buried at Madingley were crew members of British-based American aircraft while most of the others interred at the cemetery died in the invasions of North Africa and France, in the training areas of the United Kingdom and in the waters of the Atlantic.

Around the ceiling of the memorial chapel of the American Military Cemetery in Madingley, Cambridge, may be found the following inscription:

> IN PROUD AND GRATEFUL MEMORY OF THOSE MEN OF THE UNITED
> STATES ARMY AIR FORCE WHO FROM THESE FRIENDLY ISLES FLEW
> THEIR FINAL FLIGHT AND MET THEIR GOD. THEY KNEW NOT THE HOUR
> THE DAY NOR THE MANNER OF THEIR PASSING. WHEN FAR FROM
> HOME THEY WERE CALLED TO JOIN THAT HERIOIC BAND OF AIRMEN WHO HAD
> GONE BEFORE. MAY THEY REST IN PEACE.

This verse encapsulates concisely what it meant for airmen of any nationality to fly off into combat and never return. Of course, many of those non-returnees subsequently found their rest in known and marked graves whilst others have not yet returned. Others still, as we have seen in this book, are still returning.

Just beyond the Visitors' Building is a 72ft flagpole on a tall platform whose base is inscribed with the following quotation from John McCrae's poem, *In Flanders Fields*:

TO YOU FROM FAILING HANDS
WE THROW THE TORCH –
BE YOURS TO HOLD IT HIGH

The great mall beyond, with reflecting pools bordered by roses, stretches eastward from the flagpole platform to the memorial at the opposite end and along the south side of the mall are tablets listing those who are still unaccounted for on what is known as the Wall of Missing.

Wall of Missing

It is this commemoration, of course, that is of interest within the context of this book and of the names recorded. The overwhelming majority are personnel from the 8th and 9th air forces.

As with the RAF's missing on the memorial at Runnymede, the United States Army Air Force has commemorated its missing who were lost in north-west Europe on the Wall of Missing at the American Battle Monuments Commission's Madingley military cemetery. Here, on a long wall of Portland Stone, are engraved the names of 5,127 US servicemen (predominantly airmen) who have no known grave.

Unlike the Runnymede Memorial, where casualties are grouped alphabetically according to rank and have no date of death or indication as to unit, the Wall of Missing records the date of death and assigned unit. Where those listed have since been discovered or their burial places identified, their names are marked with a rosette. Certainly, a good many rosettes may now be found on the memorial wall and whilst the numbers of previously missing American aircrew discovered in the UK have been relatively few there have been a number found on mainland Europe – some in the reclamation of the Dutch Polders and others in France and Germany. In a number of cases these have been actioned by CILHI teams. Of course, the names of Robert Hymans and Elwood Raymond (see Chapter Seven) may be found here, too, although there are other names that have given rise to speculation as to their fate and location. Take for example the case of 2nd Lt William B Montgomery.

When the crash site of a USAAF B-24 Liberator was identified at Park Farm, Arundel, by the former Wealden Aviation Archaeological Group there were initially no clues as to the date of the crash, its unit or the crew. At that point nothing had been located in local archives to pinpoint this information, although witnesses talked of seeing a line of parachutes strung out across the sky before the crash. All they could recall was that it had been "…about two weeks after D-Day". Another witness who had worked on the farm, however, recalled picking up an American identity tag at the crash site marked with the name Montgomery. Not unnaturally, it was a name that resonated with the farm labourer and it was a clue to start working with. Of course, these were pre-internet days and the rather non-specific and random request to the US authorities drew no information whatsoever based upon the vague information to hand. However, during a visit to the American cemetery in 1972 the author searched for any burial there that might be linked.

There were none.

Nevertheless, there were two casualties named Montgomery on the Wall of Missing and one of them stuck out; 1st Lt William B Montgomery of the 844th Bomb Squadron, 489th Bomb Group. He had been lost on 22 June 1944 (two weeks after D-Day) and, significantly, his assigned unit flew the B-24 Liberator operating out of Halesworth in East Anglia. Montgomery had been the pilot of the B-24 (42-94826) and along with his flight engineer, T/Sgt John Holoka Jr, no trace of him was ever found. One other crew member, the co-pilot, is recorded as dead and he was F/O John J Crowther who now lies buried in a New York State cemetery.

During the very early 1970s the crash site was excavated by the Wealden group who recovered three engines and a number of .50 cal machine guns and the numbers on these weapons tallied with the gun numbers recorded on missing air crew report # 7750 which detailed the loss of Montgomery's aircraft due to flak on a raid over St Cyr, France. From the cockpit area were recovered two armoured seats which would have been for the pilot and the co-pilot, although no trace of any occupants of the aircraft were seen or found. However, and given the 'missing' status of at least two crew members, the site and all relevant details have been passed to the US authorities for potential official investigation. Perhaps, even yet, two more names on the Wall of Missing can one day be marked with a gold rosette.Unlike the names recorded on the Runnymede Memorial, most of the 5,127 names on the Wall of Missing at Madingley can be considered as 'cases pending'. In the words of President Reagan:

"I renew my pledge to the families of those listed as missing in action that this nation will work unceasingly until a full accounting is made. It is our sacred duty and we will never forget them."

List of casualty names now excluded from the Runnymede Memorial

THE FOLLOWING IS A list of names of those RAF casualties commemorated on the Runnymede Memorial who were previously listed as missing with no known grave but who are now accounted for. These are all casualties sustained during operations in the north-west Europe theatre and includes names of the RAF and Commonwealth air forces personnel whose graves have subsequently been located or where the remains of the casualty concerned have since been found and identified and accordingly given a marked grave. In some cases names have been removed from the official list because an entry was found to be in error or, in a few instances, the names or dates of death etc were found to be improperly or incorrectly listed. Whilst these names are no longer on the CWGC register (*per se*) for the Runnymede Memorial it does not necessarily follow that they will not be found still engraved on the respective memorial panels. It is not the policy of the CWGC to physically remove these names when the casualty has otherwise been accounted for. This will only be done when individual panels are replaced for maintenance purposes in the fullness of time.

This is not an officially compiled listing and it is possible that there may therefore be some omissions. The author would therefore be pleased to have notification of any additional names in order to complete or up-date this appendix. The list of names is continually being added to as yet more casualties are found or identified as will be seen elsewhere in this book.

NB: The full casualty details for those listed below (including grave locations, next-of-kin and relevant squadron or unit) may be obtained from the Commonwealth War Graves Commission website at: http://www.cwgc.org/debt_of_honour.asp

ALEXANDER R W Sqn Ldr	21 Sept 1944	BELL M H Plt Off	9 Sept 1944
ALLEN D H Fg Off	18 May 1940	BENNETT R J Flt Sgt	8 Dec 1944
ALLISON W R Wt Off	2 July 1942	BENTZ W B Plt Off	13 May 1944
ANDERSON M H Plt Off	10 May 1940	BERESFORD H R A Flt Lt	7 Sept 1940
AVER F A Sgt	29 Jan 1944	BIRD P R S Plt Off	11 May 1941
BACON B A Sgt	13 May 1943	BLACK J W Flt Sgt	7 Nov 1941
BANKS R C Sgt	2 Mar 1945	BLACK C T Sgt	7 Nov 1941
BARBER C B Plt Off	24 Apr 1942	BOAL H J Flt Sgt	31 Jan 1944
BATTY A V Plt Off	14 Oct 1942	BOND A C Fg Off	7 Dec 1942
BELL J R Sgt	16 June 1943	BOSTON J N Sgt	24 Mar 1944

BOWKER A Sgt	3 Mar 1944
BOWLER W H Plt Off	4 Sept 1942
BREEN J G Wt Off II	12 Jun 1943
BREMNER J Sgt	20 Jan 1944
BRIGSTOCKE A L Sgt	18 Mar 1942
BRIMBLE J J Sgt	14 Sept 1940
BRISBANE W C Fg Off	17 April 1943
BROTHERHOOD L Sgt	14 Oct 1944
BROWN B J W Sgt	18 Aug 1943
BURBRIDGE A G Sgt	13 June 1941
BURDETT J C Sgt	24 Mar 1944
CAIN T LAC	5 June 1940
CAMM P O Sgt	3 Jan 1944
CAMPBELL J P Plt Off	11 May 1941
CAMPBELL J S Sgt	5 Sept 1943
CARMICHAEL J S Con	5 Sept 1943
CARR J T LAC	10 April 1941
CARTER T Sgt	21 April 1943
CAWTHORP R T Fg Off	8 Mar 1945
CHALK F G H Flt Lt	17 Feb 1943
CHAMBERS R E Plt Off	29 Sept 1944
CHISHOLM R S Fg Off	13 June 1941
CHRISTIE J C G Sgt	12 Aug 1941
CLIFTON L Sgt	31 Jan 1944
COCHRANE A W Sgt	28 April 1943
COLLIER R J Sgt	31 Aug 1941
COOK C Sgt	8 Dec 1944
COOPER N L Sgt	24 Mar 1944
COWHAM S W Sgt	28 April 1943
CRESSMAN C H Fg Off	21 Sept 1944
CURTIS R Flt Lt	24 Mar 1944
CUTTS J W Plt Off	4 Sept 1940
DE SAINT AUBIN C A J Fg Off	19 Oct 1944
DEED S V Sgt	20 Dec 1942
DEEN K Flt Lt	30 Aug 1941
DODD R T Sgt	31 Aug 1941
DONALD J Sgt	20 Dec 1942
DOULTON M D Fg Off	31 Aug 1940
DRAKE G J Plt Off	9 Sept 1940
DRCKA J LAC	13 July 1941
(Originally listed incorrectly as Drocka)	
DURSTON I G Flt Lt	29 Jan 1944
EALES W N Fg Off	20 Dec 1942
EGAN E J Sgt	17 Sept 1940
ELLIS J H M Sgt	1 Sept 1940
FAWKES J Sgt	29 Aug 1944
FOX T T Plt Off	4 April 1942

Since the Runnymede Memorial was dedicated by HM The Queen during 1953 well over two hundred names have been deleted from the official list of those commemorated there. Listed here are casualties who have since been accounted for, and include Flt Lt F G H Chalk DFC, a Spitfire pilot of 124 Sqn who had been lost over Northern France. During the 1980s Frederick Chalk was found in the wreckage of his Spitfire, BR585, and subsequently buried at Terclinthun Cemetery, France, during 1989. On the outbreak of war he had joined the Honourable Artillery Company, later transferring to the RAF where he became an air gunner. He was awarded the DFC in June 1941. In 1942 he was accepted for pilot training and subsequently joined a Spitfire squadron, being lost on 17 February 1943. Chalk had been a notable cricketer, having first captained the Oxford University side and subsequently been Captain of Kent Cricket Club. His is just one name out of over 20,000 missing aircrew, but he is now a casualty who can be accounted for.

FRANCIS C D Plt Off	30 Aug 1940
FRASER G G Sgt	24 Oct 1942
FRY H L Flt Lt	29 Jan 1944
GARRET K Flt Sgt	25 May 1941
GAVEL A D Fg Off	17 April 1944
GILCHRIST H G Fg Off	14 Aug 1944
GILDERS J S Sgt	21 Feb 1941
GILL P R Flt Sgt	29 Jan 1944
GILLESPIE J R Plt Off	7 Oct 1944
GRAY T H Sgt	7 Nov 1941
GREEN L C Flt Sgt	7 Nov 1941
GREEN C Sgt	13 May 1943
GREENSIDES A Flt Sgt	13 June 1941
GRIBBEN T Sgt	13 June 1944
HALES T A LAC	18 Sept 1944
HALL A E Cpl	21 Sept 1944
HAMILTON W C Fg Off	24 Oct 1942

HARDCASTLE A V J Plt Off	13 June 1941	MAYCOCK R Sgt	18 May 1942
HARLING J E Sgt	27 Aug 1944	McAULEY M Fg Off	14 Aug 1944
HARRISON F A Plt Off	14 Oct 1944	McAVOY J Flt Sgt	14 Mar 1945
HART F J Sgt	27 June 1941	McCORMACK L G Sgt	31 Aug 1941
HARTLEY M Sgt	16 Feb 1944	McCUAIG D K Flt Lt	28 Sept 1944
HAWKINS H C LAC	10 May 1940	McDOUGALL C A Fg Off	12 June 1943
HAWTHORN R T Flt Sgt	7 Dec 1944	McELLIGOTT J J Plt Off	19 May 1940
HEALY D E Flt Lt	25 Sept 1942	McFEETORS A S Plt Off	14 Oct 1944
HEFFERNAN A F Sgt	24 Oct 1942	McLEAN H J A Fg Off	25 Feb 1945
HENDERSON A Flt Sgt	2 Mar 1945	McLEOD W C Plt Off	24 Mar 1944
HENDERSON J L Flt Sgt	7 Dec 1944	McLINTOCK W S Fg Off	21 Sept 1944
HEPWORTH R Sgt	24 Mar 1944	MENZIES J W Flt Lt	6 July 1944
HICKS D F Sgt	31 Jan 1944	MILES J T N Fg Off	24 Oct 1942
HOLMES R E AC2	4 Sept 1942	MILLER C E Sgt	7 Oct 1944
HOPKINS R A Flt Sgt	25 May 1941	MIRON A E Flt Lt	17 Aug 1944
ISAACS L D Cpl	10 May 1940	MITCHELL S R Sgt	30 Oct 1939
JANNEY W H Flt Lt	14 Oct 1944	MOORE C R Fg Off	10 May 1940
JARVIS N Sgt	31 Aug 1941	MOREY W Flt Sgt	13 May 1943
JEWETT J S Flt Sgt	4 Sept 1942	MORTIMER A Flt Sgt	20 Dec 1942
JONES P R Plt Off	14 Oct 1944	MULFORD W E Sqn Ldr	12 June 1943
JONES T Sgt	19 May 1940	MULLENGER S G Sgt	9 Nov 1941
JONES W J Sgt	31 Jan 1944	MURRAY G W Plt Off	2 June 1942
KAUER J Flt Sgt	23 Dec 1944	NUTALL N H Sgt	11 May 1941
KEHOE J E Sgt	9 Nov 1941	O'MEARA J P Wt Off	17 June 1944
KELLY C LAC	26 Nov 1944	OTTER R S Sgt	4 Sept 1942
KELLY F J Cpl	25 May 1947	OYSTON L Sgt	8 Dec 1944
KEMP H K Plt Off	11 April 1944	PALMER C J E Flt Lt	3 Jan 1944
KILLBY K N Sgt	2 June 1942	PARKIN C AC2	22 April 1940
KILLNER W H Plt Off	14 Oct 1944	PARTINGTON J W AC1	23 Jan 1942
KIRKBY G D Flt Sgt	4 Sept 1942	PEARSON G W Sgt	6 Sept 1940
KNIGHT E P Sgt	7 Oct 1944	PENMAN G B Fg Off	15 Aug 1942
KNIGHT T B LAC	14 Mar 1945	PITT F F Wt Off	19 Aug 1944
KNOWLES E J Fg Off	24 Mar 1945	PLUMB S P Sgt	11 May 1941
LANGSTON P Flt Lt	24 Oct 1944	PORTER H R Sgt	7 Oct 1944
LATHAM M Sgt	20 Feb 1944	PRICE C M Flt Sgt	31 Jan 1944
LEACH G C S Sgt	31 Aug 1941	PROSOFSKY A W Plt Off	29 July 1944
LENTON K F Flt Sgt	8 Dec 1944	PUGH T P Wg Cdr	2 Aug 1943
LEWIS R F Flt Lt	8 Dec 1944	PURMAL V R Plt Off	3 Jan 1944
LIVERSUCH R J Sgt	2 July 1942	RAMSAY J B Plt Off	18 Aug 1940
LLOYD E Plt Off	7 Nov 1941	READER G S Flt Sgt	17 Sept 1944
LUCAS E R Sgt	11 May 1941	REIDY W P Sgt	20 Mar 1945
LUDLOW R L Plt Off	29 Jan 1944	RENAUD G K Fg Off	29 July 1944
MacIVER A M Sgt	29 July 1944	RICHARDS J C Sqn Ldr	21 April 1943
MAGUIRE D J Flt Sgt	14 Aug 1944	RIDLEY J AC1	27 Sept 1941
MALLINSON L H AC2	4 Sept 1942	ROACH F Plt Off	13 May 1944
MASON D W Plt Off	18 June 1944	ROGERS R A J Plt Off	11 July 1943
MAWDESLEY W J Fg Off	2 June 1942	ROUND A K Fg Off	25 May 1941

RUSHMER F W Flt Lt	5 Sept 1940	THURSBY R A Flt Sgt	9 Aug 1944
RUSSEL H Flt Lt	16 June 1944	TOYE J W A LAC	28 Feb 1945
SCAFE W J Flt Lt	7 Sept 1942	TRASK C R Plt Off	5 Mar 1943
SCOTT E Sgt	27 Sept 1940	TURNBULL B E Fg Off	7 Oct 1944
SCOTT G W Sgt	7 Aug 1942	TURNER R A G Sgt	24 Mar 1944
SCOTT J S Flt Sgt	24 Mar 1944	USHER R H W Fg Off	8 Dec 1944
SCRIMES F J B Flt Sgt	2 June 1942	VAN WYMERS R Flt Sgt	29 Nov 1944
SHAND W P Wg Cdr	20 April 1943	WAKELIN W J Sgt	24 Oct 1942
SHARROCKS G Sgt	7 Oct 1944	WALKER G W Fg Off	27 Sept 1942
SHAW R S Sgt	13 May 1943	WALLINGER W Sgt	13 June 1944
SHERWOOD R C Flt Sgt	15 Mar 1944	WALSH R AC2	3 Sept 1947
SIDWELL R S Sgt	21 April 1943	WALTON J H Flt Sgt	25 June 1943
SIMPSON R G V Sgt	25 May 1944	WARBURTON A Wg Cdr	12 April 1944
SMEE J K Sgt	5 June 1942	WARD D R Sgt	8 Aug 1944
SMIK O Sqn Ldr	28 Nov 1944	WATTS R H Plt Off	21 Oct 1943

Note: Post-war Smik was promoted to general in the Czech Air Force. It was also discovered that he had been wrongly buried as Fg Off Taymans, a Belgian pilot, who had been killed on 28 November 1944 (the same day as Smik) when Taymans's body was found in 1965. Thus, Smik's name became an addition to the Runnymede Memorial rather than a deletion)

		WEBB A P Sgt	24 Mar 1944
		WEIR W B Plt Off	9 April 1945
		WHEELER S W Sgt	24 Mar 1944
		WHELLAMS R A Sgt	21 April 1943
SMITH E Wt Off	27 Aug 1944	WHITE J Flt Sgt	5 May 1943
SMITH F A S Sgt	11 May 1941	WILKIE J L Plt Off	2 June 1940
SMITH H B Sgt	24 Oct 1942	WILLSON W V Sgt	24 Mar 1944
SMITH H L Flt Lt	11 June 1944	WILSON W W Flt Sgt	5 Feb 1943
SMITH J D Plt Off	4 Sept 1942	ZADOROSNY S E Plt Off	18 Dec 1944
SMITH N H Sgt	12 Sept 1941		
SOMERS L W Fg Off	25 June 1943		
STANEY W T Sgt	2 June 1942		
STEIN A G Fg Off	29 June 1944		
STICKLAND V J Sgt	16 April 1941		
SUMMERHAYES J W Plt Off	13 May 1944		
SUTHERLAND J W A Flt Sgt	29 Jan 1944		
SWITZER L J Wt Off II	6 Feb 1943		
TABOR W T Flt Sgt	4 Sept 1942		
TAFFENDER W C Fg Off	13 June 1941		
TALBOT H J Plt Off	25 May 1941		
TAYLOR A L Sgt	24 Mar 1944		
TAYLOR D T Flt Sgt	24 Oct 1942		
TAYLOR J G Sgt	24 Oct 1942		
THIBAUDEAU J E A Flt Sgt	5 May 1943		
THOMAS G AC2	27 Sept 1941		
THOMAS G Fg Off	7 Dec 1944		
THOMPSON J D Sgt	7 Nov 1941		
THOMSON D M Plt Off	5 July 1944		

*Note: For recording purposes the CWGC consider that World War 2 began on 3 September 1939 and ended on 31 December 1947. The 1947 date allowed casualties who had later died of injuries sustained during the conflict to be covered, as well as including those who had died on active service in the immediate post-war period, often whilst undertaking duties related directly to the recent conflict.

NB: For further details of the Runnymede Memorial, see Finding the Few; *for details of the German military cemetery in the UK, see* Finding the Foe.

Selected Bibliography

The following books and publications were amongst those principally referred to by the author during his preparation of this work.

Chorley, W R	*RAF Bomber Command Losses*	(Midland Counties 1997)
Commonwealth War Graves Commission	*The War Dead of the British Commonwealth & Empire: Runnymede Memorial Registers Parts I to XV*	(CWGC 1953)
Cornwell, Peter	*Battle of France: Then And Now*	(After The Battle 2008)
Franks, Norman	*RAF Fighter Command Losses 1939-45*	(Midland Counties 1997)
Freeman, Roger	*Mighty Eighth War Diary*	(Jane's 1981)
Goss, Chris	*Luftwaffe Bombers Battle of Britain*	(Crécy 2000)
Hadaway, Stuart	*Missing Believed Killed*	(Pen & Sword 2008)
Halley, James J	*The Squadrons of the RAF & Commonwealth 1918-1988*	(Air-Britain 1988)
Obermaier, Ernst	*Die Ritterkreuztrager Band 1*	(Verlag Dieter Hoffmann 1970)
Lake, Alan	*Flying Units of the RAF*	(Airlife 1999)
Loucky, František	*Mnozí Nedolet li*	(Ziva Minulost 1989)
Martyn, Errol W	*For Your Tomorrow*	(Volplane Press 1998)
Plesman, Albert	*A Flying Dutchman*	(Up-Front 2002)
Ramsey, Winston G	*Battle of Britain Then And Now*	(After The Battle 1980)
Ramsey, Winston G	*Blitz Then And Now (Vol.1)*	(After The Battle 1987)
Ramsey, Winston G	*Blitz Then And Now (Vol.2)*	(After The Battle 1987)
Ramsey, Winston G	*Blitz Then And Now (Vol.3)*	(After The Battle 1987)
Sheehan, Susan	*A Missing Plane*	Berkley Books 1986)
Swift, Earl	*Where They Lay*	(Bantam 2003)
Waters Yarsinske, Amy	*No One Left Behind*	(Dutton Adult 2002)
Wynn, Kenneth	*Men of The Battle of Britain*	(CCB 2000)
Zeng L, Stankey D G, with Creek E	*Bomber Units of The Luftwaffe*	(Midland 2007)

Index

Places

Squadrons and Units

Airfields and Bases